Praise for Top Maui Restaurants

"We just got home on Friday from an amazing week in Maui and I wanted to tell you that we only ate at restaurants listed in your guide! It was so great because they came with a little 'assurance' that we were not going to be scammed! Your info was invaluable to us and I will definitely hold onto it and make sure I tell everyone I know who is going to Maui to get the newest version. Thanks again for making our trip a wonderful dining experience!"
– JEANI ADAMS, ANAHEIM, CA

"I love ur book. We just left maui and I used ur book for the second year in a row. U and your wife have the best advice."
– ALISON, SENT FROM HER VERIZON WIRELESS BLACKBERRY

"My family has recently returned from Maui (we stayed at Kaanapali Beach Hotel – wonderful!). Your book was our bible and we are so fortunate to have had your expertise.

Your reviews allowed us to sample some of the exquisite offerings of Maui and our experience would not have been complete without trying your recommendations."
– DEBORAH RISHELL

"Mahalo for your great guide! We've just returned from our fifth trip to the island in five years, and we used our guide for the first time on this trip. What a great time and money saver! It was nice to have some information about places that weren't there last year (Fred's), and places we've been by in the past and hadn't tried before (Joe's). This guide is worth every penny, and I bet you guys have a lot of fun researching it. Let me know if you need a helper - I come from a long line of good eaters!"
– SAMANTHA MAR, SEATTLE, WA

"Just wanted to let you know that I've been to Maui over 20 times and this is the first time I've bought the guide. It is excellent! I'm recommending it to my friends here and on the mainland."
– MIKE DINSTELL, MORAGA, CA

"My husband and I just got back from Maui Saturday and we found your guide to be very informative! We tried several of the places listed and found each one to be excellent. However, I do have a comment to make about it . . . you should have recommended that we each get the soufflé at Roy's! I didn't want to share!!! (But I did). Thanks again for an excellent resource. We would have missed out on some great food if not for your guide!"
– MELANIE AND WILLIE HARRELL, ROXIE, MS

"My sister Carol and I visited Maui recently with no clue on how to pick restaurants . . . I loved the folksy and down-to-earth reviews, they get right to the quick about each place and what to expect . . . We were trying to watch our pocketbooks a little, too, so it was very helpful in that department . . . I can't recommend it enough."
– SUSAN THERIAULT, PLAINVILLE, CT

"Just a note to thank you for the *Top Maui Restaurants* guide. My husband I used it extensively and found some great food - your guide was very helpful. Merry Christmas and Mahalo for the guide."
– GAE SELLSTEDT, VANCOUVER, BC

"I ordered your guide on-line. It is excellent. We are from Calgary, Alberta and have been to Maui twice but not for over 10 years, so your guide will come in handy when we visit again in April."
– TERRY & SUSAN WINNITOY, CALGARY, ALBERTA

"We have been home for just two weeks and it seems like we were never away. Your Maui guide was very helpful and we all especially enjoyed Buzz's and Cafe O'Lei."
– GENE MIRANDA, FLORHAM PARK, NJ

"Thank you so very much . . . *Top Maui Restaurants* is very helpful for planning a rehearsal dinner next June. We will be spending a week in Maui, staying at the Four Seasons, celebrating a wedding. Your service has been exceptional. Thank you again!"
– KELLY BOLDY, NOBLESVILLE, IN

Top Maui

RESTAURANTS

— 2010 —

From Thrifty to Four Star

Indispensable Advice from Experts
Who Live, Play & Eat on Maui

by James Jacobson
& Molly Jacobson

Published by:
Maui Media, LLC
www.MauiMedia.com

Top Maui Restaurants 2010 From Thrifty to Four Star
Indispensable Advice from Experts Who Live, Play & Eat on Maui
By James Jacobson and Molly Jacobson

ISBN 978-0-9752631-6-7

www.TopMauiRestaurants.com

We welcome your comments and suggestions. Please address them via email and send them to editor@TopMauiRestaurants.com.

Cover and Text Design by Dawn Lewandowski of Partners Image Coordinators • 1-877-535-1155

Dedication

To my father, Kenneth Jacobson, who taught me
the joy of good eating and how to love with a full
heart. Those gifts inspire me today, and inspired
this book. *Ich liebe dich*.

– JAMES JACOBSON

To my aunt, Sandy Lovejoy, who taught me to
trust myself and listen deeply; to my grandmother
Ruth, whose kitchen inspires me to this day; to
my hanai mother, Rhea Barton, who taught me
to feed myself, to set big goals, and to speak my
clearest truth. I miss you all and love you very
much. Thank you for everything.

– MOLLY JACOBSON

Finally, we dedicate this book to the joy we take
in each other, and to our marriage.

Contents

C

D

E

F

G

H

I

J

S

T

U

V

W

Register This Book!
(We'll Even Bribe You Twice)

As strange as it may sound, we really would like you to register this book so that we can let you know about important updates: new restaurants, closed restaurants, big changes at one of our favorite (or least favorite) places. Things change in the Maui Restaurant scene and that is why we want to keep you informed and updated.

This is a *free service* for our readers, but even so, we know that it takes a little effort to go over to a computer, type in a web address and fill in a few fields.

That is why we are going to offer you an ethical bribe. Actually, two bribes:

Win a $25 Gift Card

Every month from December 2009 thru December 2010, we will be giving away a $25 gift certificate for Amazon.com in an online sweepstakes we are running. When you register that you are an owner of ***Top Maui Restaurants 2010*** using the special link below, you will be entered to win in that month's sweepstakes.

Get a Trial Membership to TopMauiTips.com

This membership site for people who are planning their vacation to Maui has been in the works for three years and was finally opened to the public in December 2009. The site is loaded with articles that are packed with useful, actionable tips to get the most out of your trip to Maui. Whatever activity you are considering, whatever questions you have, chances are they are addressed in this thoroughly-researched membership site. And now, you can have a complimentary trial membership when you register this book.

Register your book today at:
www.TopMauiRestaurants.com/2010

How You Can Keep Up to Date on the Maui Restaurant Scene

Restaurants come and go here on Maui and we are dedicated to helping our readers navigate this ever-changing environment. There are a number of things that we have done and are planning to do that will help you get the most out of your Maui vacation.

We have recently launched our blog www.MauiRestaurantsBlog.com where you can read the latest dining news and also rate your personal experiences at any restaurant in Maui. Every restaurant has its own page and you can read what other diners have to say and see how others have rated each restaurant. (For our restaurant reviews, however, this book is the only place that you will be able to read what we think.)

There has also been some discussion about an Internet-syndicated radio show, but as of press time, we don't have details. When we know more, we will send an email to everyone who is subscribed to our list. To subscribe, register online using the link below.

We also host occasional reader appreciation Mai Tai parties at our home in South Maui. This is a great chance for us to get to talk with our readers and for our readers and other Maui foodies to talk with us…all while enjoying one of Molly's delicious Mai Tais. If you are in town when we host one of these parties, you are invited. You just have to RSVP to one of our invitations.

To receive those invitations—and other Maui-oriented information—from us, please register your copy of *Top Maui Restaurants 2010*.

To register your book, please visit
www.TopMauiRestaurants.com/2010

Introduction

A Magical Meal on Maui

This book is born of desperate necessity and soul-searing, passionate love. It has taken five years to write, decades to research, and was inspired by a glorious Maui sunset and an unforgettable meal.

The story is so magical and romantic you might not believe it. Even my own mother can hardly believe it happened to me. But everything I'm about to tell you is true. And it could not have happened anyplace else on earth but Maui.

Five years ago Jim and I met on a beach on Maui. With our first glance, we were catapulted into an intense love affair. We each gasped a little in recognition of our connection; it felt downright mystical. Our hands took the initiative and reached for each other. As they intertwined for the first time, Jim murmured "Where have you been all my life?" (Yes, he really said that.)

I couldn't answer. I could only stare, like a wide-eyed child, then look away at the sky above his head still streaked with my first Maui sunset. The first quarter moon was already bright and two stars popped out as his eyes twinkled.

He asked, "Are you hungry?"

I nodded, my head heavy on my suddenly weak neck. I was hungry. I was also struck dumb and a little dizzy. My arms tingled just above the wrist. Was my circulation cut off? But he persisted: "Do you like sushi?"

This snapped me out of my moonstruck state. My head cleared and I spoke crisply, "No, I don't. I *love* sushi. But I have to warn you, I think most of what passes for sushi shouldn't be fed to a stray cat."

> *"I don't 'like' food. I love food. If I don't love it, I don't swallow."*
>
> – Ego,
> Restaurant Critic,
> *Ratatouille*

Jim smiled and drew me to his side. We turned and faced the distant island of Lana'i, arms wrapped around each other, pulling our quickly beating hearts close together. Watching the sky shift from pink to indigo to velvet, he said, "That's my girl. I knew you'd drift in someday." The waves crashed louder and louder until they were all I heard.

When time started again, Jim took me to my first Maui restaurant. Following the petite hostess in her silk kimono through a large, lusciously draped room filled with long-haired beauties and a piano player pouring honey-sweet music all over the floor was like walking into my most private dream. We were seated at a table along the rail on the wraparound lanai (porch). Two waiters immediately hustled away for our drinks.

We toasted each other, tinkling our white porcelain cups brimming with warm sake. The miso arrived and we drank the deep, rich, hearty broth straight from the bowl. We told our life stories and held hands in between plates of fish and bowls of rice. Our fingers and our chopsticks cradled the tender pink and yellow and white morsels before delivering them to our tongues, where they quivered a little before giving up their sweet ocean flavors.

Every once in a while I pinched my thigh beneath my napkin. Was this really happening?

We stayed until the pianist had retired, other diners had departed, and the lights were dimmed. As they cleaned and stacked and cleared, the servers brought us cool water, tiny coconut creams, and refreshing green tea, assuring us that we should stay until we were ready to go. It was clear to all of us that magic was happening, and no one wanted to interrupt it.

On the drive back to the beach, heavy perfume from plumeria trees lining Wailea Ike Drive rushed through the open windows. I asked Jim "Is this heaven?"

He smiled and said "I think so." I had never felt so content, relaxed, and beautiful.

After we parted for the night, I called my girlfriends back on the east coast and woke them up one by one. As I giggled and swooned and stammered my way through the story of my first Maui evening, dozens of stars sprang from their places in the black sky above my car and streaked across the ridges of Haleakala in the most glorious meteor shower I'd ever witnessed.

Our *Top Maui Restaurants* review guide was conceived on that magical night, but we didn't have an inkling of it yet.

Two months later, firmly established in our new love affair and still discovering the depths of our mutual passion for food, Jim and I were driving by "our" restaurant when we saw a "Now Closed" sign over the door.

I was shocked. How could this paragon of fabulous dining, unbelievable ambiance, and stellar service have thrown in the towel?

Jim shook his head sadly and a weary expression crossed his face. By this time we had eaten in many of the restaurants reviewed in this guide, and he explained carefully that each one of them − no matter how wonderful − were in imminent danger of closing due to the heavy overhead and high turnover inherent in the Maui restaurant scene.

Restaurants on Maui, he explained, open and close overnight like tropical flowers. For as many superb restaurants as there are now, several times that number had failed since 1990, when he first arrived.

The following week we took a beach walk after breakfast. I noticed a beautiful restaurant practically on the sand and asked him why he hadn't suggested going there for dinner yet. He wrinkled his nose and said "It's not worth it."

I was skeptical, and pressed him. I was hungry for Italian, I said, and I wanted a special night out to celebrate our two-month anniversary. Waiters in formal-wear seemed like the perfect touch, and according to several of my guidebooks, it was one of the best restaurants on the island. Jim gave up with an affectionate shrug, and we booked a table for that evening.

To my surprise and growing horror during the meal, Jim was right. I like to focus on the positive, so I won't go into detail here. I will leave it to your imagination until you read the review for yourself on page 134.

After we left I declared "Why didn't anyone warn me?! We just spent over $200 on a meal that wasn't worth half that – at a restaurant I never would have **bothered** with back home in New York!"

The next day we were still talking about it, and the next, and the next. Watching my consternation grow at the "inaccuracy" and "unreliability" of tourist guides, Jim's author wheels started turning. The problem, he decided, was that I was relying on dining guides, not dining reviews.

What's the difference? A whole heck of a lot.

Dining Guides, in our opinion, are next to worthless. Primarily descriptive, they are designed to tell you the Who, What, Where, and When of a restaurant. They leave out the essential How and the crucial Why.

A Dining Review, on the other hand, is written by an actual person (or in this case, two persons joined at the hip) with actual opinions and actual (hopefully good) advice. A good review does not just *describe* the restaurant. It also helps you decide if you want to eat at the restaurant.

We noticed that most dining and tourist guides feature restaurant guides, not practical, honest, restaurant reviews. And unfortunately, the few reviews we did find were not written by people who know food.

Jim and I, on the other hand, know food. We both come from food-obsessed families and are excellent home chefs. We've eaten in the best restaurants in America, Europe, and Asia – not once or twice, but repeatedly.

We were even obsessed as kids.

My aunt was a restaurant owner and natural foods chef, so I grew up knowing about and eating healthy, organic food prepared to taste absolutely delicious. I started baking at the age of seven, and made all family birthday cakes, including my own. I cooked for my family when my mother returned to work, and I learned firsthand how challenging it can be to focus amidst chaos and infuse love into the food. I also learned how magical food is when you do it right, and how a good meal can pull a fractious bunch together.

Later I lived in Boston and then New York City, where I ate at the best restaurants (not necessarily always the most expensive) every single day of the week for eight years (I'm not kidding). I took cooking classes, read cookbooks from cover to cover (even though I wasn't cooking myself – I'm a perpetual student, and wanted to understand what the chefs were doing in my favorite restaurants). I've always had friends who loved good food – and my four years in New York City taught me what New Yorkers have known for a long time: food can be the best form of entertainment. Even when I moved to Montana – not known for its high cuisine – I made a point of learning as much as possible about grass-fed beef, local produce, and the wonderfully sweet, wild-tasting huckleberries the bears love almost as much as we do.

Jim's obsession with food started at his grandmother's kitchen table, at age five. He would study her cooking, trying to capture her recipes on paper. She was a high French and German cook who had never written anything down, so his notes (he still has the "recipe book") include "Stir until arm grows tired," and "Pour flour into one of Grandma's hands, two of mine, until it overflows just a little." To this day he speaks in German when he makes us breakfast.

When he started his business consultancy he worked with restaurant owners so he could get complimentary meals (we have a strict anti-comp policy for our guide – much to the chagrin of our accountant). This allowed him to dine at the best restaurants in Washington, DC, where he was born and raised. He has taken cooking classes everywhere he's lived and traveled – including Le Cordon Bleu in Paris – picking up hundreds of techniques, ingredients, and culinary mindsets. He's even studied Ayurvedic Indian cuisine with Mother Teresa's personal chef.

Once he realized the desperate need for a genuinely insightful, useful, honest, advice-oriented Maui restaurant review, Jim suggested we draft a review of "our" two restaurants: the dreamy-but-closed Japanese place and the too-well-marketed-to-die-a-natural-death Italian joint.

And that's how *Top Maui Restaurants* was born. The more we wrote, the more we wanted to write, until soon we had over fifty reviews. We shared them with a couple of friends who were coming to Maui, and they called them "invaluable."

We started selling our guide to people researching their Maui vacation online. (We still do.) Over the years the guide increased to over 200 pages. During that time, many people asked if there was a book version available. They didn't want to print out 200 pages from their home computers. We always shook our head dismissively and said "Who needs another travel book to Maui?"

But the demand kept coming, and we finally gave in for the 2008 edition of the guide. This, the 2010 edition, is still the definitive dining review guide to Maui.

We get mail everyday from readers who have just spent time on Maui and used this book. Their stories about the memorable meals they've had are touching and spur us to create an even better guide for next year.

We've also started a brand new blog dedicated to Maui's restaurants. You can visit us there at www.MauiRestaurants-Blog.com. That's where we keep readers like you up-to-date on our latest food adventures, share recipes, and alert you to changes in the restaurant scene here on Maui. Each restaurant has its very own webpage on the blog, and we worked hard to implement a reader-review feature. If you love a restaurant (or not), you can go to that restaurant's page, write your own review, and rate it on the same 5 Star system you'll see in the reviews in this guide.

Everyone who visits Maui feels the magic that flows through this place. It's not just paradise on earth, not just white sand beaches, endless skies, warm breezes, swaying palm trees, lush rainforests, green volcanoes, whales, dolphins, and rum drinks.

There's something else at work here. We don't want to get too woozy, but Maui can make you kind of …woozy. It's so …delicious. Like a coconut warm from the sun, cut open and spilling its milk down your throat, it's sweet. When you come here, you relax on some deeper level and life starts looking more manageable. Parts of you that may have been dormant wake up. Life looks …good.

We want you to relax on your vacation, and then relax some more.

Stressing out about food – about when, where, how much, or what to eat – should not be on your agenda. Let us guide you. We write these reviews as if we were writing to our friends, and we would never recommend a place that we wouldn't send our best friend to.

We've included the very best, from Thrifty to Four Star. In case you think we're always positive, we've also included some ringers and some restaurants that market themselves well enough to attract your attention but are not worth your time or money.

We take no prisoners when we write. If the place looks dirty, we say so. If the food is overcooked, we point it out. If the dessert is brilliant, we cheer and ooh and ahh. The better the restaurant, the pickier we get. But we don't expect a banana bread stand by the side of the highway to rise to the standards set by Four Star restaurants.

For the first four years, we were completely anonymous, because no one on Maui even knew who we were (we never sold to locals). Now, of course, some of the better (smarter) restaurateurs recognize us, but we stick to our no-comping standards and refuse to take advertising from restaurants (even though some want us to).

We eat out an average of eleven times every week, rotating through restaurants to update our reviews. Over time, we've refined our methods for researching and writing reviews to a science.

When we first visit a restaurant, I excuse myself at least four times to discreetly capture my detailed notes in "private" in a bathroom stall. Jim, meantime, taps away on his iPhone, sending emails to himself with his notes. During the meal, we ask lots of questions of the servers, the busboys, and the hostess, trying to pick up as much information as possible about food preparation, the owners, the chef's philosophy, and the way they operate their business. If they ask us why we're so interested, we open our eyes wide and say "Because we love food so much!"

We often tape our "car conversations" immediately after the meal, so we can catch our first joint impressions about the food and the restaurant.

We write our first draft of the review as soon as possible, but only after we've been to a restaurant at least twice, and usually three or more times. We return to the restaurant over and over to refine our opinion and keep things "fresh." If we hear about a change in the chef, a new menu, or a renovation, we make a visit to check it out. If a friend or a reader emails us or calls to let us know about a problem, we make a trip to investigate.

We eat about six disappointing meals every week to make sure that you don't have to. The result? Well, we've gained some weight, there's no denying. And we've gotten into some full-scale shouting matches that turned out to be nothing more than bad-food-induced temper tantrums.

And we've spent a heck of a lot of money on food that would make you cringe, since we don't take complimentary meals (and never will).

Our friends think we're nuts. They're happy to help by dining with us at certain places, and they report their own dining experiences back to us, but they flat out refuse to eat at many of the restaurants we have to review. But if they happen to work with visitors, they always ask us about our new favorites. Why? Because the number one question they field from visitors is "Where should we eat tonight?"

You won't be asking that question. You'll be spending your time on Maui lazing by the pool, trailing your fingers in the tidal basins, or snorkeling.

Thoughts of where to go to dinner may

enter your mind, but they'll quickly be answered by flipping through this guide.

At least, that's our hope. After all, Maui can be magic – as our story shows – and we wouldn't want its romance lessened in any way for you, our food-obsessed readers.

In 2007 we were married on Lana'i. One day during our honeymoon, we caught a glimpse of Maui and knew we were looking at the beach on which we met those years ago. We imagined looking back through time at our former selves at that magical moment and embraced as we had then, drawing each other close and feeling each other's hearts beating with the ocean waves. We thought of our home, just one block away from that beach, and sighed with contentment and happiness.

It's our most sincere hope that you will have a magical time while you are on Maui, too. This book should help.

Jim and I wish you shooting stars and glorious sunsets, and very, very good eating.

Warm Aloha,

Molly Jacobson
Kihei, Maui, Hawaii
December, 2009

How to Use This Guide

This guide is designed with ease of use in mind. It is organized into two major sections, with plenty of indexes to help you find what you're looking for. The major sections are as follows:

Restaurant Reviews

There are nearly four hundred restaurants on Maui, and while we've eaten at the vast majority of them, we cannot include them all in this guide.

(Space in the book is precious. However, each restaurant on Maui has its own webpage – where you can review and rate it yourself – on www.MauiRestaurantsBlog.com. If you are curious about a restaurant not reviewed, check out their page on the blog and see what other diners think.)

We review nearly two hundred restaurants in this section, all of which we think are important. Restaurants are important for one of the following reasons:

1. **They are restaurants we recommend.**

2. **They are restaurants we do not recommend but that you ask us about.** We used to leave these restaurants out entirely (that's why we named the book *Top Maui Restaurants*) but then we received so many questions about these places that we had to include their reviews to be of service to you. Some of these restaurants spend a good deal on advertising, which is why so many are curious about them. In other cases, the restaurant may once have been quite good – even *Top* – but has since fallen in our estimation. We feel it is worth letting you know that.

Restaurants are reviewed in alphabetical order. After the main review, we list the restaurant's address, region of the island, and nearby landmarks. We also tell you what to expect for parking, give you the phone number, tell you which meals are served, and list the hours of operation as of publication time. If the restaurant has a website, we also list that.

There are also several symbols associated with each review. The key to those symbols is below.

Top Maui Tips

We get asked a lot of questions about Maui that have nothing to do with restaurants. In order to cut down on the number of personal emails we have to answer (or have our customer support team answer), we have included the answers to the most-asked questions in this section of the book.

You'll find out:

• Where we shop for groceries

• Where we would host a wedding or rehearsal dinner

- Where we go for champagne brunches
- What "Local Food" and "Plate Lunch" mean

And those are just some of the food-related questions. In addition, we cover:

- Driving tips for Maui roads
- What to do as soon as you get off the plane
- The must–do's for foodie activities
- What driving the Road to Hana really entails, and how to prepare for it like a local
- Whether Haleakala at sunrise is really worth it, how to prepare, and what to eat afterwards
- Where to see movies on Maui, including a film festival you shouldn't miss
- How to find out about concerts, dance recitals and other cultural events
- How to find out about the night life on Maui
- Why you should consider a daytrip to Lanai
- What it takes to move to Maui

Ten Days on Maui

If we only had ten days on Maui, where would we eat? In this section, we name our Top Ten recommendations for both the budget-minded and the "Money is no object" crowd.

Easy Reference Indexes

There are several indexes that list our restaurant recommendations for easy reference. The indexes are:

- Recommended Restaurants by Budget
- Recommended Restaurants by Location
- Recommended Restaurants by Food Craving

Please note that these indexes do not list every restaurant that is reviewed, but only the restaurants we consider worth visiting.

There is also a comprehensive General Index which lists all of the keywords we could think of that you might want to look up.

Key to Symbols Used in This Book

 Restaurants with this symbol are designated a *Top Maui Restaurant.* These are restaurants we would visit even if we weren't reviewing them (as of publication – for our latest experiences check our blog at www.MauiRestaurantsBlog.com).

A restaurant that has a great view and not–so–great food cannot get this symbol, but a restaurant that serves terrific food in a dumpy location can. That's why you will see that some "3 Star" restaurants get our Top symbol, while some "4 Star" restaurants do not.

Not every restaurant is perfect, of course, so you should read the review to get our full impression of the restaurant. Any of these restaurants can have "off" days, and we cannot guarantee that you will have the same experience we have had, or that you will share our taste in food, but in general we feel confident in recommending them to visitors and locals alike for the food.

 Restaurants with this symbol are noteworthy in some way. We don't consider them Top, but we like them enough to recommend them for certain things. Read the review to get the full story.

If a restaurant does not have either of these symbols, assume that we do not feel strongly enough to recommend you visit, but we felt it was important to review them. This is usually because readers have asked us about them or, in some cases, because we used to recommend them and no longer do.

The restaurant scene changes constantly on Maui, so we ask for your help in keeping everyone up-to-date. Please review and rate restaurants at the new www.MauiRestaurantsBlog.com so that everyone can benefit. Sometimes a tip from a reader that a restaurant has improved – or fallen off the wagon – can prompt us to make a visit to refresh our thoughts. This also helps fellow diners who want to hear what other readers of our book think about local restaurants.

Ratings

We thought long and hard before we created our 5 Star Restaurant Rating system, and we have changed it from previous years so that it matches our new blog at www.MauiRestaurantsBlog.com.

It's very difficult to pin down a restaurant into a single Star rating. No matter how thoughtful we are, a shorthand system like this never tells the full story.

On the other hand, many readers love Star ratings. It helps them to see at a glance our general impression of a restaurant.

To be fair and accurate, we chose to create five separate Star Rating Categories: Food, Ambiance, Service, Love, and Value.

Each restaurant can earn up to five stars in each category. Then we average the scores across the five categories to come up with an Overall Star Rating. The highest possible Overall Rating is 5 Stars, but no one has earned it (yet).

You will notice that sometimes the Overall Rating for a restaurant is average – say 3 Stars – and yet we still give it a Top recommendation. This is because we personally care more about the food than anything else. We will eat in a hole-in-the-wall if the food is good, and most of our readers feel the same way.

The Overall Star Ratings are useful, but we don't intend them to rule any of your decisions. We hope you pay more attention to the individual Star Ratings, which are more useful in making decisions that are in alignment with your own preferences and restaurant selection criteria.

For example, if you're planning your anniversary, you probably want a place that scores high on ambiance as well as food. If you're just looking for a good meal, maybe you don't care at all about ambiance.

Here are the categories.

Food

This rating reflects how we judge the quality of food and the skill with which it is prepared. Restaurants lose Stars for commercial food service ingredients (with local produce, beef, and fish plentiful on Maui, we don't think there's much room for second-class ingredients), lousy recipes, unskilled prep work, and over- or under-cooked food.

Love

This rating reflects how much "love" we feel the kitchen cooks into the food. Some restaurants are serving inexpensive food, but it is so well made that you can "taste the love" in it. Other restaurants are serving very expensive food, but you can tell that the people who made it don't care if it's cold, tastes good, or looks good. Love is hard to describe in words, because – like the emotion love – it is primarily experiential, something you "know when you feel." Remember how you felt when someone who loved you fed you something that tasted good? The feeling of being cared for and thought about is what we're trying to capture in this rating. That feeling can come through in a restaurant meal when the people in the kitchen – and when it's a really loving restaurant, in the front of the house – genuinely care about how you, the diner, will enjoy their food. They pay attention, and they get it right.

Overall Score

This number reflects the five categories averaged out. If you start comparing restaurants to each other, you will see why our system works: there are Top restaurants in every price range. Keep in mind that the Top designation is given pri-

Ambiance

This rating tells you about the environment of the restaurant. Generally this rating will reflect how upscale it is. Beach shacks may score as low as One Star (although a clean beach shack would get Two Stars and one with a gorgeous view might get 5 Stars), while high end restaurants could get as many as Five Stars. Many restaurants with gorgeous views get to keep their Five Stars even if they have other flaws in décor, because we can't stop marveling at the scenery and think the primary impression is "Wow." Restaurants lose points for dirt, being stuffy in the heat, too windy, or in poor condition, among other reasons.

Service

This rating reflects how we feel about the service, from phoning for a reservation through saying good night on the way out the door. Restaurants lose Stars for indifferent or pretentious service (we think each is bad), slow service, and sloppiness or lack of courtesy.

OVERALL:
3.5
out of 5 stars

Value

This rating reflects how good a deal the restaurant represents when we take the previous ratings and the average cost of the restaurant into account. A beach shack that quickly serves up bone-sucking good $5 ribs might get 5 Stars for Value, while an expensive restaurant with pretentious service and so-so food might get 3 Stars for Value (or fewer). Accordingly, an expensive restaurant with stellar service and fabulous food and ambiance could easily get a value score of 5 Stars.

marily for food, which is why a restaurant with a lower number score could still be one of our favorites (for us, it's ultimately about what's on the plate).

What's most important to recognize is everything is relative. The real value in this scoring system appears only when you compare restaurants to one another.

As restaurant reviewers, we stand by our opinions, but we don't expect everyone to agree with us. As objective as we try to be, our personal preferences can't help but be part of our experience.

Like most restaurant critics, we feel that reviews should be seen as conversation starters, not as absolute pronouncements. Restaurants change, get better, get worse, and we as diners change, too. What was fabulous a few years ago may no longer be as exciting to us.

This is why we worked really hard to include a restaurant review feature on our blog, where readers can give us their Star ratings in each category, and we all get in on the conversation. Please go to www.MauiRestaurantsBlog.com, when you're ready to review and rate restaurants.

Cost

You may be surprised by how differently people perceive whether a restaurant is "Inexpensive," "Moderate" or "Expensive." After years of trying to educate people about our definitions, we've given up, and now just tell you how much entrées cost.

For every restaurant you will see one or more dollar signs. These measure only the **average cost of the entrées** on the regular menu, **not** the daily specials, the sides, the appetizers, the desserts, the drinks, tax, or tip. These dollar signs do not signify the cost of the entire meal, just the entrées that are on the menu.

$ The average entrée price is $10 or less

$$ The average entrée price is $10–$20

$$$ The average entrée price is $20–$35

$$$$ The average entrée price is $35 and up

Amenities

Certain restaurants have special features that we know you're looking for. These are usually covered in the review, but also through the use of symbols:

 The restaurant has a sunset view. Because the sun moves through the sky as the seasons change, the location of the sunset can vary. If you are set upon seeing a view of the sun setting over the water (not behind a nearby island) as you eat your dinner, make sure you check with the restaurant to see if this is possible at the time of year you are visiting.

 The restaurant is either right on the water or there is an unobstructed view (for example, a beach walk or street) of the water.

 The restaurant serves alcohol. The review usually indicates whether there is a full bar or just a beer and wine list.

 The restaurant is near Kahului Airport (OGG). (Readers want to know where to eat before or after catching a flight.)

 The restaurant offers a children's menu and/or is loved by children. If this symbol does not appear, assume that the restaurant is geared more for adults than children. This does not mean that your well-behaved child who is experienced at dining out is unwelcome, please check with the restaurant.

 Reservations are recommended. If this symbol does not appear, assume that generally, you do not need to make reservations. In some cases, the restaurant will not take reservations. During very popular travel times like Christmas week, Spring Break, and the summer months, nearly every restaurant will be very busy, so you might want to call for reservations, even if this symbol is not there.

 The restaurant has made some level of effort to include vegetarian options. There is only one all-vegetarian, full-service restaurant on Maui (Fresh Mint).

All others with this listing have either a separate vegetarian menu or are considered vegetarian-friendly because they are willing to modify their meals or methods for vegetarians or vegans. If this is a concern for you, please notify the restaurant ahead of time so they can note your preferences for the kitchen.

 American Express accepted

 Discover accepted

 MasterCard accepted

 Visa accepted

CASH The restaurant accepts cash only.

A Note about Accuracy:

Travel information of any kind is subject to change at any time, especially information about restaurants on Maui. Restaurants open and close virtually overnight here, and we cannot guarantee that any reviewed in this book will still be open when you arrive. We also cannot guarantee the hours, prices, or menu won't change between now and then. Just in the time that it took for us to finalize this edition – in the last two months – two restaurants closed and we had to take them out at the last minute.

All information is accurate at publication, but for the latest updates, we suggest you head to www.MauiRestaurantsBlog.com.

FYI: How We Review Restaurants

Every once in a while we get asked about our methods. They're not secret; in fact, they're what any good, ethical journalist would do in our shoes.

Every restaurant has been visited at least twice, and in most cases, three, or more, times before we write a review. We do this because every restaurant can have a stellar day, and every restaurant can have a terrible day. If a restaurant is inconsistent over time, it is hard for us to recommend them unreservedly, and we mention that in our review. We refresh our reviews on a regular basis, and certainly as close to publication time as possible.

We pay for every meal. (You'd be shocked at how unusual this is among food writers.) If the restaurant offers a discount to locals or has a special running, we take the discount (we're ethical, but not dumb). At times we have been comped a dessert or an appetizer by our server. Very rarely is this because we have been recognized as critics; usually it is because we are good customers. To this day, some of our very favorite restaurants clearly have no idea that we write about them. We wrote a feature story for a local magazine last year and one of the several restaurants we visited insisted on hosting us. Because we were writing for another publication and had visited that restaurant many times already, we accepted the meal, but excluded that experience from consideration when writing our review in *Top Maui Restaurants*.

We dine under cover when possible. We used to be able to be completely "under cover," and most restaurants on Maui still have no idea who we are. But Maui is a very small island, and there is less than two degrees of separation between us and most restaurateurs. When everyone goes to the same movie theaters, shops at the same Costco, and goes to the same beaches, it's easy to get to know others. The good restaurateurs Google themselves and find out that we're writing about Maui restaurants. And because we have so many other projects going in our business, some have put two and two together and do recognize us when we walk in the door (even after we use a different name for the reservation).

As we discovered this year when we were outed at a very expensive restaurant (see the *Merriman's* review), there is not too much a restaurant can do to improve their performance if they do recognize us. They can't send out for good food, instantly train their servers, or spontaneously clean the windows.

808 Deli *(American)*

This little deli tucked next to **Fred's Mexican Café** features sandwiches, paninis, hot dogs, salads, and breakfast sandwiches. Paninis are made to order (which you factor into the wait time) and we like them because they're not so cheesy that they sploosh all over your hand when you bite into the grilled sandwich. The hot dogs are kosher and come with a wide array of toppings. Sandwiches include deli meats, tuna salad and chicken salad. There is also locally-made gelato (not as good as **Ono Gelato,** but closer to the beach). A good choice to take to the beach or on a long drive is the $10 boxed lunch, which includes sandwich, chips, cookie (homemade), and a drink.

Address: 2511 S. Kihei Rd., Kihei, South Maui
Location: Across from Kamaole Beach Park II
Meals: Breakfast, Lunch
Hours: Daily 7am–5pm
Parking: Lot, Street
Phone: 808-879-1111
Website: www.808deli.net

A Saigon Café *(Vietnamese)*

A Saigon Café is one of our favorite restaurants, even though it features run-down decor, is difficult to find, and the waiters can't seem to stop telling cheesy jokes. We ignore the barely acceptable ambiance, and return our focus to the food, which is some of the freshest and most delicious on Maui.

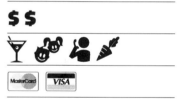

What's on each plate is well-prepared Vietnamese classics, including a superlative pho, deeply flavored with beef, yet still light on the tongue.

There's a deep commitment to fresh food here. We've never seen a wilted lettuce leaf. We've never bit into a piece of mint without that snap from a just-picked sprig. The fish is fresh and the shrimp are plump and pink. Some of our favorite dishes include the crispy, spicy Dungeness crab, and the chicken and shrimp braised in a brown sauce in the traditional clay pot. If you like fish, ask the waiter what they have that day for whole-fish preparations. They can wok-fry or steam fish — either style is delicious, so follow their guidance on which preparation to use on whichever fish they have that day. The wok-frying leaves a thin crust on the outside, which hides the tender chunks of flesh underneath and protects them from drying out. The steamed version with ginger and garlic shuts our other senses down so that picking the fish off the bones becomes a meditation.

We also love their "burritos." A stack of rice paper and a bowl of warm water are served first, followed, in short order, by a platter of raw shrimp, chicken, beef (or some combination), sliced cucumbers, pickled carrots, bean sprouts, fresh mint, and lettuce leaves. A fondue pot containing a light broth, pineapple slices, vegetables, and herbs bubbling over a carton of sterno appears next. The waiter will show you how to assemble your burrito, but essentially you drop your protein into the fondue to cook it while you dip your rice paper

continued on next page

A Saigon Café *(continued)*

into the warm water to soften it. Then you pile vegetables, sprouts, mint, rice noodles, and hoisin sauce onto the sticky paper, and once your meat or fish is cooked to your liking, you place it on the bed of fresh food and carefully wrap the thin, stretchy rice paper around the whole thing. We like to place our burrito in a lettuce leaf to make it easy to bite. Delicious and fun, we leave it to the authorities to decide if the sterno presents a fire hazard.

There's no sign on the outside of this restaurant, and the inside could use fresh paint, retiling, new booths … well, a big renovation. Some find the brusque, jokester waiters rude, but fans like us think of them as the "show" and laugh along with them. If your cell phone disappears during dinner, don't worry. It will reappear with the bill.

All jokes aside, the servers provide brisk, efficient service and are knowledgeable about the food they serve. The wine list is nothing special, but they have the usual Asian beers that complement the cuisine. We like their lemonade, which is sweet and made with both limes and lemons. We recommend skipping the Thai dishes and the desserts, (a five minute drive gets you to **Thailand Cuisine** for the first and **Bistro Casanova** for the second).

Reviewing restaurants can be grueling work. After days of eating so-so meals that have lightened our wallets, added paunch to our waistlines, and flattened our taste buds, we make a trip to **A Saigon Café** to soothe our palates and remind us of how wonderful food can be.

Address: 1792 Main St, Wailuku, Central Maui
Location: This is "under" the highway overpass in Wailuku. As you drive into Wailuku on Kaahumanu Ave., look for the neon shooting stars and the pink building to the right of the highway overpass as you drive over it. Turn right on Central Avenue at the KAOI Radio Station intersection. Take your first right onto Nani St. Drive to the first stop sign. Turn right onto Kaniela St, and the restaurant is on the left.
Meals: Lunch, Dinner
Features: Outdoor Seating, Take-out, Bar Seating
Hours: M–Sa 10am–9:30pm and Su 10am–8:30pm
Parking: Lot, Street
Phone: 808-243-9560

Alexander's Fish & Chips *(American)*

Alexander's used to be our favorite place for fish and chips, but new owners seem to have killed the magic. As you probably know, fish requires close attention to get perfect; it can go from tender and delicious to rubbery and tasteless in mere seconds. The fryer cooks let their minds wander a little too often, and we suspect the "secret" to the "secret batter" has been lost. Ribs are no longer what they once were. The outdoor location in Kihei used to be spotlessly clean for a beach fish shack, but that's no longer the case. The mall location has too much competition to hold its own. This is a loss for the Maui food scene. If you're in Kihei and hankering for fish and chips, check out **Coconut's Fish Café** or even **Eskimo Candy**. If you're in Kahului, take the ten minutes to go to Paia and visit **Paia Fish Market**.

OVERALL:
2.2
out of 5 stars

Alexander's Fish & Chips *(continued)*

Address: 1913 S. Kihei Rd., Kihei, South Maui
Location: Across from the Whale in Kalama Park
Meals: Lunch, Dinner
Hours: Daily 10:30am–8:30pm
Parking: Lot
Phone: 808-874-0788

Address: 275 W. Kaahumanu Ave. Kaahumanu Center, Kahului, Central Maui
Location: In the mall's food court on the second floor
Meals: Lunch, Dinner
Hours: M-Sa 10am–9pm; Su 10am–6pm
Parking: Lot
Phone: 808-877-5556

$

Alive & Well *(Organic/Vegan)*

 This small health food store has a good salad bar, sandwiches, sushi, bakery items, and of course, groceries. Good for vegetarians wandering Kahului or those looking for a break from rich food. Also, excellent advice on vitamins and nutrition in the well-stocked supplement section. Dennis and Mona, the owners, host a fascinating and informative weekly radio show called *Alive and Well* on 1110AM (check the website for current day and time, or call the store).

Address: 340 Hana Hwy., Kahului, Central Maui
Location: on Hana Highway near BJ's Furniture
Meals: Breakfast, Lunch, Dinner, Snacks & Treats
Hours: M-F 9am–7pm; Sa 9am–6pm; Su 10am–4pm
Parking: Lot
Phone: 808-877-4950
Website: www.aliveandwellinmaui.com

  OVERALL:
3.2
out of 5 stars

Aloha Deli *(American)*

They serve sandwiches, burgers, and the infamous Coney Island "Nathan's" hot dogs.

(We put that in quotes because if you've ever gone to Nathan's Hot Dogs in Coney Island in Brooklyn, especially after a rackety ride in the Cyclone roller coaster, you probably put quotation marks around the "Nathan's" hot dogs sold elsewhere, too. Especially those sold on Maui.)

You can sit inside at the few chairs or take out. Pretty good smoothies and decent breakfast wraps, but stay away from the bagels. This is an inexpensive option at the Maui Ocean Center and very near the Ma'alaea Harbor, where many tourist boats depart.

continued on next page

$

  OVERALL:
2.6
out of 5 stars

OVERALL:

3.4

out of 5 stars

Aloha Deli *(continued)*

Address: 300 Ma'alaea Rd., Ma'alaea, Central Maui
Location: Maui Ocean Center
Meals: Breakfast, Lunch
Hours: Daily 6am–5pm
Parking: Maui Ocean Center parking lot
Phone: 808-249-2708

Aloha Mixed Plate *(Local/Plate Lunch)*

Aloha Mixed Plate is a Maui institution for which we have mixed feelings. The turquoise-walled, tin-roofed restaurant lounges on the waterfront in Lahaina next to its better dressed big sister, ***Old Lahaina Lu'au.*** If you're looking for a sampling of lu'au food without the hefty ticket to the show, ***Aloha Mixed Plate*** at night might be a good bet for you, when you can "listen in" while eating nearly the same food.

If you go during daytime hours, you will see one of the best waterfront views on the island. The gentle lapping of the water, the boats coming and going, and the sunset view make for an idyllic scene. Unfortunately, despite pretty good Happy Hour specials, you can't consume alcohol on the seating area closest to the water. If you want to have a cocktail, you'll need to sit on the upper lanai where the bar is located.

The restaurant takes its name from the Hawaiian tradition of "plate lunch" or "mixed plate", which comes from the days when sugar plantations carpeted the islands and workers of several nationalities shared their food with each other on lunch breaks. Chinese workers brought noodle dishes like chow fun, Japanese brought their teriyaki and rice, and Filipinos brought adobo or slow-simmered pork. Koreans brought ribs, and the Hawaiians contributed their kalua pig. Plates were passed and each worker would take a portion from each dish, ending up with the "mixed plate" that perfectly reflects the melting pot that is Hawaii.

Rice and macaroni salad (two scoops rice, one scoop macaroni) always come on the plate to fill in the spaces. At ***Aloha Mixed Plate***, you can get all of the above dishes in many different plate lunch combinations, plus coconut prawns, Hawaiian classics like the salty lomi lomi salmon and the silky poi, sandwiches, and burgers, all at very reasonable prices.

The prices are key to this joint's attraction. There is nowhere else that serves fair-priced plate lunch *and* has an oceanfront location *and* offers tableside service *and* serves drinks (for $5.50, you might not mind that the mai tai features a lot of pineapple juice). So while we do not feel that the local food served at ***Aloha Mixed Plate*** is quite as good as, say, ***Da Kitchen's***, we think you get a good value given the outstanding location. Service is slow and not particularly attentive, but we are usually looking out at the ocean anyway, and the restaurant's laid-back vibe is definitely very Maui.

Address: 1285 Front St., Lahaina, West Maui
Location: Next to Old Lahaina Lu'au and across from Lahaina Cannery
        Mall
Meals: Lunch, Dinner
Hours: Daily 10:30am–10pm
Parking: Parking lot.
Phone: 808-661-3322
Website: www.alohamixedplate.com

Amigo's *(Mexican)*

They say the family that cooks together stays together. We don't know how much "together time" the brothers who own these busy Mexican taquerias get, but we're glad they're cooking for us. The three locations – one in a backwater North Kihei strip mall, one in the back of the Wharf Center in busy Lahaina, and one in Kahului across from McDonald's – all serve up good quality Mexican dishes spiced with plenty of what we call Love.

Let's talk about Love, just for a moment. When we say a dish has a high Love quotient, what we really mean is that the person (or persons) who prepared the dish was deliberate, thoughtful, and skillful.

We also mean the food tastes good.

We also mean … oh, *darn it!*

We mean lots of things. Love in food is one of those ineffable, indefinable "you know it when you taste it" things, like the difference between good art and great art, or where erotica crosses a line and becomes pornography.

Anyway ... we feel – or taste – the Love in the food at ***Amigo's***. These guys have love for their food, their families, their culture, and for their customers. You can tell by the way you're greeted when you walk in. The smiles are warm, the advice on what to order is sound, and they bring the chips (freshly fried) quickly. (You get your own salsa from the bar, which features a wide selection, all made in house.)

We like the chili verde, or green chili sauce served over pork. The sauce brings both full sweet flavors to the tongue and sneaking heat to the tonsils, just like it should. The pork is tender and flavorful. We also like the enchiladas, which feature fresh corn tortillas and generous fillings. You get a choice of red or green sauce for the top. We tend to get the red chili because we're often getting the green on another dish.

They have good burritos, flautas, chimichangas, and of course, tacos (flour or corn). We also like the chile relleno. A mild green pepper is stuffed with cheese, dipped in egg batter, and fried. The whole concoction is served with guacamole, pico de gallo, and ranchera sauce. The result is a crispy shell around a tender pepper that yields to the rather decadent cheese. The combination plates feature several house favorites and are a good value. They also come with the excellent spicy Spanish rice and delicious, perfectly seasoned beans, which taste like a family recipe (a good one).

continued on next page

Amigo's *(continued)*

This is very good, fast Mexican food for take out or dining in. If you choose to stay, they have bottled beer and generous margaritas to go with the daily specials.

Address: 41 E. Lipoa St., Kihei, South Maui
Location: Just off South Kihei Road in the Lipoa Center.
Meals: Breakfast, Lunch, Dinner
Hours: Daily 9am–9pm
Parking: Lot
Phone: 808-879-9952

Address: 333 Dairy Rd., Kahului, Central Maui
Location: Across from McDonald's on Dairy Road
Meals: Breakfast, Lunch, Dinner
Hours: M-Sa 8am–9pm; Su 9am–9pm
Parking: Lot
Phone: 808-872-9525

Address: 658 Front St., Wharf Cinema Center, Lahaina, West Maui
Location: In the back of the Wharf Cinema Center across from the Banyan tree.
Meals: Lunch, Dinner
Hours: Daily 9am – 10pm
Parking: Lot, Street
Phone: 808-661-0210

Anthony's Coffee Co. *(Coffeehouse)*

Anthony's is a Paia institution, and just about everyone stops in for a cup of joe at some point. *We* stop in for the decadent coffee ice cream-blended "Anthuccinos". Tasty breakfasts and pastries (muffins, donuts) make this a good stop before you drive to Hana (they open waaaaaay early). You can also get their sandwiches, bagels, etc. to go as a picnic lunch for your trip. There are only a few small tables and a few counter stools and benches, so if you feel like a leisurely breakfast, head elsewhere.

If you like the brew, they sell their roast (the beans are roasted in house by the owner), as well as plenty of kitschy/silly souvenir type home décor items.

Address: 90 Hana Hwy., Paia, North Shore
Location: On Hana Highway across from *Flatbread Pizza Company*
Meals: Breakfast, Lunch, Snacks & Treats
Hours: Daily 5:30am-6pm
Parking: Street
Phone: 808-579-8340
Website: www.anthonyscoffee.com

OVERALL:
3.2
out of 5 stars

$

Antonio's *(Italian)*

Spicy, homemade Sicilian classics plus many daily specials are served at moderate prices in this teensy strip mall storefront. Red-checked tablecloths drape the handful of tables, which can verge on cheesy until you realize the entire cook staff is Asian and it just seems bizarre. (That's OK, though. One of the best Italian restaurants in Honolulu has an entirely Asian staff, too – there are simply more Asians than Italians in Hawaii. A love of good cooking can be inherited from any culture.)

Everything is homemade, and we think the pink sauce – tomatoes, vodka, cream – is delicious. The stuffed pasta with gorgonzola, ricotta, and spinach touches our heart (and maybe puts a little extra strain on it, too). We also like the homemade sausages, tender and bursting with flavor. Daily specials usually feature a chicken, steak, and fresh fish. Many dishes are or can be made vegetarian-friendly.

Lunches are mainly burgers, sandwiches, and basic pasta dishes. The wine list is limited but reasonably priced, and the tiramisu is lovely. Worth a stop if you're on the South Side looking for a moderately priced homemade meal. The menu is more creative than *Aroma D'Italia,* but that means there's a higher risk of inconsistency, too. You may want to call ahead for reservations, as there aren't that many tables.

Address: 1215 S. Kihei Rd., Kihei, South Maui
Location: In the Long's Shopping Center
Meals: Lunch, Dinner
Hours: F–Su 11:30am–2pm; Daily 5pm–9pm
Parking: Lot
Phone: 808-875-8800

OVERALL:
3.2
out of 5 stars

Aroma D'Italia Ristorante *(Italian)*

We live a few minutes away from Foodland Plaza in Kihei, and we're glad we do, because this little shopping center also houses the police station (so you feel safe), *Cuatro* (one of our favorite new restaurants on Maui), *Sansei* (great Pacific Rim food, including sushi), and *Aroma D'Italia*, our favorite affordable Italian on the island.

The corner location means they can screen in their outdoor patio and put up fairy lights, which effectively masks the parking lot from view. If it doesn't work for you, sitting inside the restaurant is a comfortable choice. Some find the lacey curtains, plump-Italian-chef salt and pepper shakers, travel posters, and the *Eh, Paisano!* -style music a little too much, but we think they work. This is a family-owned restaurant with homemade food, and if it is dressed a little like your Italian-American grandma, that's OK. Grandma makes good pasta.

Actually, Chef Winder makes good pasta. He also makes good marinara sauce, good meatballs, good (but very cheesy) lasagna, good sausages, and many other Sicilian classics. His daily dishes are worth looking into, as well.

OVERALL:
4
out of 5 stars

Aroma D'Italia Ristorante *(continued)*

The fresh fish is usually perfectly and tastefully prepared, and the lamb and beef specials are similarly tasty. Ingredients come from local and organic (when possible) sources, and we haven't had anything on the menu that disappointed. Oh, except the garlic bread, which they still can't seem to keep from burning at the edges.

The wine selection changes regularly to flow with the seasons, and it's limited but very thoughtful. Good pairings for popular dishes are noted on the list itself, and there is plenty of guidance from the knowledgeable and enthusiastic staff. The Italian sodas are perfectly flavored, bouncy on the tongue and creamy going down. Italian and American beers are also available, as is a homemade tiramisu for dessert.

Service is very good, and many of the servers have been working here for a while, which is the sign of a good gig on Maui. This is a clean, affordable restaurant serving good food with a family style, and our favorite for a reasonable Italian dinner.

Address: 1881 S. Kihei Rd., Kihei, South Maui
Location: Kihei Town Center, Foodland's shopping center
Meals: Dinner
Hours: Daily 5pm-9pm
Parking: Lot
Phone: 808-879-0133
Website: www.aromaditaliamaui.com

OVERALL:

3

out of 5 stars

Ba-Le Sandwiches *(Vietnamese)*

One of the blessings of living in Hawaii is that the fast food options include Asian cuisines, which are generally lighter, fresher, and healthier than typical mainland fast food. Whether we go to **Ba-Le** for the *pho*, the noodle dishes, or one of their hearty sandwiches, our wallets stay about the same weight, and our bellies thank us.

Ba-Le means "Paris" in Vietnamese, and believe it or not, this company makes great French bread – for Hawaii. (It's very hard to develop a good crust here, the clean air means less bacteria, which in turn means soft crusts.) You'll often see **Ba-Le** bread and cakes sold in local grocery stores on Oahu, even at picky, upscale Whole Foods.

These eateries feature a wide variety of hot and cold sandwiches made with their rolls and stuffed thick with proteins and pickled vegetables. Most sandwiches cost under $7, which is a very good price on Maui. Meanwhile, the Vietnamese classics are also quite good. The pho is well seasoned and beefy, the noodles wide and slippery. The noodle dishes feature well seasoned grilled pork, lemongrass chicken, fried spring rolls, and many other fresh proteins that are prepared to order. The ever-present pickled daikon radish and carrots provide good balance with a little sour flavor.

This is not fine dining, but it is reliably good eats, and with several locations island wide, they're easy to find.

Address: 1221 Honoapiilani Highway, Lahaina, West Maui
Location: Food court, Lahaina Cannery Mall
Meals: Breakfast, Lunch, Dinner
Hours: Daily 10am–9pm
Parking: Lot
Phone: 808-661-5566
Website: www.ba-le.com

Address: 270 Dairy Rd., Kahului, Central Maui
Location: Food court, Maui Marketplace
Meals: Breakfast, Lunch, Dinner
Hours: M–Sa 9am–9pm; Su 9am–7pm
Parking: Lot
Phone: 808-877-2400

Address: 247 Pi'ikea Ave., Kihei, South Maui
Location: Pi'ilani Village Center, near Safeway
Meals: Lunch, Dinner
Hours: M–Sa 9am–9pm; Su 9am–8pm Parking: Lot
Phone: 808-875-6400

Address: 1824 Oihana St., Wailuku, Central Maui
Location: Close to the overpass.
Meals: Lunch, Dinner
Hours: Daily 9am–9pm
Parking: Lot
Phone: 808-249-8833

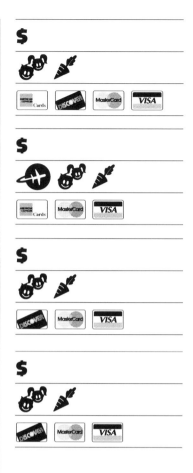

Bamboo Bar & Grill *(Thai / Sushi)*

Bamboo is a local hangout at the 505 Front Street shopping complex with a big bar, pool tables, and a menu that covers everything from Thai to Vietnamese to Sushi, and none of it well. Breakfast, lunch, dinner, and late night dining are available, along with noisy, blaring TV's. You can dine at the bar or choose sticky tables. Not recommended unless it's late and you want a bite, a drink, or some company and some noise.

OVERALL:
2.2
out of 5 stars

Address: 505 Front St., Lahaina, West Maui
Location: In the 505 Front Street shopping complex
Meals: Breakfast, Lunch, Dinner, Late-Night
Hours: M–Sa 8am–10pm; Su 8am–9pm
Parking: Street.
Phone: 808-667-4051

OVERALL:

2.6

out of 5 stars

Bangkok Cuisine *(Thai)*

This is a small restaurant with crowded tables and a forgettable atmosphere. The food is inconsistent in preparation, generally bland, and even at its best not nearly as good as *Thailand Cuisine* a few blocks away. Even so, *Bangkok* has its fans. We think it's partly *because* of the blandness – if you grow up in Hawaii, your palate generally doesn't experience the intense heat that Thai conjures. It could also be the large menu, and the "hands off" service that some folks here prefer.

Address: 395 Dairy Rd., Kahului, Central Maui
Location: Near FedEx-Kinko's on Dairy Road
Meals: Lunch, Dinner
Hours: Daily 11am–9:30pm
Parking: Lot
Phone: 808-893-0026
Website: www.bangkokcuisinemaui.com

OVERALL:

4.4

out of 5 stars

The Banyan Tree *(Pacific Rim)*

The Ritz Carlton Resort in Kapalua was completely closed for renovations in 2007. When it re-opened, the head chef at the signature restaurant, *The Banyan Tree*, was lured to Oahu with the promise of his own restaurant. While we loved Chef Jojo's work, we are very happy with his successor, Chef Ryan Urig, who has been with *The Banyan Tree* since 2003 and is enthusiastically serving the restaurant's goal of being not just an excellent resort restaurant, but an excellent restaurant.

Chef Ryan has stayed true to the ethic of high quality, local ingredients brought together in dishes that reflect global cuisines with Hawaiian touches. He has also recently introduced an amazing value for an otherwise very expensive restaurant – a three course dinner for $50 and a good wine list filled with $50 bottles of wine. The entrée choices – tenderloin, chicken, trout – are not the most decadent items on the menu, but they are excellent dishes in their own right.

(Note: this special menu may not be available when you visit, please inquire ahead of time.)

Let's focus on the food, shall we? We usually don't review the bread on Maui, since it nearly always ranges from just passable to disappointing (as we've said elsewhere, it's the clean air – no bacteria = no crust). However, the tradition at *The Banyan Tree* of serving the Egyptian spice mix *dukkah* with the sesame bread must be mentioned. The bread is soft and pleasant and a perfect transportation device for the *dukkah*. We often find ourselves finishing the entire loaf as we dip piece after piece into the dish of high quality olive oil, then into the crumbly mix of spices, nuts, and seeds. *Dukkah* means "coarsely ground" in Arabic, but we translate it as "heavenly."

Also heavenly is the delightfully playful, sweet starter which pairs Surfing Goat Dairy cheese with lavender-infused strawberries nestled in a macadamia nut tuille. If you want to compare it with another Surfing Goat appetizer, try the savory feta with roasted beets, red quinoa salad, and vinegar.

For entrees, we can't resist recommending the Snake River Kobe Beef Ribeye. The very finest restaurants on the island tend to order their meat (beef and pork) from Snake River Farms in Idaho, which raises Wagyu, the Japanese breed of cattle used for Kobe beef. This beef is buttery, delicately layered with flavor, and raises your consciousness about what red meat tastes like. While the ribeye may seem beyond the pale in terms of price, we have not once regretted ordering it.

If you've never had kampachi (yellowtail tuna) from Kona on the Big Island of Hawaii, this is the place to try it. The rich, firm fish stays succulent and wild-tasting because – although it is farmed for sustainability – it's raised in the open ocean. Please note, the preparations can change based on the seasons, but we particularly like the fresh, sparklingly-flavored strawberry mint "ratatouille" we experienced at our last seating.

As is true of most of the fine restaurants on Maui, vegetarians can often find things to eat on this menu that feel like "more than a salad."

Service is usually good, and some servers are great. However, we find it can be inconsistent. The view from the restaurant is gorgeous just before sunset, but we must warn – where the sun sets varies depending on the time of year, sometimes even behind a nearby island. If a sunset is an important component of your very expensive meal, may we suggest that you ask the hostess about this particular issue when you make your reservations.

Once the sun goes down, the Kapalua coast is absolutely dark and the restaurant's huge plate glass windows become mirror-like. We personally like this, because we are able to focus on the delicious food while looking forward to a post-meal stargazing session on the resort's quiet grounds.

Address: 1 Ritz-Carlton Drive, Kapalua, West Maui
Location: At the Ritz-Carlton Resort
Meals: Dinner
Hours: Tu-Sa 5:30pm-9:30pm
Parking: Valet, Lot
Phone: 808-669-6200
Website: www.ritzcarlton.com

Beach Bums Bar & Grill *(American / Barbecue)*

Hawaiian sports fans have to watch games during the day because we are six hours behind the mainland … so **Beach Bums Bar & Grill**, the open-air sports bar right on the harbor at Ma'alaea, gets noisy early. Plenty of fishermen and rowdy sports fans hang out here to relax, have a drink, and eat some serious smokehouse barbecue. There are also tables out on the rail (closer to the street and the harbor beyond) if you want to ignore the game and concentrate on enjoying your 'cue.

OVERALL:
3.4
out of 5 stars

continued on next page

Beach Bums Bar & Grill *(continued)*

Picture a fourteen inch white oval platter. Now picture half a chicken — dark mahogany colored from a spicy rub — laid on that platter. Lay down two long, large spareribs, also deep red brown. Add a bowl of creamed green beans with a generous sprinkling of crispy onions and a bowl of dark brown baked beans, and it looks like a meal Betty Flintstone would serve if she lived in Oklahoma.

That's where this barbecue is from (the owner worked a prize-winning barbecue joint for nearly a decade before bringing the goods to Maui), and it's top notch. The meat is smothered in a spice rub and smoked in the smoker behind the restaurant for as long as it takes (half a day if necessary) to render the flesh tender and pink inside, falling off the bone, with a deep smoky char on the outside.

To barbecue the chicken, they stand a whole chicken up "balanced" on a can of beer so the liquid infuses the meat from the inside. They rub the chicken with their spices and wrap it in bacon, and by the time it's smoked a few hours later, it is tender, juicy, and robust with flavor.

The pulled pork flakes well, has good smoke, and is dryer than we're used to here in Hawaii. But that's true in general with smokehouse barbecue, because meat and sauce are considered separate art forms in this tradition. Since the meat is smoked, it cannot be cooked in the sauce or basted with it. The sauce is added at the diner's discretion and judged on its own terms.

Unfortunately, our judgment of the house's two barbecue sauces is that neither is a winner. The "spicy" sauce overwhelms with mesquite flavor but is otherwise undistinguished. The "mild" sauce is super-sweet with a lot of guava. We don't like either on its own, but when combined with each other they make a decent sauce.

All the rubs, sauces, and sides are made in house, which we think is a good thing. The creamy green beans could use a little more salt, but otherwise are the perfect gift for Southerners with a hankering for the dish (James went to school in Charlottesville, Virginia, and this is his idea of comfort food). The beans have a good texture (not mealy, but tender), but are too sweet. The mustard on the table fixes them up. Other sides include fries (commercial-type shoestring style, but crispy), macaroni and cheese (average), and salads (nothing creative, but fresh). We do not recommend the non-barbecue sandwiches or dinner salads.

The service tends to be pretty happy-touristy. There is lots of "hey, how was your day?" and "where are you visiting from??" with toothy smiles. Generally you get your drinks fast and they check in regularly.

Our ratings are for the barbecue, not the rest of the menu.

Address: 300 Ma'alaea Rd., Ma'alaea, Central Maui
Location: Ma'alaea Harbor Shops on the lower level facing the harbor
Meals: Breakfast, Lunch, Dinner
Hours: Daily 8am–9pm
Parking: Maui Ocean Center parking lot
Phone: 808-243-2286

Betty's Beach Café *(American)*

OVERALL:
2.4
out of 5 stars

Another restaurant used to be in this plum location that overlooks the beach in the 505 Front Street shopping complex and has a gorgeous ocean/sunset view. So often the quality of food drops when the quality of the view rises, and Betty's is no exception: commercial ingredients, sloppily prepared, and expensive considering the quality. The menu ranges widely and features sandwiches, seafood, and everything in between. The u-shaped bar is kitschy-cool to look at, but we wish they would live up to the location and serve a mai tai that isn't filled with coca cola and pineapple juice. They've made a nice renovation to the restaurant, and we like the Hawaiiana décor, but they are definitely relying on what the previous owner in this location also relied upon: a full view of the **Feast at Lele** lu'au show. The view alone brings in locals and tourists, but this doesn't seem quite fair to the lu'au, which is working just as hard to serve fabulous food as ***Betty's*** … isn't.

Address: 505 Front Street, Lahaina, West Maui
Location: At the back of 505 Front Street complex, overlooking the Feast at Lele lu'au grounds
Meals: Breakfast, Lunch, Dinner
Hours: Daily 8am-10pm; Bar until 12am
Parking: Lot, Street
Phone: 808-662-0300
Website: www.bettysbeachcafe.com

Big Wave Café *(Pacific Rim/American)*

OVERALL:
3.2
out of 5 stars

At its best, ***Big Wave*** is a moderately priced, no-frills place with generous portions of good food. Lately we've noticed a shrinking in portions (a common response to the downturn in the economy here), but we still think the breakfast specials are worth $5.95 for eggs, pan-roasted potatoes, and toast on an island where that exact menu can fetch $14.95 easily. You can also get a half-order of respectable eggs benedict or a three stack of plain pancakes for the same $5.95. Hey, no substitutions, and fruit is extra – so if you want more, just order the larger plates for $8.95.

Though not on special, the macadamia nut pancakes stand proudly in a three stack, studded with macadamia nuts and bananas, and the waffles are light and fluffy.

Sometimes when we skip lunch, we go for the early bird special. It is two entrées for the price of one, every day from 5-6:30pm. When the mood in the kitchen is good, the prime rib is an excellent deal, as is the coconut shrimp entrée. (We've noticed that moods tend to translate to the quality of the food.)

The strip mall location does not inspire confidence, but the air conditioned restaurant is perfectly comfortable. If you choose outdoor seating you're usually protected from the direct sun, but the view of McDonald's always makes us cringe a little, especially at dinner (they claim a sunset view in their marketing, but the sun sets over the golden arches). To get to the

continued on next page

Big Wave Café *(continued)*

bathroom you have to walk to the mall's public restroom, which is less than luxurious. Kids like their options on the menu, however, and we're hoping that *Big Wave* cheers up and pulls through this tough time.

Address: 1215 S. Kihei Rd, Kihei, South Maui
Location: Long's Shopping Center
Meals: Breakfast, Lunch, Dinner
Hours: Daily 7:30am–9pm; bar open until 11pm
Parking: Lot
Phone: 808-891-8688
Website: www.bigwavecafe.com

$$$

Bistro Casanova *(Mediterranean / Italian)*

When a restaurant has heart and soul, you can always taste it in the food. But in the best restaurants, you can also experience it in the way the staff treats you, see it in the décor, and hear it in the "buzz" of the restaurant. Heart and soul is certainly evident at *Bistro Casanova*, the new restaurant that gutted *Manana Garage's* colorful-but-abandoned Kahului location and transformed it into a sleek, chic eatery. Sister restaurant to upcountry's institution, Casanova, *Bistro Casanova* reminds us that big-city style can blend in paradise.

Did Kahului ever need an alternative to the fast food, plate lunch, and yummy-but-hole-in-the-wall ethnic joints! The dark wood, hand-blown light fixtures, natural stone, and Mediterranean colors of *Bistro's* interior looks like a good restaurant *should* look. Meanwhile, the menu – bistro specialties from France, Italy, and Spain – has clearly inspired Chef David Gemberling.

We haven't been able to get a good steak in Central Maui in … well, in memory. But now we can, and do. The filets, rib-eyes, and t-bones are grilled perfectly and served with your choice of several sauces, from a creamy green peppercorn brandy concoction to a Marsala wine and wild mushroom, to a béarnaise (and more). Served with a side salad dressed with excellent vinaigrette, the steaks also come with *frites*.

Chef David is Belgian, and by tasting his *frites* (and his *crepes*, but more on those later) we'd guess that he has been frying potatoes since childhood. Is there anything better than a serving of crispy-on-the-outside-tender-on-the-inside hand-cut potatoes? His are seasoned with salt and a hint of – garlic? – and so good that we have taken the ones we couldn't eat home in a box. (If you're not a steak eater, you can order the *frites* as an appetizer.)

The rest of the menu features more darn good bistro food, including an excellent duck confit. A leg of duck is roasted and carefully laid on top of a bed of tender, flavorful, slightly smoky lentils. Garnished with sautéed potato disks and truffle oil (which does what truffle oil does best: taste deliciously rich), this was eaten in its entirety.

We've enjoyed the *linguine al funghi* – wild mushrooms in a creamy, garlicky pan sauce – and the calamari appetizer – lightly fried and served with a homemade tartar sauce. The paella, although everything was cooked to perfection (which is challenging in a dish combining everything from chicken to sausage to mussels and shrimp and clams and scallops), was way too salty (but to be fair, we had it within one week of their opening for dinner, and are willing to try it again once they get their sea legs).

One of our all-time favorite desserts is Crêpes Suzette, which is a crepe folded around a pool of creamy sauce laced with orange, lemon, and Grand Marnier. To do this well, the crepe must provide a slightly sweet, cushiony-but-firm texture for the zingy sauce to dance upon. There should be some crisp on the edges of the thin pancake, and the flavors should all come together to give you a little taste of pure sunshine. **Bistro Casanova,** *merci.*

On the lunch and tapas menus there are more crepes, including several savory choices. Sandwiches and panini round out the menu, as well as an extensive salad list and several pastas. If you're looking for a light meal before or after a movie, this is a good bet.

So far, we've had extremely friendly servers who tend to rush around with a slightly panicked look. Perhaps that's because they know there is too long a wait between courses and that we should have had our bread by now?

We like to give at least three months before we even step foot in a new place, let alone write a review. Here's why: the restaurant has not yet established a rhythm, and it's not really fair to judge them until they've had time to remember where the glasses are. However, we have had such good experiences at **Bistro Casanova** that we're breaking our own rule. We think these old hands – many of the staff have worked at **Casanova** for years – will get the service hustling. And if they don't, well, for shame. This menu and the cooking talent in the kitchen deserve it.

Bistro Casanova seems to have set the goal of being an upscale-but-casual, unstuffy-but-professional neighborhood place that welcomes visitors as well as locals for excellent food and great service. They plan on adding live entertainment as time goes on, and if they set excellence as their goal at every step, we predict that not only will they thrive in their new location, but that they will become one of the most successful restaurants on Maui.

Address: 33 Lono Ave, Kahului, HI 96732
Location: At Kaahumanu Street and Lono Ave., turn onto Lono and make first left into parking lot
Meals: Lunch, Dinner
Hours: M 11am - 2:30pm; Tu - Sa 11am till closing
Parking: Lot
Phone: 808-873-3650

Bistro Molokini *(American)*

The Grand Wailea is what we call the "Disneyland" resort. It's nearly cartoonish in its version of paradisiacal perfection: impossibly tall, skinny palms, golf-course-grass that is perfectly trimmed (but you never see them trimming it), and a water feature that loops throughout the grounds in roundabouts and

OVERALL:
3.6
out of 5 stars

continued on next page

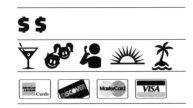

waterfalls, with hidden grotto hot tubs and swim up bars. A multi-million dollar art collection (Warhols, Picassos, nine luscious Botero sculptures, and much more) is on premises, and lush flowers spill from every corner.

Paradise like this doesn't come cheap, and if you choose to eat here, you are probably not the sort to flinch at $21 hamburgers. Good for you, because that $21 hamburger is one of our favorite items on the menu. Made with Kobe beef and enriched with truffle oil and roasted shallots, then topped with silky Gruyere cheese and super-crispy fried onions, it's a burger designed to please the Olympic Gods.

If you like fries with your beef, we love the intensely garlicky and flavorful crispy shoestrings. The onion rings, dredged in panko and flash-fried, are thick cuts of sweet Maui onion, crisp and crunchy. It's easy to make onion rings look this good, but few on Maui taste this delicious.

The menu also features lighter items like Waldorf salad, ahi wraps, fresh snapper on a bed of greens, and Maui onion soup. There are pizzas from their kiawe wood burning oven, and heartier meals like rib-eye steak and baby back ribs. The smoothies are made with ice cream and back home on the East Coast we would have just called them milkshakes. Have the bartender dowse them with an ounce (or two) of rum to really feel like you're in paradise.

The restaurant is located next to the pool, but elevated so you get the perfect view of the tops of umbrellas, the shoreline, and the ocean. On a blue-skied, clear day, there's no place we'd rather be on Maui.

So why isn't this a "Top" restaurant? Two reasons: 1. Prices are (overly) inflated by any standard; and 2. Insufferably slow service. We never go hungry to a Grand Wailea restaurant, because we will not see bread for at least twenty minutes (and sometimes longer). At this poolside restaurant, we just think they should hustle more – or hire more staff to cover the crowds.

Their neighbor, The Four Seasons, manages to provide impeccable service in their top dollar restaurants, and we're more likely to end up at *Ferraro's* for lunch than *Bistro Molokini* for that very reason.

If you are staying at the Grand and are on the beauty-and-bliss vibe the resort so amply provides – or want an excuse to tour the hotel's grounds – you'll likely enjoy your meals here.

Address: 3850 Wailea Alanui Dr., Wailea, South Maui
Location: Grand Wailea Resort
Meals: Lunch, Dinner
Hours: Daily 11am–9pm
Parking: Valet
Phone: 808-875-1234
Website: www.grandwailea.com

BJ's Chicago Pizzeria *(American)*

Chicago deep dish pizza is a beast all its own. Designed to weigh you down as you walk the cold streets of the Windy City, it comes packed into a round, straight-sided cast-iron pan lined with a crispy crust where it meets the metal, and slightly doughy where it meets the first layer of cheese. Above the cheese, the toppings are piled (and when your pizza is two inches deep, you can hold a lot of toppings), then red sauce is ladled over everything. In the end, it's got the heft of a casserole and you probably need a knife and fork to eat it. It goes well with both beer and big bold wine.

It's less obvious to have a tropical cocktail with your deep dish, but it's possible at **BJ's Chicago Pizzeria.** The fabulous sunset view of Lahaina Harbor from their second floor location is inspiring, and the live music every night helps us kick back and remember we're in the tropics despite the heavy food.

Our favorite pizza is "BJ's Favorite." It's a kitchen sink pizza loaded with homemade meatballs, pepperoni, Italian sausage, mushrooms, green peppers, black olives, and sweet onions. The red sauce is good – it's not too spicy, and doesn't compete with the many ingredients – and the crust has that little bit of crunch we like.

We also like the Buffalo wings. The huge platter piled with brilliantly orange thighs, wings, and drumsticks comes with fire on the chicken and cool blue cheese dressing on the side. There aren't many places to get Buffalo wings on Maui, so we sometimes find ourselves indulging in East Coast nostalgia while sipping a cool, light Maui Brewing Company Bikini Blonde. Service is proficient once you get a seat, but lines can form on busy nights.

Address: 730 Front St., Lahaina, West Maui
Location: Across from the sea wall, near the intersection with Dickinson.
Meals: Lunch, Dinner
Hours: Daily 11am–10pm
Parking: Street
Phone: 808-661-0700

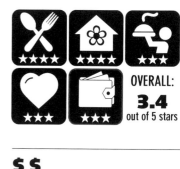

OVERALL:
3.4
out of 5 stars

Blue Moon *(American)*

Blue Moon is a local diner with lots of natural light from the plate glass windows. Big tables crowded close together create a cafeteria effect, especially with the big takeout/deli counters near the back. They feature plate lunch, seafood, steaks, burgers, and a pretty good breakfast, but the food doesn't make us jump up and down. If you're in Kihei and looking for something relatively inexpensive and off the beach road, this is a decent option.

Address: 362 Huku Lii Pl., Kihei, South Maui
Location: Near the Tesoro station off the Pi'ilani Highway
Meals: Breakfast, Lunch, Dinner
Hours: M-Sa 7:30am–8pm; Su 7:30am–3pm
Parking: Lot
Phone: 808-874-8600

OVERALL:
2.8
out of 5 stars

OVERALL:
3.4
out of 5 stars

$ $

Brigit & Bernard's Garden Café *(German)*

This cozy little restaurant is tucked away in the industrial zone amongst fishmongers, body shops, and window glass dealers. It is very popular with locals for the focus on lunch and a few evening meals. The food might be worth poking around for if you're passing through central Maui during lunchtime or in the evening. The little "biergarten" is fenced in and surrounded by fairy lights, so it feels like a European oasis in the middle of industrial gothic.

Many German dishes like Wiener schnitzel are featured, and we especially like the Jaeger schnitzel. You can get very good bratwurst and bockwurst, although some of our Euro-friends wish they came as sandwiches in addition to plated meals.

Potatoes au gratin are cheesy and layered in thin, but hearty tasting slices. There are a lot of daily specials. If it's not on the menu, ask for the pork loin in their hearty port wine sauce. The rack of lamb is another decent choice. Skip the desserts, but indulge in the excellent beer selection. Reservations recommended only because it's such a small place.

Address: 335 Hoohana St., Kahului, Central Maui
Location: On the bend of the street, just off Alamaha.
Meals: Lunch, Dinner
Hours: Daily 11am-2:30pm & 5pm-9pm
Parking: Lot
Phone: 808-877-6000

OVERALL:
3.8
out of 5 stars

$ $

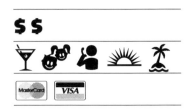

Bubba Gump Shrimp Co. *(American)*

Our cynical, snobby past selves (the ones we left behind – kind of – when we moved to Maui years ago) would have shuddered to think we would recommend a chain restaurant that is **designed** to be a tourist trap … but we can't help ourselves.

If you like shrimp, don't mind paying prices that are nudged just a little higher than they should be, and if you won't hate yourself in the morning for contributing to their shameless commercialism (or being tempted to buy a t-shirt), **Bubba Gump's** is worth checking out.

First of all, it's on one of the best pieces of Front Street real estate: directly on the water with an outrageous view of the harbor, Lanai, and sunset. We like to sit on the rail, and we wear clothes we don't care about too much – because we get sprayed nearly every time.

Every shrimp dish we can remember ever eating is on the menu, as well as OK steaks, pretty good fish dishes, and fried chicken that we like. But we usually order the shrimp sampler: a wired rack with arms holding paper cones filled with several different preparations … this and the strawberry lemonade makes us as happy as *Forest Gump* when he runs without his braces. The overflowing bucket of peel-and-eat shrimp inspires one friend to spend lazy Sunday afternoons here with her sweetie.

If you haven't ever been to this theme restaurant paying homage to the 1994 classic Tom Hanks movie Forrest Gump, the incredible location and the friendly, efficient servers that keep the place running may be worth your stop. Everywhere you look there are details that tie into the movie; our favorite being the license plate-sized signs on each table. When you sit down, the green sign reads "Run, Forrest, Run!" When you're ready to order, or if you want to get your server's attention, flip to the red sign that reads "Stop, Forrest, Stop!" This system gets their attention so quickly that we sometimes muse it ought to be mandatory for all Maui restaurants.

The portions are the same whether you are there for lunch or dinner, and we like to eat mid-afternoon to avoid the crowds. We also like that our friends with kids can take their little ones here and totally relax, knowing theirs will not be the only table emitting spontaneous giggles and shrieks.

Address: 889 Front St., Lahaina, West Maui
Location: Right on the seawall on Front Street
Meals: Lunch, Dinner
Hours: Daily 10:30am-12am
Parking: Street
Phone: 808-661-3111
Website: www.bubbagump.com

Buzz's Wharf *(American/Pacific Rim)*

Buzz's is a Maui landmark, but we're feeling like they're phoning it in lately. Located on the wharf in Ma'alaea, their great views – especially during whale season – are consistent, and they're still using the same good ingredients, but the Love factor is slipping.

The prawns they serve are no longer exclusive to their restaurant and we've had New Caledonia prawns at several other places that are just as good. Their Tahitian preparation, which is a baked dish using vermouth, dill, and parmesan cheese, has not been duplicated (that we've seen), and is still our favorite. The sweet (lobster-like), exceptionally tender shrimp are perfectly set off by the slightly puckery sauce. Only five come on a plate, but if we ate more than that, we'd expire of a heart attack on the spot.

Fish dishes are generally OK, but the prices are no longer just high; now they seem downright expensive (loss of Love does this to a place). If you're in Ma'alaea and have your heart set on fish, this is the place to go if the ***Ma'alaea Grill*** doesn't open back up (plans as of publication were sketchy).

Address: 159 Ma'alaea Boat Harbor Rd., Ma'alaea, Central Maui
Location: Ma'alaea Harbor Village, down on the water
Meals: Lunch, Dinner, Pupus
Hours: Daily 11am-9pm
Parking: Lot
Phone: 808-244-5426
Website: www.buzzswharf.com

OVERALL:
3.4
out of 5 stars

$ $ $

OVERALL:
3.4
out of 5 stars

$

Café Des Amis (Mediterranean / Indian)

This little bohemian Pa'ia café has expanded well beyond their ten indoor tables to the formerly empty lot next door, making it into a fairy lit garden café. The addition of the outdoor seating area, enclosed by a tall wooden fence, makes it much easier to get a table than it used to be, which is lovely. We're not sure that they've added staff to accommodate the bigger space ... but the point of *Café Des Amis* has never been quick service, and you should avoid eating here if a leisurely pace drives you crazy or if you're blood sugar is tanking.

What you should come for are the reasonably priced crepes, curries, and smoothies made from healthy, fresh ingredients. This menu is not extensive, but it's not meant to be.

We like the super simple cilantro crepe with rice, and also the more hearty fresh tuna with potatoes. The lentil tomato crepe is basically an Indian dal wrapped up in a French crepe, and it's lovely. When we order the brie and apple crepe, we ask them to leave out the avocado, which turns the creamy texture of the brie into mushy ick in our mouths. All savory crepes come with a small green salad (undistinguished, but fresh). The breakfast crepes with eggs are served all day long and make a good, light dinner. For dessert, try the Maui cane sugar crepe with lime juice: crispy, tart, sweet.

Curries are good, and come in a few mild flavors. We ask them to take the heat up a notch or two, and the shrimp is our favorite. Each curry is served in a big bowl – nearly a serving bowl – with rice ladled next to the curry. If you like wraps and don't so much want rice, the curry wraps come with vegetables. The fruit smoothies are very fresh and creamy, and the baristas know what they're doing at the espresso machine.

This is a good place to stop when you're in the mood for something light but satisfying, and a great place to see Paia town neighbors hanging out with each other. The mismatched chairs (some of which are positively rickety) and possibility of being showered upon (Paia gets some misty rain most afternoons) just reinforce the gentle non-conformist mystique of eating here. If you're sick of resort dining, *Café Des Amis* – with her fresh-from-windsurfing-servers – likely has the cure.

Address: 42 Baldwin Ave., Paia, North Shore
Location: Across from Mana Foods
Meals: Breakfast, Lunch, Dinner, Snacks & Treats
Hours: Daily 8:30am-8:30pm
Parking: Street
Phone: 808-579-6323

Café @ La Plage (American)

This little panini shop makes perfectly pleasant sandwiches for breakfast and lunch with fresh ingredients. We like that even though you order at the counter and they bring the food, they actually check back with you to see if you have everything you need. For essentially a takeout/internet place, that's a nice touch. Everything is made with care and attention, and the espresso drinks are very good. We skip the shave ice and the bagels, though. This is a good place for breakfast before the beach, and an excellent choice for a beach lunch or a beach break.

Address: 2395 S. Kihei Rd., Kihei, South Maui
Location: In Dolphin Plaza across from Kamaole Beach Park I
Meals: Breakfast, Lunch, Snacks & Treats
Hours: M-Sa 6:30am - 5pm; Su 6:30am-3pm
Parking: Lot
Phone: 808-875-7668

OVERALL:
3.6
out of 5 stars

Café Kapalua (American)

This delightfully simple American menu at decent prices (for Kapalua) is a welcome addition to the resort's dining options. Ingredients are sourced as locally as possible – in their own Kapalua Farms, for example – and the flavors are clear and fresh. We miss **Vino**, which used to be here, but if the wide open restaurant with beautiful, green golf course views can't support a dinner restaurant, this is a good use of the space. Try the breakfast burritos, and we also like the special espresso drinks.

Address: 2000 Village Rd., Kapalua, West Maui
Location: in the Kapalua Adventure Center
Meals: Breakfast, Lunch
Hours: Daily 7am - 3pm
Parking: Lot
Phone: 808-665-4386
Website: www.kapalua.com

OVERALL:
3.6
out of 5 stars

Café Mambo and Picnics (Mediterranean)

After years of sampling *Café Mambo's* offerings, there are a few specific reasons we come to this funky, noisy, casual eatery.

1. The Crispy Duck Fajitas
2. The Happy Hour Burger and Beer Special
3. The Smoothies

We'll start with the crispy duck, which is rendered in its own fat and sautéed with a sweet sauce. The result is a luxurious concoction of caramel colored, tender shredded meat that is crispy and succulent, salty and sweet.

OVERALL:
3.8
out of 5 stars

continued on next page

Café Mambo and Picnics *(continued)*

Whether you eat it on top of a bed of fresh greens (the salad), on a bun (the burger), or rolled in a flour tortilla with homemade salsa, guacamole, black beans and feta cheese (the fajita) is entirely up to you. All three preparations work for us, depending upon how hungry we are. The fajitas for two are large enough for four, while the single serving is large enough for two if you're getting other items.

The crispy duck is worth our 25 minute trip to Paia.

A designated driver may be necessary if you're going to visit during Happy Hour. The special price – at publication $3 – on some of the most popular tropical cocktails and favorite beers – brings in lots of locals, as does the sensibly priced Burger and Beer special. Currently, for $9.95 you get a Maui Cattle Company burger with fries (or a green salad), and a beer. That is a very good deal for Maui, but we warn you now that if you like your burger less-than-well-done, please let them know that. Otherwise it's left on the grill too long and becomes a candidate for hockey practice.

If you're in the mood for something a little lighter, the hummus platter can be the perfect starter for a large group or an entire meal for one or two. The bright yellow hummus (cumin) is positively silky in texture, and when dipped with a warm pita triangle, mounds perfectly on the bread with a nice little tail hanging off. No mealy texture – our personal pet peeve – just creamy, earthy garbanzo flavors highlighted with warm, bright spicy tones. While you will see many other things on the menu, we recommend sticking to the appetizers, the fajitas, and the sandwiches. Although the paella is an honest effort, it is beyond this kitchen, and several of the other more expensive items are similarly too ambitious. Although we've focused on the duck, we must say that many vegetarian and vegan friends consider this the most vegan-friendly restaurant on the island, because many items can easily be slightly modified to remove the offending meat and dairy without losing flavor or style.

The smoothies are made with ice cream, so … well, isn't that enough?

Breakfasts are good and include waffles, pancakes, omelets (a little over-done), hearty egg platters, and good burritos. Many of our readers recommend their boxed lunch for a road trip to Hana. The baristas work with Illy coffee, which is a good, moderately priced brand (if you're thinking everyone should be serving Kona coffee by default, check your wallet and see whether you really want to spend $6 on every cup you buy).

There are free screenings of classic and cult classic films at Café Mambo on certain nights (call for a schedule). No food, but drinks and desserts are available. If you want to have dinner and a movie, the kitchen closes at 9pm, right before the movie begins.

PS: Did we mention the crispy duck?

Address: 30 Baldwin Ave., Paia, North Shore
Location: Across from Mana Foods
Meals: Lunch, Dinner
Hours: Daily 8am–9pm
Parking: Street
Phone: 808-579-8021

Café Marc Aurel (American)

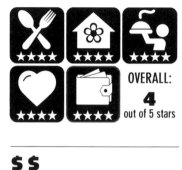

OVERALL:
4
out of 5 stars

$ $

The crowd at **Café Marc Aurel** varies wildly depending upon what's happening on the tiny "stage" at the back of the room. We've seen woo-woo New Agers chanting sanskrit, soul singers belting out the blues to stomps and whistles, belly dancers, hopeful, crooning singer songwriters, and many other large and small acts. Everyone is welcome, and the place is often packed when the music is hot (or mellow).

The dark paneling, brick walls, and wrought iron café tables and chairs are decidedly un-Maui, but the tattooed waitresses and laid back vibe is. The art on the walls is all made by locals, and usually priced to sell. We come here when we're in the mood to remember bohemian joints in our birth cities.

The *hui* – the Hawaiian word for "community" – which owns **Café Marc Aurel** has kept its focus through a rather tumultuous transition. Marc Aurel, the founder, had to leave Maui a couple of years ago, quite suddenly, leaving the waitresses to keep the place going, sans the eponymous owner. They made it work by buying in to the business and continuing on with barely a hitch – and Marc Aurel supervises from afar and continues to stop in on his yearly trips.

If you visit during the day, we'd stick to coffee or espresso, which is good, especially given the dearth of excellent espresso nearby, and skip the pastries. After 4pm this becomes an excellent place for *pau hana* – which translates as end of workday drinks but can include a light meal, too.

The wine list remains very good, and the servers are knowledgeable and well worth consulting. To go with your bottle or flight, we recommend the simple but luxurious cheese and meat platter. We love looking at an actual cheese platter and picking our favorite *fromages*.

If you're looking for something heartier, we recommend the sandwiches, especially the Margerit, which is a mozzarella, tomato and basil sandwich on a crusty baguette. The tacos featuring hummus are also excellent. We'd skip the pizzas and the salads, but we wouldn't skip the coup d'etat dessert, which presents three scoops of vanilla ice cream drizzled with chocolate syrup and then submerged in espresso and crowned with whipped cream. On an island where truly good desserts are hard to find, this simple consortium is both decadent and delicious.

Café Marc Aurel is a little bohemian oasis in the heart of our county seat, and is doing good work. You can get their performance schedule at their website, and if you want to participate in an Open Mic Night make sure to get there early to sign up – the list fills fast.

Address: 28 N. Market St., Wailuku, HI 96793
Location: On the same block as the Iao Theater
Meals: Breakfast, Lunch, Dinner
Hours: M–Sa 7am–9pm
Parking: Street, Lot
Phone: 808-244-0852
Website: www.cafemarcaurel.com

OVERALL:

4

out of 5 stars

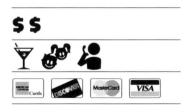

Café O'Lei *(Pacific Rim / American)*

Café O'Lei in Kihei is located in one of the most unlucky restaurant locations on the island, where several previous places opened and then mysteriously closed in rapid succession. It could have just been the steep flights of stairs to the second floor of Rainbow Mall, but some speculated that the place was haunted. Apparently, it's not, because *Café O'Lei* is packed even during this tough tourist slump. Chef Owners Dana and Michael Pastula have a magic formula that they apply to every restaurant: consistently good food is delivered at reasonable prices by hustling servers.

For starters, we recommend the baked Maui onion soup. Maui onions are exceptionally sweet, and we find that most Maui restaurateurs have put little time into thinking through how to keep the soup from becoming cloying and sugary. A liberal use of fresh thyme and brandy go a long way toward darkening and deepening the flavor. Good gruyere cheese tops the soup and then a puffed pastry crust forms a ballooning, crackly roof. The presentation is dramatic, the soup earthy, slightly sweet, and gratifying.

Another good starter is the Manoa lettuce wraps. The chef combines chicken with water chestnuts, ginger, and hoisin sauce, and you spoon the mix into tender, fresh lettuce leaves and eat them like a burrito. With the coming of *Flatbread Pizza Company*, we no longer go for the flatbreads at *Café O'Lei*, although they do have a good pizza oven (inherited from a former unlucky restaurant). The tower appetizer consists of three plates stacked with coconut shrimp (usually OK, sometimes a little greasy), tempura fried ahi rolls (a little much with the coconut shrimp) and lightly battered calamari rings.

One of our absolute favorite dishes is the braised shortrib. The cut isn't always the best, but the preparation makes up for it. The rib meat falls off the bone, cloaked in a deeply flavored ginger-shoyu glaze with sesame oil to smooth the flavors and siracha (red chili paste) to hit the top notes and singe the back of the throat with some heat. It comes draped over steamed rice, but we usually get the mashed potatoes instead. The chefs aren't afraid of butter, and neither are we.

Other good choices include a seared ahi in a spicy ginger butter sauce and light wasabi aioli, as well as jumbo shrimp laced with garlic butter sauce, basil pesto, and chopped macadamia nuts. Both of these entrees are under $20. Nightly specials usually feature a fresh fish, and are reliable in their preparation.

If your table is craving sushi, it's pretty good. You can sit at the bar, and there are usually sushi specials. Desserts are focused on delivering more quantity than quality, so we usually skip them. The exception to this is when they have the banana lumpia concoction, which they do very well. The wine list is not particularly impressive, but they have a good beer selection and some pretty strong martinis.

If you can't visit for dinner, lunch is a very good value, and you'll be sitting in a packed restaurant amongst a gaggle of locals (realtors love this place). All sandwiches are under $10 and come with salads, and the fish dishes come with rice and salad. The tempura fish and chips lunch is a particular favorite. The fish is mahi-mahi battered in a light, crispy tempura and deep fried to a golden glow. Another good choice is the blackened mahi-mahi (Cajun-style) with papaya salsa. This item shows up at dinner, too, but it's only $9 at lunch.

When the tourist economy is roaring, lines can form, so we recommend reservations or calling ahead. The Kihei location is our fail-safe restaurant to take anyone who is not used to spending a lot on dinner out. The up-scale casual ambiance, fair prices, generous portions, and abundance of tasty dishes make this place a safe bet for people making this their "nice night out" or those who want a break from the resort prices.

The Wailuku location has more limited hours, but a similar menu. The Dunes at Maui Lani location can handle special events, and is the home of the restaurant's catering service.

Address: 2439 S. Kihei Rd., Kihei, South Maui
Location: Turn into the Rainbow Mall – which has a great many rainbow flags outside of it – and walk to the front of the building and climb the stairs.
Meals: Lunch, Dinner
Hours: Tu-Su 10:30am-3:30pm & 4:30-9:30pm; Sushi bar until 9:30pm
Parking: Lot
Phone: 808-891-1368
Website: www.cafeoleirestaurants.com

Address: 62 N. Market St., Wailuku, Central Maui
Location: Next to the Iao Theater
Meals: Lunch, Dinner
Hours: M-F 10:30am- 3pm; Th-Sa 5pm- 8pm
Parking: Street
Phone: 808-986-0044
Website: www.cafeoleirestaurants.com

Address 1333 Maui Lani Parkway, Kahului, Central Maui
Location: At the Dunes at Maui Lani golf course
Meals: Lunch, Dinner
Hours: Tu-Su 7:30am- 7:30pm; M 7:30am- 4pm
Parking: Lot
Phone: 808-877-0073
Website: www.dunesatmauilani.com

Cane and Taro *(Pacific Rim / Sushi)*

Cane and Taro is D.K. Kodama's new restaurant in a newly renovated, prime Ka'anapali location (the dumpy *Rusty Harpoon* used to be here). His success with *Sansei, Vino* (closed now) and his Oahu restaurants *The Counter* and *d.k. Steakhouse* make us think that as this restaurant gets its act together it will be as reliably delicious.

continued on next page

Cane and Taro *(continued)*

At press time, however, his chefs haven't mastered all of his dishes yet, with the exception of his sushi. The service is very good (as it usually is in his restaurants). Drinks are delicious, too.

The menu combines the favorite items from all three of his current restaurants, and it reads like someone is throwing wild 95-mile-per-hour pitches at you – we keep thinking "What? How can they do great meatloaf *and* pull off the kampachi sashimi in ponzu sauce?"

Since the restaurant has only been open a month at this point, we are only including this review as a courtesy to you – not as a well-formed opinion (this is also why we have not given it any star ratings). We like to give a restaurant several months to sink or swim financially and work out the kinks before we even eat there, but D.K. Kodama is an important Hawaii chef, and we felt you should know that he has new digs. As this restaurant gets its legs we'll be talking about it on www.MauiRestaurantsBlog.com.

Address: 2435 Ka'anapali Pkwy, Ka'anapali, West Maui
Location: In the old **Rusty Harpoon** location, right above **Hula Grill**
Meals: Breakfast, Lunch, Dinner
Hours: Daily 8am-4:30pm & 5pm-10pm
Parking: Lot
Phone: 808-662-0668

Capische? *(Italian)*

OVERALL:
4.6
out of 5 stars

Capische? is one of a handful of Maui restaurants that could compete in the fiercely competitive markets of San Francisco, New York, Chicago, or D.C., and we deeply appreciate them for running their business as if every meal – and every diner – counts.

[This is a tourist area, so many restaurants get a lot of "one-night stands" – diners who will only visit once – and this can cause restaurateurs to lose their motivation to give every night their all. In contrast, in markets where there is a strong local foodie culture and local diners make up the regular customer base, restaurateurs cannot afford to offer badly constructed recipes, sloppy execution, glacial service, or inferior ingredients. They must be consistently good to survive, and in some markets, consistently great.]

Capische? remains our favorite place on Maui for a romantic, no-holds-barred (read: very expensive and very special) dinner.

The hotel itself has a spectacular water feature that welcomes you with a koi pond at the entrance and then falls to flow underneath the hotel (Yes! Underneath!) into pools farther down the property. Unless you have already dined here and are somehow bored with the gemlike setting, we highly recommend making your reservation for just before sunset so that you can really appreciate the ambiance and read your menu (the restaurant is very dim after dark).

Every table is outside, and most are on the rail overlooking the garden, the resort's villas, and finally, the lush volcano slope rolling down to the Pacific and the islands of Kaho'olawe, Molokini, and Lana'i. For a completely different feel, ask for a seat in the fragrant herb garden. And for the most intimate, exclusive experience, ask for reservations in their private dining room, **Il Teatro** (more about that in a minute).

The menu is creative and fresh Northern Italian with some French influences. While there are several standards that consistently please, it changes with the seasons and with the availability of local produce. Fresh ingredients prepared perfectly are the key to the menu's outrageous success, which is why Chef Owner Brian Etheredge cultivates a vegetable garden at his home in addition to his herb garden at the restaurant, and brings in much of his produce from Hana Fresh in Hana and Michael McCoy, a farmer in Kula. Local fishermen know to stop by with that morning's catch.

There is as much care and attention put into the appetizers at **Capische?** as into the entrees, and we often end up ordering more than one. The kitchen is happy to split appetizers on two plates and bring them as separate courses. We have several favorites worth mentioning to you.

The Caesar salad: a head of Romaine lettuce is quartered and left undefended before the onslaught of shaved parmesan cheese and homemade croutons. This is drizzled with a garlicky, creamy sauce with a shot of balsamic vinegar to pucker it up. The garlic croutons are lightly dusted with parmesan cheese and are actually crunchy – not stale – which tells us that they are made very recently, as bread goes stale quickly in Maui's climate.

Another favorite is the beef carpaccio braciola. Beef tartare is sliced thin, pounded thinner, and used to coat the bottom of a platter. An herb and greens salad is tossed thoroughly with tangy mustard vinaigrette and mounded with diced onions and fried capers (heavenly salty-crunchy capers) on top of the beef. Taken together the flavors dance a tango on your tongue – spicy and sultry, warm with that ineffable ingredient we call Love.

NB: The first time Molly ate this (in a rolled version, which you might request) she blushed and couldn't speak for several minutes. When she did, she said, "Either the chef is deeply in love with me, or he is deeply in love with this dish." It was like a scene from *Like Water for Chocolate.*

If the ahi bruschetta calls to you, answer. Perfectly seared ahi reclines on a slice of garlic toast while olives, capers, and a divine truffle aioli tumble onto the plate.

It's hard to choose a favorite item, but we must also recommend the kabocha pumpkin gnocchi. Bathed in lavender brown butter, it's perfectly salty-seared, and literally – we hate using such trite language, but it's the best way to say it – melts in your mouth. (We promise to not use that phrase again in this book.)

The caprese salad tastes so fresh we wonder if the basil and tomato were literally picked that hour, and the quail saltimbocca – wrapped in applewood bacon and laced with brown butter sauce – inspires one to bad table manners.

Although other restaurants focus almost exclusively on fish, we nearly always end up ordering at least one fish entrée at **Capische?** because here the

continued on next page

Capische? *(continued)*

exquisite Hawaiian species are deeply respected. We've never had a piece of fish anything other than perfectly cooked. To this day, the best fish of our life was an opakapaka (pink snapper) poached in olive oil barely floating in a pool of parsley pesto, topped with a salad of micro greens. The olive oil carefully sealed off the tender flesh and let it blossom into full flavor. The parsley pesto – a beautiful bright emerald – was fresh, light, and the perfect complement to the snapper. Chef Brian and Chris Kulis, his *sous chef*, know how to let the fish's natural flavors shine without mucking it up with too much other … *stuff*.

If you're in the mood for meat, the choices usually include Snake River Farms Wagyu (American Kobe) beef and Kurobuta (the Kobe beef of pig) pork. While not local, it is the best, and we never regret ordering it from this kitchen.

We are not as big a fan of the pastas as some of our readers are, but that is more a function of how much else there is to enjoy, rather than a reflection of the pastas themselves. A perennial favorite is the signature cioppino of Kona lobster tail, shrimp, scallop, clams, fish, and king crab legs simmered in a savory, rich tomato saffron broth and ladled over *al dente* capellini pasta.

The servers are knowledgeable and many of them spend some time in the kitchen themselves, so do not be afraid to ask their opinion about the menu. Some will offer it whether solicited or not – we're not the only ones who have encountered service that suddenly veers away from relaxed and friendly to slightly panicked – but regardless of individual mannerisms, they are well trained in the menu and can be relied upon for advice. They also hustle, and this is still one of the few places on Maui where if we ask for something, we get it nearly immediately. After dining here, we often have to remind ourselves to ratchet our service expectations down a notch or two at the next evening's restaurant.

The award-winning wine list should be shopped, and room in your evening's budget should also be reserved for one of their drop-dead delicious martinis. We're afraid that we still do not love the desserts here, although we make exception for the sorbets made in house. You might not have room for anything more, anyway.

We spend at a minimum one special occasion every year at **Capische?** and if you are celebrating, are ready to spend some money, and don't want to feel hurried (like you would be at **Mama's Fish House,** for example), this is our favorite choice.

For a truly exceptional experience, ask about **Il Teatro**, the private dining room off the herb garden, where the chef will cook a five course dinner for you personally at tableside. The opportunity to watch either of these Culinary Institute of America grads in action is spendy but worth it if you consider yourself a "foodie." Wines can be paired with each course. The room has two tables of four, so depending upon how many other people are interested – or how big a party you have – it may or may not be available when you want to go. If you book a table at **Il Teatro**, you might consider hiring transportation to complete the fantasy evening.

Capische? is not the most Hawaiian of restaurants, and granted, you can get great food like this elsewhere on the mainland or in Europe. But you can't get food like this in more than a handful of restaurants on Maui, and nowhere else do you get this view and ambiance combined with the hospitality that Chef Brian and his crew exude. Despite our telling everyone we know about how much we love *Capische?* this is still one of Maui's best kept secrets – even among locals – and the best restaurant on island.

Address: 555 Kaukahi St., Wailea, South Maui
Location: at the Hotel Wailea, this used to be called the Diamond Resort
Meals: Dinner
Hours: Nightly 5:30-9:30pm
Parking: Valet
Phone: 808-879-2224
Website: www.capische.com

Cary & Eddie's Hideaway Buffet *(Local/American)*

This oceanfront restaurant used to be a *Chart House.* Now, it's not. While very popular with some locals for their buffet lunch and brunch loaded up with Hawaiian and local dishes, it's not popular with us. It's designed for – and perfect for – tourists who want to debark from the nearby cruise ship and then go right back on board without exploring too far.

Address: 500 N Puunene Ave., Kahului, Central Maui
Location: Right on the water, at the intersection of Puunene and
            Kaahumanu
Meals: Brunch, Lunch, Dinner
Hours: Tu-Sa 11am-9pm; Su 8am-9pm
Parking: Lot
Phone: 808-873-6555
Website: www.hideawaymaui.com

Casanova *(Italian)*

Casanova is an upcountry institution and a gathering spot for the local community. The kitchen sends out good food, the service is kindhearted and friendly, and the live music and dancing schedule is packed. The emphasis is not on giving you "the best night of your life," but we have had many good nights here, and three of our readers have reported spontaneous marriage proposals. There is some undercurrent of enthusiasm and happiness that is catchy.

[An example of this is the opening of their promising sister restaurant *Bistro Casanova*. To open a new place during the worst economy in Maui history certainly takes a hopeful outlook.]

The *Casanova* menu is Italian and everything is made from scratch. Consistently tasty items include the *carpaccio di bresaola*, which is thinly sliced beef

OVERALL:

2.2
out of 5 stars

$ $

OVERALL:

3.6
out of 5 stars

$ $

continued on next page

Casanova *(continued)*

rolled with fresh arugula, parmesan cheese, and a lemony olive oil dressing. There are some good flavors here, although we wish a little sharper pepper taste (capers?) were present. We like the *ravioli di magro al tartufo*, homemade raviolis with spinach and ricotta cheese inside and a delicately flavored sage cream sauce with a little truffle oil to enrich it. The steaks are good, and we like the fun presentation, where the mashed potatoes are shaped into a pineapple, with a little sprig of greens at the top to represent the crown.

We like pizza for a light meal or an appetizer. The wood-burning oven turns out a pretty crust, and the simpler toppings are the best. (By the way, their bread is excellent because it's this pizza dough baked in their oven.) The tiramisu is slightly heavy in texture, but the flavors are strong and rich.

The big bar area and the dance floor (this building was the USO during World War II) make the entertainment events and dancing nights popular. Make it a point to check out their schedule, there is something going on most nights of the week.

Address: 1188 Makawao Ave., Makawao, Upcountry
Location: At Makawao Avenue and Baldwin Avenue intersection
Meals: Lunch, Dinner
Hours: M–Sa 11:30am-2pm; Daily 5:30-9:30pm; Pizza until 11pm on nights with entertainment
Parking: Lot
Phone: 808-572-0220
Website: www.casanovamaui.com

OVERALL:
3.6
out of 5 stars

Cascades Grille & Sushi Bar *(Pacific Rim / Sushi)*

We rarely recommend hotel restaurants – too often they coast because they have a guaranteed customer base, and too often the food tastes like a (bad) wedding banquet – but we make an exception for **Cascades Grille & Sushi Bar** at the Hyatt Regency in Ka'anapali. Even locals who live on the West side feel that the sushi here is good enough to stay after work for *pau hana* (end of workday drinks and bites).

The extravagant Pacific Rim style sushi is generally very fresh, with rolls just as fancy as at **Sansei** (if you don't want to drive to Kapalua or hit the brand new **Cane and Taro**, which features **Sansei** sushi rolls.) We especially like their hearty S.W.A.T. roll, which is 8 pieces of rolls starting with spicy tuna, avocado and cucumber inside and spiraling out to a thin layer of rice which leads to fresh salmon and green onions studded with sesame seeds and held together with a pungent ponzu sauce.

If you're really looking to push yourself – and your budget – try the ridiculously decadent Frank-da-Tank. Two crabs – soft-shell and snow – nestle amongst the cucumber inside the roll, while rice cuddles them into their little cocoon. Meanwhile blackened ahi, avocado, caviar, and a ponzu sauce enriched with truffle oil swirl around the outside. This monster roll comes with a glass of cold sake to wash it down (it should, for $31).

Generally we like onion rings that are sliced so paper thin that they melt to sugar on the tongue (so few places make them that way … sigh … the tempura at **Hakone** is perfect), so we're always surprised at how much we love the onion rings here. Sweet Maui onions are sliced into inch-thick rings, thickly coated in a well-seasoned batter, and flash-fried. Served steaming hot in a bamboo basket, they come with an undistinguished barbecue sauce and a Thai pepper sauce that knocks our eyeballs back in our heads. Sweet, spice, tang, crunch, pop goes our taste buds.

While we still like the steak – rubbed with a lavender-salt rub from up-country Maui – we've heard complaints about the "flowery" taste. Perhaps not everyone gets the concept? No matter, we like it, along with the simple red wine reduction and the meaty, local Dr. Seuss-pleasing Hamakua mushrooms. We skip fish here – too often it's tough, over-seasoned, or – horrors – both – and you can get excellent fish elsewhere on the West side.

We like their cute concept of a dinner-sized Bento Box, a complete meal that arrives on one big, apportioned platter. Six sections feature one each of: a petite filet mignon, mahi-mahi with coconut curry sauce, a green salad dressed with caramelized pineapple sauce, jasmine rice, a California roll, and miso soup. Smaller portions, but a wide taste of several good dishes.

The restaurant has hard-to-beat views from the top of the Hyatt's waterfall feature, and the setting is very romantic. Service is wonderful, efficient, and attentive or disinterested, slow, and sloppy, depending entirely upon the disposition of the waiter in question.

If you're "stuck" in Ka'anapali, are used to the jacked up prices (sorry, but everything's overpriced in Ka'anapali) and want a nice meal out, this is a better option than most on the strip.

Address: 200 Nohea Kai Dr., Ka'anapali, West Maui
Location: at the Hyatt Ka'anapali
Meals: Dinner
Hours: Daily Lounge 4:30pm – 10pm; Sushi Bar 5:30pm – 9:30 pm; Dining
      Room 6pm –9:30pm
Parking: Valet
Phone: 808-667-4727
Website: www.maui.hyatt.com

Castaway Café *(American / Local)*

This quiet bungalow café has local fans because you won't pay an arm and a leg in Ka'anapali for good pancakes at breakfast, sandwiches at lunch, or fish dishes at dinner. Competent cooking and a gorgeous view, but some (including us) feel the service is hit or miss. However, if you're stuck in Ka'anapali and want a break from the resort restaurant prices, this is a good option.

OVERALL:
2.8
out of 5 stars

continued on next page

Address: 45 Kai Ala Dr., Ka'anapali, West Maui
Location: at the Maui Ka'anapali Villas and Resort
Meals: Breakfast, Lunch, Dinner
Hours: Daily 7:30am–9pm
Parking: Public Lot, then walk to the beach and you will see the restaurant on the beachfront at the Villas
Phone: 808–661–9091
Website: www.castawaycafe.com

OVERALL:
2.4
out of 5 stars

Charley's Restaurant & Saloon *(American)*

Charley's is a Maui institution, and its relaxed ambiance (especially since a major renovation after a devastating fire), expansive menu, friendly service, and reasonable prices would be enough to take us most of the way to happy. The fact that Willie Nelson plays on a regular basis should take us over the top, but we just can't ignore the fact that whenever we stop in for anything other than breakfast, we want to delegate the meal-eating to someone else.

We know plenty of locals who love Charley's and make it their favorite meeting place. Nostalgia dies hard, but die is must for us. Go for the live music and the drinks in the bar, and an appetizer or two while you listen – but there is much better food (and drinks) on the corner at *Milagros* or down the street at *Flatbread*. Breakfasts are better, but we'd still prefer *Anthony's* or *Moana Bakery* or *Mambo Cafe.*

Address: 142 Hana Hwy., Paia, North Shore
Location: Right across from Indigo
Meals: Breakfast, Lunch, Dinner
Hours: Daily 7am–10pm
Parking: Street, Lot
Phone: 808–579–9453
Website: www.charleysmaui.com

OVERALL:
3
out of 5 stars

Cheeseburger in Paradise / Cheeseburger Island Style *(American)*

If you're in the mood for a big, sloppy cheeseburger and a basket of fries in a restaurant structured for ticky-tacky Hawaiiana silliness, a *Cheeseburger* restaurant might be your thing. While we find the nearly-trademarked "sassy" service (everything in this restaurant has a trademark – why not the service?) a little too real (read "impertinent"), some diners get a kick of out the teasing.

[We're not opposed to sassy waiters – read the review for *A Saigon Café*. We're also not unilaterally opposed to chain or theme restaurants – read the review for *Bubba Gump's*.]

The Lahaina location has stunning views of the harbor from their two floors of open-air dining rooms. Live music can be heard down the street

and does much to draw in the customers for those hour-long waits. But kids love the noise and the water and the food, and if you've got them, you'll be happy they're happy. (But they might like the *Cool Cat Café* just as well, and that's got a slightly better burger.)

The Wailea location at the upscale Shops at Wailea open-air mall is much more sedate, although the waits can get long since this is the only moderately priced mall restaurant. Both locations have plenty of room for their cute t-shirts, tiki mugs, and cheeseburger-shaped earrings.

Cheeseburger in Paradise
Address: 811 Front St., Lahaina, West Maui
Location: right on the sea wall, you can't miss it
Meals: Breakfast, Lunch, Dinner
Hours: Daily 8am-10pm
Parking: Street
Phone: 808-661-4855
Website: www.cheeseburgerland.com

Cheeseburger Island Style
Address: 3750 Wailea Alanui Dr., Wailea, South Maui
Location: at The Shops at Wailea,
Meals: Breakfast, Lunch, Dinner
Hours: Daily 8am-10pm
Parking: Lot
Phone: 808-874-8990
Website: www.cheeseburgerland.com

China Boat /
China Bowl & Asian Cuisine *(Chinese/American)*

China Boat and its sister restaurant, *China Bowl*, serve mainstream Chinese dishes to mainland tourists. While the food is definitely "Americanized" Chinese, it is generally cooked competently. Considering Hawaii has a rich Chinese immigrant history and there are some wonderful Chinese restaurants on Oahu, we think that these restaurants might be better if their audience were more knowledgeable about the cuisine. (When diners eat, they are voting with their dollars… so we think we get the restaurants we deserve.)

OVERALL:
2.8
out of 5 stars

If you are from a city with top notch Chinese, you may want to go for Thai, Vietnamese, or Japanese restaurants while on Maui. If you really enjoy Americanized Chinese or have a nostalgic craving for it (we do, sometimes), the daily specials generally offer some good choices at China Boat and China Bowl.

China Boat
Address: 4474 Lower Honoapiilani Rd., Lahaina, West Maui
Location: In the Kahana Gateway Center
Meals: Lunch, Dinner
Hours: Daily 11am-2 pm & 5pm-10pm
Parking: Lot
Phone: 808-669-5089
Website: www.chinaboatandbowlmaui.com

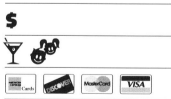

continued on next page

China Bowl
Address: 2580 Keka'a Dr., Ka'anapali, West Maui
Location: In Fairway Shops
Meals: Lunch, Dinner
Hours: Daily 11am–9:30pm
Parking: Lot
Phone: 808-661-0660

Cilantro *(Mexican)*

Cilantro hits the spot when we're in the mood for fresh, inexpensive Mexican. Located kitty corner to Foodland in Lahaina, we love to buy some beer at the market and head here for a quick, satisfying meal rounded out by our own BYOB choice of beverage.

The gleaming exhibition kitchen is staffed by friendly chefs who work the tortilla presses (they make their corn tortillas by hand), grills, and cutting boards in full sight while you place your order at the counter. Giant jars of chilies and bins of fresh produce serve as reminders that sometimes the best food is fresh and simply prepared.

Succulent roasted chicken provides the basis for some of our favorite dishes. The chicken is marinated in herbs and citrus before it is rotisserie-roasted. The constant spinning and the perfect balance of acidity leaves the flesh tender and pleasantly astringent. The Mother Clucker Flautas are particular favorites. Two flour tortillas are rolled up with secret spices and the delicious chicken then flash fried and smothered with *crema fresca* and mellow roasted jalapeno jelly. The tortillas end up crispy, while the chicken stays hot and melts into the crème and almost-sweet jalapenos. Delicious.

Cilantro chefs know how to work a grill and how to treat fish's tricky protein with respect. The day's catch has good grill marks and is perfectly done. Our favorite so far is a flaky opakapaka on a bed of garlicky, spicy jicama slaw.

Salads are very good, fresh, and big. If you want a protein, you can add pork, chicken, steak, fish, or grilled shrimp. Try the margarita-reminiscent tequila-lime vinaigrette.

The chips are crisp and not too greasy, and the salsa bar features choices ranging from mild to crazy hot and including green tomatillos. This is a very casual taqueria (paper plates and plastic utensils), clean, boisterous when busy, and brightly painted. For a cheap lunch or inexpensive dinner for two to ten, it's a dearly loved Maui institution and well worth your while.

Address: 170 Papalaua St., Lahaina, HI 96761
Location: Near Foodland
Meals: Lunch, Dinner
Hours: M–Sa 11am–9pm; Su 11am–8pm
Parking: Lot
Phone: 808-667-5444
Website: www.CilantroGrill.com

Cinnamon Roll Fair *(American)*

Just underneath Denny's you'll find **Cinnamon Roll Fair,** a teensy store-front counter stocked with a few baked goods, including muffins and trays of sticky, gooey rolls with many, many spirals dripping cinnamon. They have a choice of toppings they'll put in little plastic takeaway cups, and many times we are jealous of vacationing people who are eating there, as if they are entitled to eat just a cinnamon roll for lunch, simply because they are on vacation.

Address: 2463 S. Kihei Rd., Kihei, South Maui
Location: In the Kamaole Center
Meals: Breakfast, Snacks & Treats
Hours: M–F 6am–6pm; Sa–Su 6am–5pm
Parking: Lot
Phone: 808-879-5177

OVERALL:
3.4
out of 5 stars

$

CASH

CJ's Deli & Diner *(American)*

CJ's is a down home restaurant hoping to cater both to locals and visitors with comfort food at reasonable prices. Keeping in mind that everything in Ka'anapali is overpriced, they generally succeed.

We like the breakfasts best, especially for families who need a break from the resort prices. Pancakes and French toast and omelets are the best bets. Lunch and dinner entrees are problematic, but we do think the Hana Box Lunch is a good deal. For $12 you get a deli sandwich with the lettuce, tomato, and toppings wrapped separately so your bread doesn't get soggy. You also get chips, a drink, and a brownie. This is not a bad deal. If you need a cooler, they'll loan one to you for a $5 deposit, which you can keep for the length of your stay. They'll even give you free refills on ice (good inducement to get you to come back for another meal).

If you're on the West Side and facing the dearth of inexpensive breakfast options, this could be your best bet.

Address: 2580 Keka'a Dr., Ka'anapali, West Maui
Location: In the Fairway Shops
Meals: Breakfast, Lunch, Dinner
Hours: Daily 7am–8pm
Parking: Lot
Phone: 808-667-0968
Website: www.cjsmaui.com

OVERALL:
3.2
out of 5 stars

$

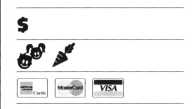

OVERALL:
4
out of 5 stars

$

Coconut's Fish Café *(American)*

Just as Maui institution **Alexander's Fish & Chips** tanked in quality, **Coconut's Fish Café** opened up to fill the gap. Thank goodness!

Coconut's is convinced that a fish shack doesn't have to serve unhealthy food, and it manages to convince us, too. Substituting coconut milk for much of the mayonnaise in both the cole slaw and the tartar sauce turns out to be a good choice, although some may find it a hint too sweet.

The fish burgers here are perfectly grilled and taste as good as the ones at **Paia Fish Market.** They're dressed much the same, too, with tomato, cheese, coleslaw, tartar sauce, on a sesame or whole wheat bun. The mahi-mahi is, naturally, flaky and a little sweet, while the ono, our favorite, is firmer and a little more savory.

If you prefer no bun, they offer a wonderful alternative: brown rice. The rice is perfectly cooked and seasoned, and the grilled fish on the rice with the slaw on the side is a lovely, healthy lunch.

Of course, you could also add fries – perfectly serviceable shoestring commercial spuds dressed with a seasoned salt – for a couple more dollars.

We also like the fish and chips, which are decidedly different than elsewhere on island. In order to live up to their healthy goal, the restaurant has decided to batter the fish in what is basically Italian bread crumbs. This results in a very light, seasoned batter that effectively seals in the juices, but also makes the dish taste a little like the fish sticks we ate as kids. If you like your fish in a heavy batter and enjoy that crisp sound when you bite it, you would do well to stick with the grilled fish burgers. The shrimp and calamari are fried in the same breadcrumb batter and the same advice applies.

The restaurant is filled with light, very clean, and features custom-built surfboard shaped tables. This is a delicious, healthy, slow-cooked-but-fast-food option in Kihei.

Address: 1279 S. Kihei Rd., Kihei, South Maui
Location: in the Azeka Mauka Marketplace
Meals: Lunch, Dinner
Hours: Daily 11am-9pm
Parking: Lot
Phone: 808-875-9979

Colleen's *(American / Pacific Rim)*

Colleen's is an upcountry favorite for comforting meals any time of day or night. Big portions and generally well-prepared classics are served in a clean, high-ceilinged, open, noisy joint.

The breakfast omelets are reasonable and tasty at $8.50, and the Eggs Benedict come in several different styles – from ham, bacon, lox, veggie, crab, mahi-mahi, and ono – all ono (good). The tofu vegetable wrap is a favorite, as is the prosciutto tapas plate. Add a latté (very good) and you're all set for the day. At lunch, you can't go wrong with a big salad topped with the mahi-mahi or ono. Or if you're really hungry, get the beef burger (Maui Cattle Company beef, hormone free) and add fries and a pint of beer, all for $10.95.

At night the restaurant keeps the lights low and puts out votive candles and bluesy jazz. The wild mushroom ravioli is good, as is the creamy, comforting penne with vodka sauce and chicken. You might also try the seared ahi or the New York strip steak. The wine and beer list is short but decent. They make their own bread daily, and the espresso is excellent.

This is a great alternative to Pa'ia if you want to stray a little off the beaten path but still hang with the upcountry crowd. Right next door is Studio Maui, a yoga center and the site of many classes, workshops, and events to sustain your spiritual side.

Address: 810 Haiku Rd., Haiku, Upcountry
Location: Haiku Cannery
Meals: Breakfast, Lunch, Dinner
Hours: Daily 6am-9pm
Parking: Lot
Phone: 808-575-9211
Website: www.colleensinhaiku.com

Cool Cat Café *(American)*

The **Cool Cat Café** is a fifties-themed restaurant with a great location on the top floor of the Wharf Cinema Center. There is typically a long wait to sit, but once you have a table, we find the service speedy. There is a lot of seating both inside (yech) and outside (breezy, if a little crowded in places). The menu has pretty good burgers, pretty good sandwiches, not so good fries or onion rings, and nice thick milkshakes. We like the Porky Pig, a kalua pig sandwich that looks undistinguished on its roll, but is surprisingly tasty (sweet and a little hint of sour), with good cole slaw on the side.

A full view of the banyan tree blocks most of the harbor and the ocean, but you definitely feel like you're getting a view. Live music and a full soda fountain and bar help to round out the relax-you're-on-vacation vibe. They heavily promote themselves via other merchants (you'll be offered a coupon to **Cool Cat** at least once as you walk down Front Street), but that doesn't mean they're not worth stopping in, if you're in the mood for a slightly overpriced, but comforting meal.

And if you want fifties-type memorabilia, like I Love Lucy handbags or rhinestone studded hair doodads, this is the place to come. Or you can just get a Cool Cat Café t-shirt to take home.

continued on next page

Cool Cat Café *(continued)*

Address: 658 Front St., Lahaina, West Maui
Location: Upper floor of the Wharf Cinema Center
Meals: Lunch, Dinner
Hours: Daily 10:30am–10:30pm
Parking: Street, Lot
Phone: 808–667–0908
Website: www.coolcatcafe.com

$ $

AMERICAN EXPRESS Cards **CASH**

Costco Food Court *(American)*

We had to think long and hard about including Costco's food court in this edition. But ultimately, we decided that you should know that we eat here occasionally when we're in Kahului and just want a quick bite to eat. So do most Maui residents (almost everyone has a membership to Costco, which makes living on Maui a lot more affordable than it would be without it).

The pizza is heavy duty and one slice is like three everywhere else, and the hot dogs are Kosher franks. You can't argue with the prices (a hot dog and coke is still $1.50 here just like at every other Costco), and if you're a member you're going to be glad you don't have to pay $8 for a gallon of milk.

In addition to their food court, you might want to check out their refrigerated foods section, much of which has local food. Their vegetables are surprisingly local (and very often organic), and the La Brea bread they sell in their bakery is the best "supermarket" bread on Maui.

You can also get lots of books on Maui, plenty of Hawaiian chocolate and macadamia nuts to bring home as gifts (all packaged for travel).
One of our top tips for visiting friends is to check out Costco as the first stop after picking up the rental car. Pick up tasty treats, sunscreen at deep discounts, and beautiful fresh leis at the best prices around.

Address: 540 Haleakala Highway, Kahului, Central Maui
Location: At the intersection of Dairy Road and Haleakala Highway
Meals: Lunch, Dinner, Snacks & Treats
Hours: M-F 11am – 8:30pm; Sa 9:30am – 6pm; Su 10am – 6pm
Parking: Lot
Phone: 808–877–5248
Website: www.costco.com

Favorite **NEW** Restaurant

Cuatro Restaurant *(Latin / Asian Fusion)*

Cuatro Restaurant, which is *Sansei's* new sister restaurant in Kihei, is a nearly perfect square. This may seem trivial, but this *feng shui* fact seems significant to us. The sense of balance, harmony, and intimacy can also be found in the food, the wine list, and the service. Rarely are we as excited about a new restaurant as we are about *Cuatro*. Quite simply, we love everything about it.

The food is a Latin-Asian-European fusion that makes liberal use of cilantro, truffle oil, balsamic vinegar, chilies, and butter (and many other things). In most dishes you can taste the four corners of the globe – and yet those far flung flavors don't fight with each other. The cuisine offers an easy approach for the spice-wary, with plenty of choices for those who are more adventurous.

A good example is the spicy tuna nachos appetizer. Six wonton, crisp and fresh, are laid on top of baby greens. A spicy tuna mixture that *Sansei* fans will likely recognize is scooped on top of each wonton. Next comes a layer of truffle aioli, then a cilantro pesto heated up with kochujang (a red chili pepper paste from Korea), then an avocado relish. Each serving ends up being either two perfect bites or one big mouthful of East-West Love.

The pupu steak is another good starter, and sized generously enough to be a small entrée. The steak is marinated until tender and then sautéed with earthy local mushrooms in a spicy teriyaki sauce. The sauce also features a little truffle oil, which melts the spice to the salty, and transitions the mushrooms to the meat. The end result is a cohesive taste experience that, in our opinion, is what good fusion is about: the sum must be equal to much more than the individual ingredients, and the different cuisines must marry each other, not threaten divorce.

The fresh fish of the day changes, of course, but can be prepared in one of four styles, each unique. You cannot go wrong with a fresh piece of mahimahi sautéed with rock shrimp in a classic lemon caper butter sauce, but we like the more adventurous "house" preparation. Try a fish like ono or ahi blackened with Mexican spices, served over rice pilaf in a cumin-oregano beurre blanc with an avocado pico de gallo. Heat in the back of your throat, yes, but the rich beurre blanc and creamy avocado smoothes it all out.

Our favorite fish preparation, however, is the "Mauiterranean Grill." Garlic mashed potatoes are spread in a bed on the plate, with perfectly grilled vegetable slices on top – eggplant, onions, and whatever else is fresh. The fish is rubbed with what's almost a steak rub, grilled, and topped with tomato-caper relish. The basil beurre blanc is not enough – it would be just spicy citrus and creamy nutty flavors. Where's the sweet to balance this out? It's in the balsamic syrup drizzled over the fish and the plate.

A very good meat entrée is the marinated pork. Pork is so easy to dry out, and so often rendered like sawdust, that we hesitate to order it. But this is so tender, juicy, and flavorful after its marinade and grilling session (Chef really knows how to grill) that we will order it again and again. Sweet green chilies in the *chili verde* sauce give way seamlessly to the sneaky heat in the back of the throat, and overall it's a satisfying dish. Another good choice is the roasted chicken breast. Stuffed with green chilies, ham, and a little pepper-jack cheese and then swathed in a southwestern butter sauce, it's perfectly tender and juicy. Is there anything better than a perfectly roasted chicken?

Dessert pickings are slim; there is only a dish of locally-made ice cream with local fruit and caramel sauce. While, on the one hand we appreciate the honesty of not offering dessert if you can't do it well, it's a hole in the repertoire of what, otherwise, is a nearly perfect dining experience.

continued on next page

Cuatro Restaurant *(continued)*

The wine list is very small, but carefully selected, and there are some bottled beers available. The keiki (children's) menu is simple: grilled fish, chicken, or steak, plus veggies and potatoes or rice. They can also get pasta with butter and cheese, or a cheese quesadilla.

The service is friendly and proficient, and they know the menu well. The nearly exhibition style kitchen gives you glimpses of the action through the Asian-style door panels (the closer you sit the more you can feel the energy of the grill). You will not have trouble getting a server's attention in the small room. There's an early bird special everyday from 4-6pm: 25% off food (as of publication, please call to verify).

Cuatro Restaurant operates like the best of city restaurants: proficient, energetic, confident, and hospitable – and it doesn't need a view to entertain you. Along with ***David Paul's Island Grill, Cuatro*** is our pick for favorite new restaurant.

NB: Catering and private dining are also available. If you are planning a wedding on Maui, put ***Cuatro*** on your list of places to check out.

Address: 1881 S. Kihei Rd., Kihei, South Maui
Location: in the Kihei Town Center near Sansei
Meals: Dinner
Hours: Daily 4pm–10pm
Parking: Lot
Phone: 808-879-1110
Website: www.cuatromaui.com

Da Kitchen *(Local/Plate Lunch)*

A major distinguishing feature of good local food is that you get a great deal of it. Engaging with mixed plate could be called "eating until you are sore," and it's practically a sport in Hawaii.

Local food is not to be confused with Hawaiian food. Hawaiian foods are traditional to these islands and include items like lau lau (any protein cooked in a ti leaf), lomi lomi (salt-cured salmon) and poi (taro or other root pounded into a nutritious paste).

Local food, on the other hand, is the best or favorite dishes from each of the cultures that make up the local population. Over the centuries, that has included Hawaiians, of course, but also Chinese, Japanese, Filipino, Koreans, and Portuguese or Brazilians. The favorite foods from each culture make their way into what we call Local Food. Just like visitors to New York should make a point to try the native's bagels, visitors to Hawaii should try Local Food. It is not fine dining, but skipping it is like skipping a lobster shack on the Maine Coast or a pig palace in Georgia.

We recommend ***Da Kitchen*** for your particular adventure. The restaurants are clean, the food is good, and the portions are Hawaiian-sized so you can split them and still have leftovers.

OVERALL:
3.4
out of 5 stars

$

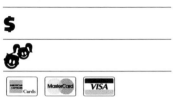

Every order comes packaged for takeout, but if you want to sit and eat in the restaurant, there are plenty of chairs. You'll get your napkins and utensils with your order (the exception is the new Lahaina location, which is a sit-down restaurant with table service).

The combination plates are a good place to start. The kalua pork is good, as is the beef and chicken teriyaki. These dishes are often overly salty, but they are also meant to be eaten with the accompanying "two scoops" of rice and scoop of macaroni salad, which makes the seasoning more reasonable. Chicken katsu – breaded cutlets – is often too bready and not enough chicken. We prefer the chow fun to the crispy noodles, and the ribs are pretty good when they are available.

There is no charm to either the ambiance or the service, but if you're looking for a good meal at great prices and want to know "where da locals eat" *Da Kitchen* is da place.

Address: 425 Koloa St, Kahului, Central Maui
Location: Near K-Mart and the Airport
Meals: Lunch, Dinner
Hours: M-F 11am-8:30pm; Sa 11am-4pm
Parking: Lot
Phone: 808-871-7782
Website: www.da-kitchen.com

Address: 2439 S. Kihei Rd, Kihei, South Maui
Location: In the Rainbow Mall
Meals: Lunch, Dinner
Hours: Daily 9am-9pm
Parking: Lot
Phone 808-875-7782

Address: 658 Front St., Lahaina, West Maui
Location: Bottom level of the Wharf Cinema Center
Meals: Lunch, Dinner
Hours: Daily 11am-9pm
Parking: Lot (validated), Street
Phone: 808-661-4900

Dad's Donut Shop *(Bakery)*

OVERALL:
3.4
out of 5 stars

Tucked into Harts Corner in Wailuku, *Dad's Donuts* is an unassuming concrete slab lanai with a rail, two tables, and a takeout window. Compact little donuts nestle in protective paper cupcake liners. The fat little bundles are made from a family recipe, turned out in an old-fashioned crank donut dropper. They come in plain, cinnamon sugar, and powdered sugar. The firm, cakelike texture and tender tooth are perfect. The cinnamon sugar variety, in particular, hits a nostalgic chord. There are also a few glazed varieties for those with a sweeter tooth. Owner Chris Hart, former Maui County Planning Director, grew up in his father's bakery in upstate

continued on next page

OVERALL:
4.4
out of 5 stars

Dad's Donut Shop *(continued)*

New York and is using his Dad's precise "formulas" to make his family's donuts, muffins and cinnamon buns.

Address: 1910 E. Vineyard St., Wailuku, Central Maui
Location: At Hart's corner
Meals: Snacks & Treats
Hours: M-F 6:30am-2pm; Sa 6:30am-12pm
Parking: Street
Phone: 808-244-3303
Website: www.dadsdonuts.com

David Paul's Island Grill *(Pacific Rim)*

The last meal we had at Chef David Paul Johnson's table started with a bean soup so hearty and creamy that we actually scraped the bottom of the bowl. We would have licked it if the wine critics for the *Wall Street Journal* weren't sitting in plain view of our table (it turned out not to be them, but that's a funny-embarrassing story destined for a www.MauiRestaurantsBlog.com post).

The soup was made with black beans, earthy-sweet and tender, completely pulverized by a blending that lasted, according to the waitress, for at least fifteen minutes. The texture of the soup was a silky smooth cream. The *crème fraîche* dollop on top, when mixed in, gave a wonderful tangy counterbalance to the warm spices in the soup. Every once in a while, a dish is both perfectly balanced in flavor – earthy, sweet, spicy, pungent, salty – and also is utterly simple and straightforward. In other words: perfect. This soup is one of those dishes.

David Paul is known for bold flavors and fresh ingredients, and his menu changes with the seasons and the available produce, so the soup may not be on the menu when you visit. Every time we've been, it looks like a completely different menu, although there are always at least three or four favorites from his previous menu at *David Paul's Lahaina Grill.*

[Contrary to what many seem to believe, David Paul left the *Grill* nearly a decade ago, but the restaurant kept his name and many of his dishes. In late 2007 it dropped his name to become simply *Lahaina Grill*. David Paul then opened *David Paul's Island Grill* in the summer of 2009. The similarity in name between the two restaurants, his founding of *Lahaina Grill* and his current use of the same loopy spiral he once used at the first restaurant – has led to understandable confusion. The bottom line: David Paul has not been on Maui for a long time; he is back; he is cooking at *David Paul's Island Grill* on Front Street.]

As mentioned, the menu is extensive, and if it seems too much to wade through the descriptions of each dish, you might try the Tasting Menu, which includes that evening's nine featured items as a four course menu. It usually includes the dishes Chef is most excited about that evening, with the most seasonal ingredients and the nicest combinations of flavors. The trick is that the whole table must order the tasting menu, presumably for the kitchen's timing. It's an excellent way to sample a wide range of dishes without having to choose. Some substitutions can be made — for instance, we usually can convince them to include our favorite Triple Berry Pie on the dessert course. Although some find the portions too small, we find the meal more than enough food (how can you not be satisfied with four entrees?). At $45 per person at press time, this is a very good value.

It is hard to comment on specific dishes without running the risk of disappointing you later if they're not there, but we have to write *something*, so here it is:

We love the cool, spicy watermelon gazpacho. When you sip the nearly-clear pink liquid from the lip of the martini glass, the first to step forward is the intense watermelon, concentrated and sugary, which gently transforms itself to savory and then leaves a spicy backsplash that is intense but terribly satisfying. We also have enjoyed the butternut squash raviolis stuffed with mascarpone cheese and topped with a small piece of lobster. The decadent textures combined with the luxurious flavors … we can't decide if this belongs as a pasta, a main course, or a dessert (or all three).

Do not overlook his salads, which are just-picked fresh and include an excellent diced roasted beet dish. Also, if you are torn between two dishes, ask if they can both be served as half portions. The kitchen has some flexibility and can do this for items that don't require a cut of meat.

Not every dish is perfect, and we doubt they could be, given how wide-ranging the menu is. Our quarrel is mainly with one of the duck dishes, which is perfectly cooked — tender, juicy, falling off the bone — but somehow not as successful a flavor profile as we expect. One of David Paul's chief talents is giving a "taste bud tour" as James calls it: bringing different flavors together to fill each taste zone with activity, like he does with the bean soup we describe above. But his spicy orange duck, for example, was either spicy or sweet, depending upon the bite. The sweet edged toward the cloying, while the spicy tasted strongly of rather burnt Chinese Five Spice.

An insistence on sustainable food sources and local purveyors leads David Paul to use the beef and lamb available from Hawaiian ranchers, and that can lead to an uneven experience. We've had a few cuts that were less than perfect … however, that's true for every restaurant on the island which uses local beef. Maui needs a really good butcher, pronto.

Other than the food, there is a good wine list with dozens of wines by the glass. You can also visit their wine cellar to shop on your own and see the labels (all bottles are priced). This is a really fun way to pick your poison, and it makes good eye candy on the way to the elegantly appointed bathrooms.

The classy, contemporary restaurant — totally overhauled by David Paul — is absolutely beautiful. The muted blues, greens, and mustards on the walls, the natural slate tiles on the lanai, the big mirrors, the exhibition kitchen, and the big square white plates remind us of upscale casual eateries in our old haunts. The view, however, is all Maui. If you sit on the open air lanai you will see one of the best wide-open views of Lahaina Harbor.

continued on next page

David Paul's Island Grill *(continued)*

Service is the only real issue we have with ***David Paul's Island Grill.*** While each server we've encountered is both knowledgeable and helpful, there is something seriously off about the timing at this restaurant. It feels like every course comes four to five minutes (and sometimes longer) later than it should, and while water is poured immediately by the hostess, the first drinks and the bread come late. This could be caused by a slow kitchen, or a staff that hasn't yet set a successful rhythm, or both ... but in any case, it's a noticeable flaw and one that we've heard consistent complaints about from readers. The restaurant is still relatively new, and we hope that this improves over time.

Come to think of it, we do have one other issue with ***David Paul's Island Grill.*** This being one of our two favorite new restaurants (***Cuatro*** is the other); we think it should be located in Kihei, closer to our home.

Address: 900 Front St., Lahaina, West Maui
Location: Near Warren & Annabelle's and ***Hard Rock Cafe***
Meals: Dinner
Hours: Su-Th 5pm - 10pm, F-Sa 5pm - Midnight
Parking: Validated for Lahaina Center parking
Phone: 808-662-3000
Website: www.davidpaulsislandgrill.com.

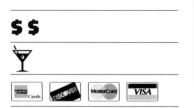

OVERALL:
3.4
out of 5 stars

$ $

Dog & Duck *(Pub)*

This little pub is quietly (or not so quietly) making people happy with good music, good food, and good drinks poured by cute bartenders. The service is relaxed and friendly, and if you're looking for a good lunch or cheap dinner, this is a great place to check out if you like pub food.

You'll find standard pub fare like bangers and mash (sausages and mashed potatoes) and corned beef and cabbage, as well as steaks, burgers, and potpies. Specials can stretch to feature island flavors, even local fish over rice with well-made and tasty sauces. While most of the ingredients are commercial, they're prepared carefully and thoughtfully.

There is a small outdoor seating area on the wraparound porch, and while extra chairs and speakers may be inelegantly stashed in the corners of the pub, the atmosphere is clean and pleasant. There are televisions throughout the room and live music some nights (call for the schedule).

Address: 1913 S. Kihei Rd., Kihei, South Maui
Location: Kalama Villages across from the Whale
Meals: Lunch, Dinner
Hours: Daily 11am-10pm, bar open until 2am
Parking: Lot
Phone: 808-875-9669

Dollie's Gourmet Pizza *(Pizza)*

This casual pizza joint in Kahana features a full bar, which makes it easy for locals and visitors to like. All told, the pizzas are fine, the service is fine, and the atmosphere is pleasant. Not a bad place to unwind without emptying your wallet in the process.

Address: 4310 Lower Honoapiilani Rd., Kahana, West Maui
Location: Kahana Manor Shops
Meals: Lunch, Dinner, Late-Night
Hours: Daily 11am–12 midnight
Parking: Lot
Phone: 808-669-0266
Website: www.dolliespizzakahana.com

Down to Earth *(Health Food Store)*

With the fast food chains packing Dairy Road, you might miss this healthy alternative, and that would be a shame. This small Hawaiian chain health food store is not the best health food store on the island, but it's the most central and it has a good takeout/prepared food counter. It's also overwhelmingly vegan and all organic.

Self-serve stations feature hot and cold items like salads, lasagna, chili, curries, millet cakes, mock tofu chicken, curried tofu (great, with apples, cashews, and raisins), and Greek salad. You pay by the pound, and can take out or eat in with the locals at the stools and tables available in the upper loft.

Address: 305 Dairy Rd, Kahului, Central Maui
Meals: Breakfast, Lunch, Dinner
Hours: M–Sa 7am–9pm; Su 8am–8pm
Parking: Lot
Phone: 808-877-2661
Website: www.downtoearth.org

Dragon Dragon Chinese Restaurant *(Chinese)*

There are very few good Chinese restaurants on Maui, and **Dragon Dragon** is pretty good for the island. If you're craving Chinese and can't get out to Kihei to visit **East Ocean**, this will do the trick.

Service is efficient, and they're usually pretty good about steering you toward the best items of the day. Any special made with fresh local Hawaiian fish is likely to be a standout. Sometimes they have a steamed whole fish with a tasty black bean sauce. Dim sum is particularly good here but served only at lunch time.

continued on next page

OVERALL:
3.6
out of 5 stars

Dragon Dragon Chinese Restaurant *(continued)*

During the holidays this restaurant has fixed price specials for groups of six or more people, but make sure you call for reservations ahead of time.

Address: 70 E. Kaahumanu Ave., Kahului, Central Maui
Location: Maui Mall
Meals: Lunch, Dinner
Hours: Daily 11am–2pm & 5pm–9pm
Parking: Lot
Phone: 808-893-1628

Duo *(American)*

Duo is so named because it is equally a steak and fish house … but it also could be inadvertently advertising it's slightly split personality when it comes to food. Both the poolside breakfast buffet and the main dinner restaurant at The Four Seasons, **Duo** bears a huge responsibility at the most exclusive resort on Maui. It must go from brightly-lit, comfy-cushioned, linger-and-read service in the morning to upscale, romantic, full service at night.

Let's start with the bright side: breakfast. The open kitchen presents a big buffet with platters of pastries, fish, cereals, covered dishes mounded with sausages, scrambled eggs, and French toast, vats of miso soup and oatmeal. You can get fresh fruit and yogurt or made-to-order omelets. If it's a holiday, they are likely featuring a more expansive champagne brunch with a seafood bar, carving station, and piles of desserts. We like coming for breakfast on special occasions – not just because the food is good (which it is, and should be at these prices), but because the service is so wonderful.

Every morning the kitchen makes a new smoothie "shooter", which is presented by the waiter during your meal. Whether it's carrots and orange juice or spinach, apple, mango, and lime, it's a well-balanced, thoughtful, healthy supplement. The servers are unfailingly pleasant and efficient, and this is one of the best places on Maui to feel true Aloha in the service. The bright-but-shady poolside location is cheerful, and you can see the ocean beyond the cabanas. It's a lovely restaurant.

When we visit for dinner, we are always struck by how it doesn't quite make the transition to luxury fine dining the way they intend it to. Perhaps it is the lighting which seems intentionally set too low so that you don't notice that the cushions are weatherproof and the hot tub is just over yonder.

The "duo" theme is repeated in the menu, which is split up so that you must pair every part of your meal yourself. The cuts of meat, the fish, the sauces, the sides are all listed separately. If you order the rib-eye, but don't order a sauce, you will get a rib-eye with no sauce. Which might suit you fine, as we find that many of the sauces are undistinguished (which is a problem when you list your sauces in two separate sections). The merlot sauce for meat is the best balanced and the best reduction.

It's almost a play on a Chinese menu – "I'll take the rib-eye from column A, the snapper from Column B, the merlot sauce from Column C, and the truffled spuds from D!" While we like the *idea* of getting to play with different flavor profiles and combinations of proteins and sauces, we still don't completely buy this concept. After all, we could buy a great cut of steak ourselves (Costco often has USDA Prime that is out of this world) and make our own sauce at home – *we* know what *we* like. When we go out, we want the Chef to feed us. That's the point of dining: to be fed. At *Duo*, we feel the diner is left to fend for themselves and too often gets lost.

This is not to say that there aren't people who are completely happy to order all six sauces for their steak or fish and "try" them all, one bite after another. We're just not those people.

The fish vary with the day and the season, but generally include ahi, a snapper, mahi-mahi, lobster, and prawns. All are prepared simply and well, and presented on a plate with your choice of sauce in a little dish. The sauces include orange-butter, pineapple-papaya salsa, lemon-caper butter, Thai red coconut curry … the pineapple papaya salsa is the best.

Sides are served family style, and are ordered separately from the proteins. There are potatoes ten different ways (again, we wish the choices were narrowed down a little), and the vegetables are generally fresh and local. If the corn "off the cob" is on the menu, order it – it's simple, but it's one of the best sides they make: buttery sweet and creamy.

Tip: ask for the truffle aioli that is normally sent out with the homemade fries (skip the fries themselves). Use it as an excellent sauce for everything – it's rich and delicious.

Our favorite appetizer is the ahi sashimi, which is significant, since all that the kitchen needs to do is correctly slice an excellent cut of fish in order to make sashimi work. We do not recommend the oily goat cheese fritters, which, although made with the excellent Surfing Goat Dairy cheese, are a crunchy mess.

All that aside, we do **very much like** the way *Duo* cooks protein. Our meat is always perfectly seared, and our fish is always perfectly flakey, never overdone. If you have never had Japanese Kobe beef, this is the place to get it. Mention that you are ordering it when you make your reservation, because they can sell out before service begins. Kobe is expensive but a worthy experience and *Duo* will cook it perfectly for you (they better at upwards of $25 *per ounce*).

Duo has an excellent wine list, with all wines grouped according to their body and characteristics rather than their varietals. Even novices can read this wine list and get a pretty good idea of what they should order. This kind of attention to detail and description would be well served on the main menu.

The servers are well-trained and attentive without being obtrusive, and they carry little pocket flashlights in case you forgot yours and need to read the menu (yes, the restaurant is that dark at night).

Overall, we like *Duo*, especially for their breakfasts and brunches. The food at night is also good, but it is expensive and we don't feel matches the value of *Spago* just upstairs, *Ferraro's* across the pool, or *Capische?* up the hill.

continued on next page

Duo *(continued)*

Address: 3900 Wailea Alanui, Wailea, South Maui
Location: Four Seasons Resort
Meals: Breakfast, Lunch, Dinner
Hours: M–Sa 6am – 11:30am; Su 6am – 12pm, Daily 5:30pm – 9pm
Parking: Valet
Phone: 808-874-8000
Website: www.fourseasons.com

East Ocean *(Chinese)*

East Ocean is like the fairytale character of the wizened old woman in rags who turns out to be a beautiful fairy god-mother. The flashing red "All You Can Eat Buffet" sign in the window, the dusty and dark curio case at the door, and the murky fish tank that makes *feng shui* masters shudder could easily fool one into thinking "good food can't be made here."

At one time, that would have been a good guess. Today, however, we count this as the best place for Chinese on Maui. We enjoy our meals here and this is one of our favorite lunch places. We also love Chinese New Year, when there are fireworks in the parking lot, drummers, and at least four colorful dancing lions parading through the restaurant, batting their long eyelashes for little red envelopes stuffed with cash.

James always orders the won ton soup if he feels a cold coming on, but it's worth ordering on any visit. Two large serving bowls are brought to the table; one filled with just-perfectly-cooked greens floating in crystal clear, well seasoned broth; the other filled with excellent homemade pork and shrimp wontons. The server places several wontons in an individual soup bowl, and then ladles the broth over the top.

The menu features many traditional dishes, but our favorite entrée has to be the salt and pepper fish. Tender slices of flounder are breaded in a light mix of salt, spice, and pepper and then deep-fried. Garnished with diced peppers, the dish is fresh, surprisingly light, but still satisfying and rich. This, over some of the very good rice, is our idea of a heavenly meal. If you prefer meat, the salt and pepper pork ribs are equally addictive.

We highly recommend the green beans and pork dish made from hearty ground pork with a spicy kick mixed with wok-fried green beans (keeps them crisp but tender inside). We also love the shrimp dish made with walnuts piled on a platter and tossed with a perfectly balanced sauce that includes tangy mayonnaise and just the right amount of honey.

If you're accompanied by picky eaters or children who don't like spices, the simple chicken vegetable dish is perfect. The vegetables are bright and crisp, and the white sauce is simple, mild, and really delicious. It's easy for a kitchen that's cutting corners to use a lot of corn starch in their white sauce and lose the flavor, but these chefs respect the food. Ask for white breast meat in any poultry dish and they'll happily substitute it for the dark thigh meat.

While we like coming for dinner, most of the best dishes are also available on the less expensive lunch menu. They offer a lunch buffet on some days, but we prefer to order off the menu. No matter when you come you'll see a heavy percentage of locals who know where the good eats are.

Service is typical for Chinese restaurants: efficient and attentive, not particularly smiley. If you have a special request, ask, as we have always found that the kitchen can do almost anything we throw at them.

You can order takeout, but keep in mind that most of this cuisine should be eaten immediately, so don't order the Peking duck (good) unless you're eating in.

Despite the rather unpromising ambiance in the entrance and the less-than heavenly bathrooms, the dining area is spacious and breezy. Tables for two and four line the walls, while large round tables fill the middle of the big room, perfect for the multi-generational families who swarm this place on weekends and holidays.

Address: 2463 S. Kihei Rd., Kihei, South Maui
Location: Kamaole Shopping Center next to Denny's
Meals: Lunch, Dinner
Hours: Daily 11am–9:30pm; Buffet F–Su 11am–2pm
Parking: Lot
Phone: 808-879-1988

Eskimo Candy *(American)*

OVERALL:
3
out of 5 stars

Eskimo Candy has been wholesaling fish to island restaurants, hotels, and grocery stores for many years. A while back they also opened a retail store and a lunch counter that serves fish plates, burgers, wraps, and ribs.

Eskimo Candy is pretty transparent about what you're eating. The Fish-n-Chips platter is advertised as "w/ frozen mahi" and "w/ frozen ono" ($6.95 each). The truth is that anyone selling you fish and chips on Maui is working with frozen fish – otherwise you'd be paying $16 for that plate – but few are so willing to say so on their menu.

Of course, no other restaurant is hoping to sell you *fresh fish* to take home, either. We would buy more fresh fish and marinated fish from **Eskimo Candy's** retail operation if the prices were lower than they are at other grocery stores (after all, there is no middleman, so why don't they cut us a break). We do like their poke (ahi sashimi with spices), but we also like Foodland's (which is open longer hours).

The bottom line is **Eskimo Candy** provides good to average, inexpensive food in a clean, get-out-of-here-quick atmosphere. Outside tables don't have a great view (the street and parking lot), but the service is helpful and quick, and kids are very happy with the fish shack atmosphere and the menu.

continued on next page

Eskimo Candy *(continued)*

Address: 2665 Wai Wai Pl, Kihei, South Maui
Location: Turn from South Kihei Road at Gian Don's, Eskimo Candy is on the right.
Meals: Lunch, Dinner
Hours: M–F 10:30am–7pm
Parking: Lot
Phone: 808-879-5686
Website: www.eskimocandy.com

$

OVERALL:
3.6
out of 5 stars

Fat Daddy's Smokehouse *(American / Barbecue)*

Fat Daddy's makes good Texas barbecue by smoking meats in their own smoker behind the restaurant and serving them up with traditional sides like macaroni and cheese, baked beans, cole slaw, and cornbread. (Everything is made from scratch.)

If you haven't had Texas barbecue, you should know that it's ***supposed*** to be bright pink inside and dark brown – charred – on the outside. The meat cures while soaking up the intense, wood smoke flavor. Once smoked, the meat is dressed with a sauce, which can be sweet or spicy, vinegary or tomato-ey, and this is served on the side or dashed over the top.

We like the brisket, the ribs, and the pulled pork. The sauce is too sweet on its own, but when paired with the meat, the woodsy char darkens the flavor and they balance each other out (use more sauce on the pork than you think you need). We like the watercress salad as a side because, while the bitter cress is used sparingly, it's nice with the sweet carrots, and the dressing is light and fresh. The cornbread we leave alone.

The plate combinations are a good value and big enough for most people to share. A full bar and several flat screen televisions makes this an excellent place to hang out with your friends and watch the game. Kids also love this place for a filling, inexpensive casual family meal.

Address: 1913 S. Kihei Rd., Kihei, South Maui
Location: Kalama Villages across from the Whale
Meals: Lunch, Dinner
Hours: W–M 11:30am–9pm
Parking: Lot
Phone: 808-879-8711
Website: www.fatdaddysmaui.com

Feast at Lele *(Lu'au)*

If a hotel lu'au featuring buffet trays full of salty, heavy Hawaiian food, fourteen strangers at your big round table, and average entertainment doesn't appeal to you, check out **Feast at Lele.** Chef James McDonald, Chef Owner of one of our very favorite restaurants, *I'O*, has created a lu'au experience you won't get anywhere else.

First of all, you and your dining partners sit at your own table, and the food is served in courses (no getting up and grazing in herds). The servers are appropriately dressed in sarongs – which, if you come from a cold climate and don't often see a lot of skin, may look like *inappropriate* dress, (nudge, wink).

The spectacle continues in the fabulous view of Lahaina's harbor at sunset (you're on the beach), and, of course, the music, hula dancing, and fire dancing. While more traditional lu'aus – including the venerable **Old Lahaina Lu'au** – are communal, **Feast at Lele** is like an exotic, romantic dinner theater.

Warning: the drinks are strong, and you should pace yourself if you don't want to start seeing eight beautiful hula dancers when you should be seeing four. The mai tais are delicious (we've heavily researched the subject and have strong mai tai opinions) and the lava flows are sweet but punchy … but we highly recommend looking at their other tropical cocktails. Chef James has a good mixologist so if something appeals, get it. Plus, they're included in the price of the evening, so … hire a cab to go back to your accommodations. Beer and wine are also available.

Each course of the evening features several plates of traditional foods from each of the four South Pacific regions that contribute to Hawaii's lu'au tradition: Hawai'i, New Zealand, Tahiti, and Samoa (the fifth course is dessert). The servers know exactly what is on each plate, and how it was prepared, and they can answer all of your questions, which is a real bonus for those interested in knowing about the food, not just tasting it.

One of the nice things about this lu'au is that the entertainment matches the courses; for example, when you're eating Tahitian food you're watching dances from Tahiti. The servers are attentive and somehow manage to give the impression that yours is the only table they have to take care of that evening.

We like that Chef James is willing to update the traditional foods – salted or grilled fish, poi, greens – with some simple touches to please our more modern palates and show off his culinary chops. While not every dish is perfectly delicious (that might not be possible given the limits of the cuisines), it's all authentic, and we appreciate it both on its own merits and as an educational experience.

We do wish the dancers were more consistent in their performances. This is a very intimate space, and there are far fewer dancers here than at many lu'aus, so if someone is having an off night, it's obvious. On the other hand, we've seen truly animated, fiery performances, too (no pun intended, but the fire dance is always fun).

If you are skeptical about lu'aus and afraid they're too "touristy" for you, we recommend **Feast at Lele**. The price tag is high, but every self-described foodie we've sent agrees that it's worth it.

continued on next page

Feast at Lele *(continued)*

Some readers have asked if going to *Feast at Lele* is a good way to get Chef James' cooking without visiting his nearby *Pacific'O* or *I'O*. No, it's not. While the traditional foods served here are certainly his interpretations, it's not really anything like either of his other restaurants (and both of those are very different from each other). All three restaurants, however, use the fantastic local, organic ingredients grown at his O'O Farms in Kula.

Address: 505 Front St., Lahaina, West Maui
Meals: Dinner
Hours: Nightly 5:30pm - 8:30pm
Parking: Lot, Street
Phone: 808-667-5353
Website: www.feastatlele.com

Ferraro's Bar e Ristorante *(Italian)*

It would be very easy for *Ferraro's* to skimp on service and food quality and simply coast by on their absolutely perfect location … which is why we are glad that this restaurant is located at The Four Seasons, a resort which refuses to rest on its laurels.

The restaurant gathers its white linen tables on several broad terraces shaded by giant umbrella tents. The view is the expansive green lawn rolling down to the ocean below. A large, columned bar built from warm stone provide sample casual dining, and tables for large and intimate parties are available. After dark, this is a dimly lit restaurant, but during the day we're grateful for the shade of the tent, because the brilliant South Maui sun shines on the waves and the view is bright indeed.

We love coming to *Ferraro's* for the less expensive lunch, because the view is so pristine, the food so lovely, and the service so wonderful. The wood-burning oven churns out good pizzas, the sandwiches are made with local ingredients (get the lobster roll), and the salads are big and bold.

When we go for dinner, we try to get reservations for sunset, which when seen from *Ferraro's*, defines the word *spectacular*. Wailea is one of the prettiest areas of the island, and the sunset view from Ferraro's is picture postcard perfect. Live music – gentle guitar, violin, or flute – is amplified just enough so that you can hear it, but still speak in a normal tone of voice and trust that your dinner companions can hear you.

The service at The Four Seasons is, to use James's word, "sterling." Friendly, knowledgeable, and relaxed, they manage to guide, inform, and help you without being obtrusive. When they say "It's no problem," you actually feel that it isn't, for them. It's lovely to be in such capable hands.

Occasionally we will be reminded that we are at a resort, not at an independent restaurant. For example, on one recent visit we ordered the excellent Caprese salad. This is a stack of red heirloom tomato slices, thin, a layer of lush mozzarella, yellow heirloom tomato slices, a good olive oil and a beautiful deep green basil puree. Our first bite was delicious, but too cold. We

OVERALL:
4.2
out of 5 stars

let it sit on the table for a few minutes to warm up a little. Were the salads assembled and then refrigerated to save time during service? Perhaps, but they could have left them out for a few minutes before serving to disguise the fact. This restaurant is one of those so-nearly-perfect places, that the little things like this appear more obvious.

The pasta dishes are lovely, and all can be split into half courses or appetizer sizes, which is convenient if you do not want an entire meal of pasta. We absolutely love the lobster linguini. It comes with a savory cream sauce and an incredibly generous serving of perfectly cooked lobster.

The bolognese has very clean flavors: not too spicy, not too sweet, not to salty. The veal, pork, and beef in the sauce are perfectly cooked and tender.

For main entrees our current favorites are the sea bass with a slightly peppery watercress butter sauce, and the ciopella di mare, a lovely tomato-saffron-crab broth that is perfectly seasoned, with scallops, shrimp, lobster, calamari, and fish. James is tempted to tip the bowl to the back of his throat.

Desserts are traditionally very good, and change regularly (as does the rest of the menu). If they have the cheesecake made with a super-light ricotta cheese and a disk of lemon gelato on top, we recommend it. The sugared pine nuts and rhubarb on the side make this dessert both refreshing and fairy-tale light.

The little things, like the excellent house bread with olive tapenade threaded through it, and the fact that coffee comes in a French press, up the ante for this restaurant making our favorites list. The wine list is good, filled with Italian bottles, but you can also order from the more extensive list at sister restaurant Duo. If you're looking for an exceptional meal in an exceptional setting, Ferraro's may be perfect for you. Parents with kids find both a familiar but sophisticated children's menu and a comfortable atmosphere because the terraced restaurant makes it easy to put the most romantic tables on a lower level.

Address: 3900 Wailea Alanui Dr., Wailea, South Maui
Location: Four Seasons Resort
Meals: Lunch, Dinner
Hours: Daily 11:30am – 9pm
Parking: Valet
Phone: 808-874-8000
Website: www.fourseasons.com/maui

Five Palms Restaurant *(American / Pacific Rim)*

Five Palms is in one of the best waterfront locations on the island. Anchoring the north end of Keawakapu Beach, the view stretches out the Wailea coast, over the water to little crescent-shaped Molokini, and beyond to the majestic red mound of Kaho'olawe. Stunning.

Outdoor seating on the lanai is your best bet, and the best bet for food is breakfast. The garden benedict – spinach and sun dried to-

continued on next page

OVERALL:
3.4
out of 5 stars

Five Palms Restaurant *(continued)*

matoes – is a good choice. So is the banana foster pancakes (rum's in that pineapple sauce), and we also like their egg breakfasts. Lunches, which are served along with the breakfast menu from morning to happy hour in the afternoon, consist of large sandwiches with well-prepared steak fries. The burger is good (order it a little rarer than you normally would). So is the spinach salad with blue cheese and bacon.

We have been known to meet friends for half-priced appetizers and drink specials in the late afternoon, but we rarely stay for dinner, which in our experience is disappointing. Service is halfhearted and slightly sloppy, but the view makes up for most of it during daylight hours. After dark, however, there is nothing to look at but the plate.

Note: the champagne brunch at Easter is highly recommended.

Address: 2960 S. Kihei Rd., Kihei, South Maui
Location: at the Mana Kai
Meals: Breakfast, Brunch, Lunch, Dinner
Hours: Daily 8am-9pm
Parking: Lot
Phone: 808-879-2607
Website: www.fivepalmsrestaurant.com

OVERALL:
4.2
out of 5 stars

Flatbread Pizza Company *(Pizza)*

There are some restaurants that approach food as a life mission, and ***Flatbread Pizza Company*** counts itself one of those restaurants. *Sustainable, organic,* and *local* are more than watchwords here; they are a business decision for the company and a life choice for many of the staff members. The resulting food is delicious, and this is one of our favorite places on Maui.

Even deep dish pizza fans tend to ooh and ahh over the thin, irregularly shaped pizzas. The dough, made with local spring water, organic flour, cake yeast, and kosher salt, is densely flavored, chewy, and crispy in all the right places. The red sauce is made fresh in-house from organic tomatoes and several organic herbs. Toppings include a maple fennel sausage made from scratch, nitrite-free pepperoni, chicken, and plenty of veggies including sweet caramelized Maui onions. You can select your own toppings or choose from one of their thoughtful combinations.

We especially like the sausage pizza with caramelized onions, sun dried tomatoes, mushrooms, mozzarella, parmesan cheese, garlic oil and herbs. It's a white pizza, but we occasionally get it with the red sauce added. Another perennial favorite is called the Pele Pesto, which features an incredible pesto made from basil, macadamia nuts, and garlic. Goat cheese, fresh tomatoes, Kalamata olives, and herbs round out the pie.

Every day features two specials, one vegetarian and one meat. These tend to showcase the freshest and most unusual local ingredients the manager has found, but most combinations (especially the meat) range from odd to unappealing. Unless a special really calls you, we recommend choosing from among the many regular combinations on the menu.

The large salads feature crisp, fresh greens, shaved carrots, chunky celery slices, and a smattering of dark green seaweed, and represent our one real quarrel with *Flatbread*. Yes, the salads are large, but they're really just a head of lettuce left slightly too wet from its washing, so that the dressing slips off and puddles on the plate. This dressing – the only one available – is a pine-apple vinaigrette that is too bright with vinegar, too sweet with pineapple, and has too little body (perhaps a dash of mustard would help). We usually skip the salad altogether for this reason (more room for pizza), or make our own dressing with vinegar and olive oil. We also skip dessert and head to *Ono Gelato* just up the street.

There's a full bar, including the tasty **Maui Brewing Company** beers on tap, and a good selection of local cane sugar sodas. The signature drink on the mainland (this is a small chain from New England) is lemonade sweetened with maple syrup. In the colder climates of the northeast it can be served warm, but in Paia it is only served with ice. The iced version is still refresh-ing – especially since so few Maui restaurants make fresh lemonade at all – but not as tasty as we remember it. We suspect that with both lemons and maple syrup being very expensive on Maui, this drink gets a short shrift.

All Paia restaurants are noisy, and *Flatbread* is no exception. The big main dining room offers lots of seating options, from huge booths to smaller ta-bles to tallboy chairs to couches and coffee tables to the bar itself. The brick oven is roaring inside, so we often sit out on the shaded lanai. Every Tuesday is packed as people turn out to support whichever local nonprofit gets 10% of that evening's sales. You might wait for as long as forty-five minutes on any given night, however, so consider calling ahead and putting your name on the list before you arrive.

Service can range from excellent and attentive to distracted and intention-ally oblivious, and we suspect that training is left to previous employers. The person who delivers the pizza to the table is usually not the server, but the pizza maker, often wearing a heartfelt expression of humble pride as they describe the pie they made just for us. There is no doubt that those who work the pizza oven – with their rippling windsurfer physiques, tattooed arms, and wild hair – are there to serve the Fire, the Bread, and maybe even the Divine in You. *(Namaste.)*

Address: 89 Hana Hwy., Paia, North Shore
Meals: Lunch, Dinner
Hours: Daily 11:30am–10pm
Parking: Street
Phone: 808-579-8989
Website: www.flatbreadcompany.com

OVERALL:
3
out of 5 stars

$ $

Fred's Mexican Café *(Mexican)*

Oh, *Fred's*, what are we going to do with you??

When you opened a couple of years ago, you used fresh, high quality ingredients, you put care into your food, and your prices were very reasonable.

Now your $2 Taco Tuesdays have gone to $2.95, we've had one too many too-fishy-tasting-fish-tacos, and the flavors in everything else on your lunch and dinner menus are just average. (Thank goodness you give out that two for one coupon in the tourist magazines for breakfast.)

We still like your breakfast, your rowdy bar scene and your competent, friendly servers. You've still got one of the best views on the island. But where did the love go??

Address: 2511 S. Kihei Rd., Kihei, South Maui
Location: Across from Kamaole Beach Park II
Meals: Breakfast, Lunch, Dinner
Hours: Daily 7:30am – 10pm
Parking: Lot, Street
Phone: 808-891-8600
Website: www.fredsmexicancafe.com

OVERALL:
3.2
out of 5 stars

$ $

Fresh Mint *(Vegan / Vietnamese)*

Fresh Mint is a crazy little restaurant in a crazy little building with a crazy shade of purple on the walls and crazy delicious vegan food that satisfies even the most carnivorous appetites.

This establishment is not run so much like a restaurant but more of a home kitchen.

Don't expect good service: it's just the owner and his wife serving and cooking, and they have trouble doing both at the same time. One of you might get your entrée ten minutes before the other one does – but that's OK, you'll want to share each one. Think of them as courses.

Don't expect a beautiful restaurant. The walls are purple (eggplant or Barney? Can't decide, depends upon the lighting), and the bathroom is through the kitchen.

Do expect very fresh food made with care. The sauces are excellent and well made, and the soy meats are cooked so perfectly that the texture fools many a meat eater. If you're a vegan, you should certainly stop in for a meal or two. If you're not, you might want to get a break from fish and steak.

Address: 115 Baldwin Ave., Paia, North Shore
Location: Past Mana Foods on the left side.
Meals: Dinner
Hours: Daily 5pm-9pm
Parking: Street
Phone: 808-579-9144

Gaby's Pizzeria *(Pizza)*

OVERALL:
3.6
out of 5 stars

Gaby's is a gathering spot for many locals on the West side because they offer big, reasonably priced pies and drinks in a friendly, open restaurant that's open late.

The pizza slices are good, but we order the better Sicilian pies, whose square proportions and thick crust remind Molly of her college days in Boston. The spicy sauce is made in-house and is very good, and we like the sausage, which is also made in-house. The clam and garlic slices are fragrant with basil, hearty, and tasty.

We like the "Makai" pizza rolls, which are a tongue in cheek nod from the Sicilian owner, Gaby, to the seafood culture that is Maui's restaurant scene. Made to look like fat sushi rolls, the chef takes pizza dough and rolls it with shrimp, crab, spinach, mushrooms, onions, mozzarella and cream cheese. It's baked and served with a pesto ranch dipping sauce and a sweet chili dipping sauce. It is just as cheesy as it sounds. If you're looking for something lighter, the "California Roll" coils feta cheese, sun dried tomatoes, pesto, artichokes, red peppers, and Maui onions.

There are deli sandwiches, pool tables, and good happy hour specials, and if Gaby is on the premises, he's likely to come out and entertain you with plenty of funny stories. Worth a stop in for a break from the high prices in Lahaina.

Address: 505 Front St., Lahaina, West Maui
Meals: Lunch, Dinner, Late-Night
Hours: Daily 11-12am
Parking: Lot, Street
Phone: 808-661-8112

Gazebo Restaurant *(American)*

OVERALL:
3.2
out of 5 stars

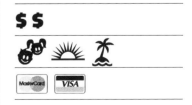

The wait for a table at ***The Gazebo*** is legendary. Unless you show up at least fifteen minutes before they open, you'll be waiting for up to an hour for a table. We like to decide when we want to eat, and then show up at least thirty minutes earlier. The free coffee bar on the deck of the pool (yes, you line up along a kidney shaped pool) helps to keep the edge off the hunger.

The tiny round restaurant has big picture windows all the way round (hence the name) and in whale season we like to sit facing Napili Bay, where the giant animals frolic in the early morning sun.

The food is average American breakfast and lunch food, and we're afraid that the view often makes it taste better than it really does (views do that sometimes). We like the omelets better than the pancakes, which – despite their many raving fans – strike us as formulaic, even with the chopped macadamia nuts and the sliced bananas on top. If you like coconut syrup, you can buy some in any supermarket on the island, get a can of macadamia

continued on next page

Gazebo Restaurant *(continued)*

nuts, and pack them for home. Put them on your own pancakes at home with a dollop of Cool Whip for the same taste, without the slightly too steep price tag.

We tend to migrate a little farther down the bay to **Sea House**, where the breakfasts are made with more care and better ingredients. We also like **Plantation House** for breakfast, which is served well into the afternoon, and we like **Mala** on weekends.

Address: 5315 Lower Honoapiilani Rd., Napili, West Maui
Location: Outrigger Napili Shores
Meals: Breakfast, Lunch
Hours: Daily 7:30am-2pm
Parking: Lot
Phone: 808-669-5621
Website: www.outrigger.com

OVERALL:
4.6
out of 5 stars

Gerard's Restaurant *(French)*

A few years ago a reader told us that he loved the food at **Gerard's**, but he felt a little uncomfortable: underdressed, overly loud. He compared it to "eating at Grandma's."

His grandmother must have been a little stern, because our experience is that **Gerard's**, while quiet, is also unfailingly well-mannered – and well-mannered folk don't make you feel uncomfortable, no matter how formal they may be. **Gerard's** produces wonderful food. The restaurant is immaculately clean, down to the corners of the windows. They have *just* the right linens and polish the silver carefully. They serve the right food at the right time with the right wine, and the service is relaxed and attentive.

The food is high French, but Gerard uses Hawaiian ingredients deliberately and with great style, incorporating them seamlessly into dishes as if they always were part of the cuisine. In addition, there are several bistro items on the menu. If you want a hearty and warming stew, you may want to try the meaty, savory, smooth *Boeuf Bourguignon*. If you want lots of flavors and textures, try the classic white bean *Cassoulet*, stocked with tender, perfectly cooked chunks of meat and sausage. *Coq au Vin* rounds out the bistro menu with its slow-braised chicken – perfect.

If you want to try several of the best dishes on the menu, we recommend going for the eight-course *Degustation Menu*. A *degustation* is a meal that is composed of many varied tastes and is eaten with the intent of concentrating on the sensual and gustatory pleasures of the food. While the courses can change, the most recent menu does include many of our favorite dishes, so we'll look at it in detail.

The first course is the foie gras medallions, perfectly seared and placed upon a round of French toast, then drizzled with poha berry compote (sweet like honey with a little sour pucker). Next course is very rich wide, flat noodles with truffle butter sauce, accompanied by a duo of plump, sweet prawns sautéed lightly in hazelnut oil. Luscious.

Third course is a tiny bowl of a chilled cucumber soup. Swirled into the smooth, creamy, pale green soup is a white thread of Surfing Goat Dairy cheese. A little ball of tomato sorbet rests in the very middle of the dish, and when you stir this all together, you get a cool, sweet, tangy taste of summer with just a titch of spice from the sorbet.

For the next course, a simple spinach salad with two seared scallops arrives. Fifth course features a beautiful piece of snapper draped in a bright emulsion of orange and ginger. The fish is tender and slightly crisp from its bath in the oil in which it roasted, but it could use a tad more salt. What saves it is the perfectly seasoned and subtly flavored braised fennel that serves as its bed and the perfect companion.

We should mention, here at *Intermezzo*, that each course is accompanied by a change of cutlery carried in silver trays, and the servers make sure that you know they're available with both explanations and anything else you may desire. The service is so quiet, professional, and genuine that it's a relief. We've never heard impossible questions like "How are the flavors?" or "Is everything tasting all right?"

Instead we hear the classic "Is there anything else I can bring you?" which is more than enough inquiry.

The sorbet intermezzo is made in house, and served in a chilled martini glass with an ounce of champagne. It's like a fizzy, elegant fruit punch.

Our favorite course is the rack of lamb. Two lamb chops (the rack has been dismantled for you) are presented with the house *potatoes au gratin*, and a *flan* made from a green vegetable (watercress, spinach). The chops are generously sized, perfectly medium rare, crusted with a beautiful salt that keeps the New Zealand lamb succulent. The flan is a tad rubbery and under-flavored, but the fluffy potato gratin, with the wonderfully melty cheese, is decadent and comforting.

The final course is a dessert from their exceptional list. Our favorite is the classic *crème brulée*, which Gerard serves chilled and crusted with at least an eighth of an inch of raw Hawaiian sugar torched into a thick, hard caramel. We must actually stab at the dessert to break this crust and get to the custard, and the result is a mouthful of cool vanilla and slightly warm caramel. My, my, my.

Another favorite dessert from a recent visit was the *Mille-feuille*, or Napoleon. A spectacular puff pastry standing seven inches high, it is layers of "thousand leaved" puff pastry alternating with lemon curd and strawberries. Light, fluffy curd, crackly sounds as you break the pastry – and we complain there are so few good pastry chefs on Maui!!?

The restaurant is located in the Plantation Inn, a gracious building well back from Front Street. There are no views to speak of, and there are three dining areas in the restaurant: inside in a very air conditioned and slightly stuffy parlor, outside on the lanai, or in a small, fairy-lit garden area. We like

continued on next page

Gerard's Restaurant *(continued)*

the porch best, where, even though the tables are very tight, we can see the dishes come out. Music plays to give quiet conversation some cover, but perhaps because of the close quarters, conversations can erupt between tables easily, and we always meet nice people at **Gerard's**.

The wine list is lovely, the service is French, and the bottom line is that if you are looking for a rowdy night out on the town, head to **Lahaina Grill** or **Pacific'O** ... but if you want a special, quiet French meal focused solely on the subtle pleasures of the palate, **Gerard's** is the place to be.

Address: 174 Lahainaluna Rd., Lahaina, West Maui
Location: at The Plantation Inn
Meals: Dinner
Hours: Nightly 6pm–8:30pm
Parking: Street
Phone: 808-661-8939
Website: www.gerardsmaui.com

Gian Don's Italian Bistro *(Italian)*

Gian Don's boasts a generous space on South Kihei Road – generous enough to house a baby grand piano for the musicians who come to play on certain nights. The service is generally good, and the solid middle-of-the-road menu reflects the restaurant's history (it was a sister to **Marco's** in Kahului and still uses some of the same recipes). There is also a tendency to stray into the "something for everyone" temptation that all tourist-economy restaurants face, and that's where they lose us.

We like the vodka rigatoni and the ravioli, but wish there were just a little more pasta in the pasta:sauce ratio. We order fish prepared in the classic preparation (olive oil, butter, garlic, onions), but stay away from most of the other preparations. We're surprised by some of the odd items that please, including the ribs, which come with an excellent homemade plum barbecue sauce, and the house salad, which is just a lovely little fresh dish. We also like the tiramisu. We don't, however, understand why, when they clearly know how to dice garlic, the garlic bread is made with garlic *powder*.

While their dinners may disappoint, their breakfast rarely does. Eating out on their bright lanai in the morning is a treat, and the offers the most consistent value.

Address: 1445 S. Kihei Rd., Kihei, South Maui
Meals: Breakfast, Lunch, Dinner
Hours: Sa–Su 9am–9pm; Nightly 4:30pm–9pm
Parking: Lot
Phone: 808-874-4041
Website: www.giandons.com

OVERALL:

3

out of 5 stars

Gianotto's Pizzeria *(Pizza)*

Giannotto's serves New York style pizza with a really crispy, paper thin crust that crunches under your teeth, and that salty cheese we haven't had since we left the Tri-State Area. Back home it would be average, and on Maui, it's nostalgic, but still average. The sandwiches, or subs, are similarly nostalgic – stuffed with fillings and a little greasy.

Frank Sinatra and Bruce Springsteen albums line the walls beside faded high school sports teams pictures and baby photos. The owner's New Jersey roots are evident in his gravelly voice and business-like attitude, but he's been here long enough to have been softened by Aloha.

The few seats inside the pizza joint are supplemented by picnic tables outside, and this is a good place to take the kids for a quick meal no one will complain about on the way to the Iao Valley.

Address: 2050 Main St., Wailuku, Central Maui
Meals: Lunch, Dinner
Hours: M-Sa 11am-9pm; Su 11am-8pm
Parking: Street
Phone: 808-244-8282

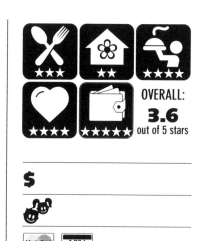

Grandma's Coffeehouse *(Coffeehouse)*

If you're upcountry and wishing you could take a break from the winding roads and get a cup of coffee, stop at Grandma's. The little shop has a few tables and chairs, homemade pastries, and everything can be made for there or to go. This little village has a cute array of look-see stores; including a lovely little art gallery, and is worth a stop.

Address: 153 Kula Hwy, Kula, Upcountry
Location: at Thompson Road
Meals: Breakfast, Lunch, Snacks & Treats
Hours: Daily 7am-5pm
Parking: Lot
Phone: 808-375-7853

Green Banana Café *(Coffeehouse)*

We like the **Green Banana** for its coffee drinks and pastries. We also like the servers behind the counter, who are genuine and put some love into their work. Let us tell you a little story to explain what we mean.

One day Molly was overwhelmed and exhausted, so she stopped in to **Green Banana** for a coffee. As she looked at the blackboard menu, her mind went blank. Everything looked equally appealing. She

continued on next page

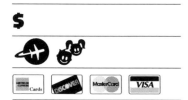

OVERALL:
4.4
out of 5 stars

Green Banana Café *(continued)*

could not decide. When she pressed herself to choose, her mind rebelled. On a day when she had been responsible for many tough decisions, her mind simply refused to make even one more.

Molly told the dark-haired server behind the counter "I'm having a really bad day, and I just want you to sell me something that will make me feel better."

The server didn't miss a beat. She brightened and said "Do you like vanilla?" Molly nodded. "How about carrot muffins?" Molly nodded. "Do you want caffeine; do you need to be alert now?" Molly nodded.

There was a bustling and a shirring sound from the espresso maker, and when the server returned, she held a tall mug filled with a vanilla latte, double shot, with an-over-the-brim cap of fresh whipped cream. She pointed to the tray of carrot muffins and asked "A lot of glaze, or a little, or medium?" Molly said "A lot, please," and the sweet angel plucked the largest, most densely glazed muffin off the tray with a long pair of tongs. She placed it on a china plate and handed it to Molly, who gazed gratefully at her as she handed over her credit card and silently made notes in her head so she would remember to write about this Caffeine and Pastry Angel.

The carrot muffin was tender and sweet and rich, delicious enough to press her fingers into the crumbs left on the plate so she could eat every last bit. The latte was creamy and deeply vanilla-ed.

Even if you are not in crisis, the pastries of all kinds have made us happy at *Green Banana*. We also adore the Acai berry bowls filled with the beautiful, exotic blue fruit, homemade granola, and yogurt. *Green Banana* is definitely worth a stop and a linger while you're shopping in Paia.

Address: 137 Hana Hwy., Paia, North Shore
Meals: Breakfast, Lunch, Dinner, Snacks & Treats
Hours: Daily 6am–8pm
Parking: Street
Phone: 808-579-9130

Hakone *(Japanese / Sushi)*

Hakone is our favorite traditional Japanese restaurant on Maui, even after losing nearly half of its dining room, several pages from its menu, and several nights of service during the recent transition of ownership from the Maui Prince to Makena Resort. The servers in kimonos are still there, and the same talented sushi chef is behind the bar. The tables are still large and polished, and the sake list is intact. The giant weekend buffet meal is no more (at least for now), but several of their best items are available every night. If you love sushi and want a traditional Japanese meal, *Hakone* is your place.

We like the miso butterfish and the salmon plate. The combination meals make a good value: in addition to the main course you get their excellent miso soup, a large green salad with a light vinaigrette, rice, and ice cream (green tea and red bean are our current favorite flavors).

We like the sushi combination platter with the day's best sashimi, a California roll (real crab, light mayonnaise), and a few pieces of nigiri. If you like to order a la carte, they have several traditional, simple rolls as well as a few of the extravagant rolls that Pacific Rim cuisine has inspired on menus across Hawaii. If you see a roll featuring snow crab tempura, order it.

Speaking of tempura, this is the best on Maui; indescribably light, crispy, and flavorful. In addition to the shrimp, carrots, sweet potatoes, and green beans, we love their impossibly-thin slices of Maui sweet onion cut into perfect rings, lightly battered and fried. When we take a bite, the onion dissolves before our teeth have a chance to do their work. While the onion and tempura evaporate in our mouths, the rest of the onion stands crisp in our hand. The melt-in-your-mouth-not-in-your-hands effect is a revelation.

We very much like the "No Like Fish" roll, which is a fat vegetarian delicacy. The Sunomono salad features real crab (not a substitute), deep green, tender seaweed and pale green cucumber.

From the quiet, proper service to the Aloha shirts hanging on the walls like ceremonial kimonos, this place provides a truly special experience, and we highly recommend it. It's still a bit expensive, but if you're looking for a quiet dinner on a Wednesday, Thursday, Friday, or Saturday, you may see us there.

Address: 5400 Makena Alanui Dr., Makena, South Maui
Location: at the Makena Resort (used to be the Maui Prince)
Meals: Dinner
Hours: W-Sa 6pm-9pm
Parking: Valet, Lot
Phone: 808-875-5888
Website: www.makenaresortmaui.com

Hali'imaile General Store *(Pacific Rim)*

What would Maui's restaurant scene be without *Hali'imaile* (Hah lee ee MY leh) *General Store*? A cornerstone of the Hawaiian Regional Cuisine movement, for two decades, this foodie oasis in the middle of the pineapple (now sugar) fields has been serving well-made, comforting, delicious meals.

OVERALL:
4
out of 5 stars

We're going to make special mention of the drinks because the bartenders here love their work and make killer cocktails (though they can be slow to deliver). The wine list is very good, and we always find something we didn't expect.

We have never walked out of *Hali'imaile General Store* unhappy with our meal. We like to start with the long-time favorite appetizer, Sashimi Napoleon. Layers of sashimi, smoked salmon, caviar, and won tons stack up on a bed of crisp salad greens laced with tobikko caviar and wasabi vinaigrette. The whole contraption looks delicate, but it's tougher than you would think to destroy it with a chopstick or a steak knife and render it into bites.

continued on next page

Hali'imaile General Store *(continued)*

The smoky, spicy, sweet flavors with the crisp, crunchy, silky smooth textures define pleasure. Although the crab pizza is "famous", we usually move on to other courses.

We like the fish dishes, which change on a regular basis with the seasons. The macadamia nut preparation is a customer favorite for a reason (it's the killer mango lilikoi butter sauce), but we also like the peppery-but-sweet Thai chili sauce on the seared ahi dish.

If you're in the mood for meat, we recommend the braised short ribs, which come with a truffle oil-enriched macaroni and cheese. We also love the baby back ribs with the spicy, tangy, sweet barbecue sauce. The mashed potatoes that come with many dishes are noteworthy for their creamy texture and buttery flavor. If you are looking for something a tad lighter, the simply prepared roast chicken dish usually features astringent asparagus extravagantly wrapped with prosciutto. (It's only a *tad* lighter.)

The desserts are as rich as the main courses, so if you have a sweet tooth, save room. While we find the pineapple upside down cake just too darn sweet, James's all-time favorite dessert is the chocolate macadamia nut pie: a chocolate pastry shell filled with caramel and chocolate and macadamia nuts, topped with whipped cream. The menu changes with the seasons, so you may not find it when you visit.

The restaurant's setting is kitchen-kitsch: bold colors, big ceramics, lots of framed photos of Chef Owner Beverly Gannon and her celebrity clients. We love the hustle and bustle of the front room of the restaurant, but the quieter back room is better for larger groups. One of the first female celebrity chefs and one of the twelve founders of Hawaiian Regional Cuisine, Bev Gannon hires servers who genuinely love food and really get to know her menu and recipes, so the service is both attentive and a celebration of your meal.

Address: 900 Hali'imaile Rd., Makawao, Upcountry
Location: Turn from Baldwin Ave. or Haleakala Highway
Meals: Lunch, Dinner
Hours: M–F 11am–2:30pm; Nightly 5:30pm–9:30pm
Parking: Lot
Phone: 808-572-2666
Website: www.bevgannonrestaurants.com

Haui's Life's a Beach *(American)*

Sometimes you just want to go to a dive and drink cheap beer and eat unimaginative nachos. The extra bonuses at *Life's a Beach* include neon palm trees, pool tables, cheap mai tais, and live music. Don't mess with the local guys with tattoos, but otherwise, have a good time.

OVERALL:
2.4
out of 5 stars

Address: 1913 S. Kihei Rd., Kihei, South Maui
Location: Kalama Village across from the Whale
Meals: Lunch, Dinner, Late-Night
Hours: Daily 11am–2am
Parking: Lot, Street
Phone: 808-891-8010
Website: www.mauibars.com

Hawaiian Moons Natural Foods *(Organic/Vegan)*

The only health food store in South Maui, this is the place to shop for a small, but careful, selection of groceries, produce, vitamins, and beauty items. Prices are high compared to other health food stores on the island, but those other stores are very far away from Kamaole Beach Park I. We think of this as a convenience store that sells health food.

The prepared foods bar is very good and well-shopped, so it turns over frequently. The hot entrees are vegetarian and the smoothies are also recommended.

Address: 2411 S. Kihei Rd., Kihei, South Maui
Location: Across from Kamaole Beach Park I
Meals: Breakfast, Lunch, Dinner
Hours: M-F 8am–9pm; Sa-Su 9am–9pm
Parking: Lot
Phone: 808-875-4356
Website: www.hawaiianmoons.com

Honolua Store *(American/Local/Plate Lunch)*

Kapalua's gorgeous coast invites some of the wealthiest of the wealthy to live and play there, and the restaurants – some of the best on the island – are as expensive as the view. That's why we like the budget-friendly **Honolua Store** for a quick break or a full meal.

Built out in a recent expansion, this place carries not only the typical groceries one might need at the resort, but many specialty items and wine, cheese, and other gourmet foods. The grill is open longer hours – right through dinner time – and serves about twice as many items as it once did. You can get sandwiches (cold or hot), burgers, fish and chips, and local and plate lunch dishes. If you're looking for a break from the resort prices, this is an excellent place to pick up a reasonably priced, tasty breakfast, lunch, or dinner.

Address: 900 Office Rd., Kapalua, West Maui
Location: In the Kapalua Resort
Meals: Breakfast, Lunch, Dinner
Hours: Daily 6am–7:30pm
Parking: Lot
Phone: 808-665-9105
Website: www.kapalua.com

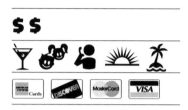

OVERALL:
3.4
out of 5 stars

$ $

Hula Grill *(Pacific Rim)*

Hula Grill is a nearly irresistible restaurant if you're walking by Whaler's Village. It's so friendly looking, with its sandy Barefoot Bar and upscale dining room menu. The late afternoon music (don't sit too close or you won't be able to hear anyone but the vocalist) and the sunset views draw us and many others like a magnet.

The appetizers and sandwiches in the Barefoot Bar are average to good, if overpriced (Ka'anapali again). The real pull here is the sand, the pretty good drinks, and the view of the beach walk (girls in bikinis, boys with smooth chests and salty hair) and the sunset.

Dinner inside is not nearly as compelling (must be the lack of view); the food becomes less interesting and more expensive. However, as one of just a handful of dinner restaurants in the resort, you may end up here at least once, and some good choices include the steaks and the fish specials. Kids like their menu, too.

Address: 2435 Ka'anapali Parkway, Ka'anapali, West Maui
Location: Whaler's Village
Meals: Dinner, Pupus, Happy Hour
Hours: Daily 5pm–9:30pm, Barefoot Bar 11am–11pm
Parking: Lot (validated)
Phone: 808-667-6636
Website: www.tsrestaurants.com

OVERALL:
4
out of 5 stars

$ $ $ $

Humuhumunukunukuapua'a *(Pacific Rim)*

Once you get the rhythm going, it's easier than you think to say ***Humuhumunukunukuapua'a*** (just sound it out, it's phonetic). But if you don't want to bother, just call it "Humu's," and everyone will know what you're talking about.

This is the signature restaurant at The Grand Wailea, and it floats in a lagoon stocked with humus (the restaurant's namesake, which translates to "fish with a nose like a pig") and many other tropical beauties. The open air restaurant has a thatched roof, a large central bar with a wraparound fish tank, and tiki torches. The sunset view is unbelievable and the setting positively theatrical.

The food is very good, the service very slow, and the prices very high. If you splurge, try the sesame-crusted mahi-mahi with the salty black-bean miso sauce, the filet, or any of the daily specials. Close your eyes when the bill comes and think of that sunset.

Address: 3850 Wailea Alanui Dr., Wailea, South Maui
Location: Grand Wailea Resort
Meals: Dinner
Hours: Nightly 5:30pm–9:00pm
Parking: Lot, Valet
Phone: 808-875-1234
Website: www.grandwailea.com

I'O *(American/Pacific Rim)*

OVERALL:

4

out of 5 stars

I'O's Chef Owner James McDonald is so dedicated to fresh, local ingredients he started his own organic farm in Kula. After nearly a decade in operation, O'O Farms supplies the vast majority of produce and herbs to his restaurants *I'O*, *Pacific'O*, and *Feast at Lele*. (We highly recommend touring the farm, 808-667-4341.)

Chef James's drive to wow the diner is evident in the evolution of his food. While *Pacific'O* stays true to his fusion roots serving the exciting, bold flavors that put him on the beach in Lahaina in the first place, *I'O*, just next door, now takes a simpler approach. Chef James' commitment to food is fundamental: extraordinary ingredients – he buys fish from fishermen who land just offshore to show him the day's catch – and prepares them as simply as possible. The clean flavors and sheer sensuality of his dishes gets us at a gut level (pardon the pun) … but it also engages us intellectually and emotionally.

In other words, *I'O* serves really good food.

Try the Thai Curry Asparagus Soup, in which the green vegetables are emulsified into silk and swirled with a spicy red pepper/tomato coulis that spirals around a generous piece of lobster. Try the crab cake that spills its solid lumps from a light panko crust with a luxurious miso aioli on the side. Don't miss the fresh and delectable green papaya cole slaw that beds the cake.

The grilled calamari appetizer is a meaty steak marinated and then grilled just until tender. Served with tabouleh, it's topped with a roasty-toasty sweet tomato dressing. Why does everyone else insist on breading this sweet fish?

One of our favorite salads is the perfectly roasted beets, drizzled with a rich pesto and kissed by creamy, salty feta cheese. Our favorite appetizer is The Mad Hatter, a beautiful puff pastry bursting with scallops, mushrooms, and chilies bathed in a lobster-flavored coconut curry. We lick the plate. With fish coming in off the water every day, the crudo ("raw") specials are always choice morsels. These small plates are perfect as appetizers or enjoy several for a light meal. The daily fish specials are excellent, including the crispy ahi.

The wine list is highly rated, and each item on the menu lists a wine suggestion. The large number of wines by the glass is a sign that the owners care about your meal enough to break open a bottle for just one serving. There aren't many tropical cocktails, but we don't mind, because the martinis are so excellent.

We obviously love the food, but the restaurant does have some issues which can interfere with a foodie's appreciation of the kitchen's efforts. The waiters generally know food, and know the menu, but they (or the kitchen?) can be very, very slow, and at times we've had a dish arrive cooler than it should be because of it. Plan for a leisurely paced meal, and keep the bread on the table.

We love the beachfront location – spectacular at sunset – and the modern

continued on next page

I'O *(continued)*

lines and colors on the interior. Despite the romantic garden seating, we choose to sit on the rail inside because **Feast at Lele**, Chef James's beautiful lu'au experience, is right next door. While we enjoy hearing the music, it can be a little loud if you're outside (of course, many people take the opposite view and choose to sit in the garden to glimpse the show through the trees). We also appreciate sitting on chairs made out of wood, rather than the decidedly downscale plastic garden chairs available outside.

You may think that you can visit any of Chef James's restaurants and get the same food, but it just isn't so. **Pacific'O** is slightly more "what you expect from Hawaii" and **Feast at Lele** is definitely traditional lu'au fare turned (way) upscale. It seems that **I'O** is where Chef James allows himself free rein to make whatever is most inspiring, and is our favorite of his three restaurants.

Address: 505 Front St., Lahaina, West Maui
Meals: Dinner
Hours: Nightly 5:30–10pm
Parking: Lot, Street
Phone: 808-661-8422
Website: www.iomaui.com

Isana Restaurant *(Korean / Sushi)*

Isana is a good Korean restaurant featuring yakiniku style barbecue, which you cook yourself on the tabletop. A sushi bar is set off to the side, and their late night half-price specials pack in the locals. Service is generally friendly, but can be brusque, dismissive, and disarmingly honest (we've been told bluntly not to order something because it's not a good dish – we wish we could remember what it is but didn't write it down). The large space holds many large barbecue tables, and there's karaoke late at night. Quite a trip.

We recommend the sushi, especially the spicy scallops dynamite, which lightly dresses tender, well-seared scallops with the spicy Japanese mayonnaise (we also like the shrimp version). The uni is usually very good, also. For Korean barbecue we especially recommend the kalb meat marinated in soy and the spicy pork loin. While the prices will seem high to those who know the cuisine, it's the only tabletop Korean on Maui.

Address: 515 S. Kihei Rd., Kihei, South Maui
Location: Across from Sugar Beach
Meals: Lunch, Dinner
Hours: Daily 11am–10pm; Sushi bar is open until 12am
Parking: Lot
Phone: 808-874-5700
Website: www.isanarestaurant.net

OVERALL:
3
out of 5 stars

$ $ $

Jacque's Northshore Bistro *(American)*

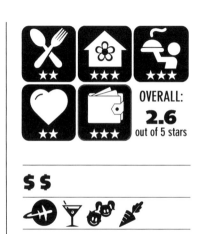

This giant lanai covered with a tin roof is known for its pretty good sushi bar, which (while currently cut way back on its hours) represents the most focused part of the restaurant.

The rest of the menu reads like a transcontinental tour. The beautiful people – surfers and windsurfers from every country – like to eat here, and every dish *attempts* a fusion of their international flavor profiles. They serve steaks, fish, pasta, and salads, and while occasionally something works really well, many items – lilikoi and green peppercorn and saffron? – confuse us, both on the menu and on the plate.

The drinks are strong – as they often are at pick up joints – and the prices on both food and drinks are fair and quite a bit lower than you'll find elsewhere on island. The service is slow but rather exceptionally good looking, and we can recommend Jacques for value.

Address: 120 Hana Hwy., Paia, North Shore
Location: Next to **Charley's**
Meals: Dinner
Hours: Nightly 5pm-10:30pm; F-Sa Sushi Bar 5pm-6pm
Parking: Street, Lot
Phone: 808-579-8844
Website: www.jacquesnorthshorebistro.com

Jawz Tacos *(Mexican)*

Jawz started out as a taco stand just outside of Makena's Big Beach, and that's still our favorite place to get their food. If you go to their sit-down restaurant in North Kihei, you'll find a slightly more refined grill on their fish and a huge salsa bar with salsas ranging from sweet to heat, diced onions, pickled carrots, sour cream, wasabi Asian sauce, and many other yummy toppings. The burritos and tacos themselves are sold to you barely dressed, so take advantage of the bar.

We like the fish (they also have steak, pork, chicken, and shrimp), but don't think this is the place to get inexpensive ahi, because when you shred and grill ahi it just tastes like canned tuna. Get the ono or the mahi-mahi instead.

Fresh-squeezed lemonade is rare on Maui, because lemons can be extremely expensive here. While Jawz has a huge vat of fresh lemonade, it's anemic (we suspect it's a cost control issue). They also make a pretty good margarita and sell Mexican beers. The happy hour specials make an inexpensive meal even cheaper, while the large tables and surfing movies on the televisions make this is a pleasant place for a quick lunch or dinner.

Address: 1279 S. Kihei Rd., Kihei, South Maui
Location: Azeka Mauka Marketplace
Meals: Lunch, Dinner
Hours: Daily 11am-9pm
Parking: Lot
Phone: 808-874-8226
Website: www.jawzfishtacos.com

OVERALL:
4
out of 5 stars

Joe's Bar & Grill *(American)*

Chef Bev Gannon has reversed the typical Wailea equation (great views, but less than great food) to give us excellent home style comfort food in a setting that – while quirky – still provides a lovely vista. Joe's is perched on stilts over the tennis courts at the Wailea Tennis Center. There's a clear view over the courts, golf course and ocean, and you can see great sunsets there.

The restaurant itself is open air and features a deep bar made of copper, wide planked floors, and large tables that are somehow still intimate. We love coming with a few good friends to commune over the big plates of steak, fish, pork loin, or our favorite, meatloaf.

(Let us tell you how good this meatloaf is: Chef Bev Gannon creates the recipes for the in-flight meals on Hawaiian Airlines, and a few years ago when the first class flyers realized that her meatloaf was being served in coach, they refused the fancier dishes created for them and demanded the coach menu.)

The meatloaf is thickly sliced from a large loaf made with moisture-retaining veggies and tender beef. The sweet-sour-spicy barbecue sauce creates the perfect combination of savory, comforting flavors. Served with steak fries or mashed potatoes, this is the manliest meal on Maui.

We also love the diver scallops, which come served as plump little islands of perfectly seared flesh on silver-dollar-sized discs of tender yellow potatoes. Beautiful deep green beans accompany the shellfish, and the whole dish is sauced with a light-but-rich shallot butter. Also try the ribs, which we love at ***Hali'imaile General Store*** as well, and the prime rib with the stunningly simple au jus.

Appetizers and salads are simple and aboveboard and very good. For example, the shrimp cocktail is excellent. The secret to this dish is not just superfresh shrimp, but the spicy cocktail sauce. Bev's version is freshly spiced with horseradish, but also lemony highlights, and a hint of sweet. We also like the simple wedge salad with homemade blue cheese dressing. The desserts are generously proportioned and straightforward, just like the rest of the meal.

One of this restaurant's quirks is that the parking lot is set up the steep hill from the restaurant, making for something of a climb after your meal (it's downhill on the way in). To address this, there's always someone in a golf cart ready to shuttle you back and forth. It's good service, which is matched throughout the meal by the staff, whom we admire as some of the best servers on the island.

With so many island restaurants – Chef Bev's ***Hali'imaile General Store*** and her new ***Seawatch*** included – serving complicated fish preparations and indulgent beef dishes, it can be a relief to get away from it all and just have some good, down-home food. Prices are moderate for Maui and certainly for Wailea, the view is good (although we have to note the thwacking tennis balls can interfere for some people), and the service is just as good as the food. We think we'll go tonight.

Address: 131 Wailea Ike Place, Wailea, South Maui
Location: Wailea Tennis Center
Meals: Dinner
Hours: Daily 5:30–9:30pm
Parking: Lot
Phone: 808-875-7767
Website: www.bevgannonrestaurants.com

Joy's Place *(Vegetarian/American)*

Joy's serves high quality sandwiches, salads, and soups to go. The ingredients are invariably fresh and local and whether your thing is nut burgers or free range turkey (roasted in-house), you'll find excellent choices.

Vegan or carnivore, we recommend trying the falafel with the homemade tahini caper sauce. Sandwiches are generally filled to bursting, and they use sprouted breads or locally-made herb breads.

Smoothies are available, as are pasta salads and soups made fresh from whatever is best in season. The prices aren't cheap, but there's a lot of love and very good ingredients, and you definitely get what you pay for.

If you're considering Subway for a beach lunch, consider Joy's as a healthier alternative.

Address: 1993 S. Kihei Rd., Kihei, South Maui
Location: Island Surf Building
Meals: Lunch
Hours: M-Sa 8am-3pm
Parking: Street
Phone: 808-879-9258

OVERALL:
3.4
out of 5 stars

Julia's Best Banana Bread *(Banana Bread)*

If you or your traveling partner has nerves of steel, you should drive around the West Maui Mountains from Kapalua to Wailuku. The views are unbeatable, the land wild and rugged, and the trade winds blowing in from the west make the air on this side crystal clear. When you hit Kahakuloa (Kah hah koo loh ah), the teensy fishing village, look for the green roadside stand. If it's before 2pm, Julia may still have some bread for you. Made with local bananas, it's succulent, moist, and sweet. Is it the best in the world, as the signs proclaim? Not necessarily … but it's delicious in its context (gorgeous scenery), and if you're driving out this way, you should get a loaf or two. The coconut candy is also very good.

If you don't want to drive out to Kahakuloa, you can order the bread from her website (*so this century*) or you can try Julia's bread at **Flatbread** in Pa'ia. They top it with chocolate sauce and macadamia nut ice cream as a

OVERALL:
4.2
out of 5 stars

CASH

continued on next page

Julia's Best Banana Bread *(continued)*

dessert. It suffers a little from the long trip, and you'll have to pay for a slice nearly what you'd pay for a loaf at her stand … but *you* don't have to make the drive.

Address: Honoapiilani Highway, Kahakuloa, West Maui
Location: past Kapalua where the highway gets very narrow
Meals: Snacks & Treats
Hours: Daily, 9am - 5:30pm or when sold out
Parking: Lot
Website: www.juliasbananabread.com

Kai Wailea *(Sushi)*

Kai Wailea opened two weeks before press time, so this is not really a review. Our first impression is we like the sushi. A lot.

Kai Wailea's sister restaurant, *Kaiwa* in Waikiki, is well-known for unique, creative sushi and Japanese dishes served in an elegant, comfortable restaurant with excellent, traditional service.

The sushi chefs at the new Wailea location are definitely making the great sushi we expect from this company. The flavors and combinations — we love the hamachi with fresh jalapeno slices — are spot on and surprising, and the presentation is elegant and exuberant. We like the creamy, but spicy, Kihei roll, the generous size of the seared ahi roll, and the sashimi presented in sculptured ice bowls. Everything — including the ginger and the soy sauce — is made in house. The beer and sake list is very good, and there is a full bar.

The location, though freshly painted, is a little brightly lit for our taste. The service is fast and competent, although sometimes a little overly enthusiastic about the new menu and what's "The best!" (One of our pet peeves for service is when waiters exclaim accolades without specificity. Why should I think a dish is *fantastic* just because you like it? I don't know you.)

This is a place to watch — we hope it gets its sea legs and is around for a long time. At press time it's too new to give star ratings, but please visit www.MauiRestaurantsBlog.com to get updates and record your own review and rating.

Address: 3750 Wailea Alanui Dr., Wailea, South Maui
Location: The Shops at Wailea
Meals: Dinner
Hours: Nightly 5pm-10pm; Late Night Happy-Hour F-Sa 9:30pm-
       12:30am
Parking: Lot
Phone: 808-875-1955
Website: www.kaiwailea.com

NEW RESTAURANT
Check MauiRestaurantsBlog.com for Updates

Kihei Caffe *(American)*

Locals and tourists flock to Kihei Caffe for breakfast. The counter is manned by the owner, who oozes true Aloha spirit, and the service is fast (with a little less Aloha).

Order inside, and then go find a seat – if you sit before you order, you actually mess with a system that works really well. (Unfortunately, if you sit before you order you may also be scolded by a server.)

This greasy spoon has a view of Kalama Park and a slice of the ocean beyond, and serves no-frills breakfast and lunch dishes. We're not huge fans of the average breakfast fare, but we come anyway because we can get in and out quickly, the coffee is good, and orange juice is fresh. The egg plates come with pretty good biscuits, and the bacon is thick and tasty. The stack of three pancakes is fluffy and filling. We recommend elsewhere for lunch.

The outdoor seating invariably puts us at the mercy of obnoxious sparrows, but that's true at any of the outdoor restaurants on the island. What we don't see anywhere else are the wild chickens that calmly forage under tables for dropped bits. The servers clear plates quickly to discourage the wildlife from feeding and to remind us that we shouldn't linger when other diners need tables.

Address: 1945 S. Kihei Rd., Kihei, South Maui
Location: Kalama Village across from the Whale
Meals: Breakfast, Lunch
Hours: Daily 5am–2pm
Parking: Lot, Street
Phone: 808-879-2230

OVERALL:
3
out of 5 stars

$

Kimo's *(Pacific Rim / American)*

This waterfront restaurant is run by a very successful family of businesses, T S Restaurants, which chooses gorgeous beachfront locations, decorates them with lava rocks, tiki torches, and lots of wood, and serves up big portions of average to good steaks, chicken, and fish dishes.

Sister restaurants on Maui include *Leilani's on the Beach*, *Hula Grill*, and a *Duke's* slated to open in Honua Kai after press time.

In general, we find the food undistinguished. Service is fine if a little forced, drinks are strong, and the location, location, location never, ever disappoints. The sunset view from *Kimo's* can make even the most average of fairly-priced food seem much more than average, and we think that accounts for much of this restaurant's popularity.

Address: 845 Front St., Lahaina, West Maui
Meals: Lunch, Dinner
Hours: Daily 11am–10:30pm; Bar is open till 1:30am
Parking: Street
Phone: 808-661-4811
Website: www.tsrestaurants.com

OVERALL:
3.4
out of 5 stars

$ $

OVERALL:
2.6
out of 5 stars

$ $ $ $

Ko (*Pacific Rim/Local*)

This well-intentioned restaurant at the Fairmont Kea Lani in Wailea has a nice casual poolside setting, which contrasts with the menu: rather complex dishes that attempt to elevate traditional local dishes (they call it Plantation Food) from peasant to high cuisine.

While there is great care and passion put into the concept, and the wine list and menu are crafted with sustainability and organic ingredients in mind, the kitchen just doesn't pull it off. The items all sound delicious, but the execution falls far, far short of what the prices demand. In our work, it's important to evaluate food on the basis of what actually comes out of the kitchen without telegraphing what we're thinking … which is why we never, ever send dishes back and we always take home leftovers (even those we don't want). This is the only place on Maui where something was so inedible (literally we could not eat it without gagging) that we had to send it back. (It was the Portuguese bean soup: so salty we guessed it could have been made with sea water.)

This restaurant really bums us out, because the concept has such promise, and we want to like it much more than we do. There are no highlights to mention, and only several really big mistakes, at hotel prices.

Address: 4100 Wailea Alanui Dr., Wailea, South Maui
Location: Fairmont at Kea Lani
Meals: Dinner
Hours: Daily 5:30.m.–9pm
Parking: Lot, Valet
Phone: 808-875-4100
Website: www.fairmont.com

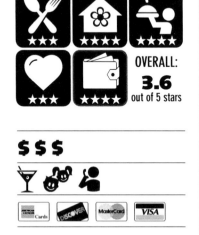

OVERALL:
3.6
out of 5 stars

$ $ $

Kobe (*Japanese Steakhouse*)

Teppanyaki is just plain fun, dontcha think? Japanese chefs juggle knives and throw fire while they prep, sear, and serve your meal tableside … it's food theater, and everyone gets a front row seat at the U-shaped tables.

Kobe is one of the only teppanyaki places on Maui, and we're glad they're here, because it's pretty darn good food, and a pretty darn good show. (Just don't sit upstairs, where the ventilation is less than adequate.)

Visitors flock here, but so do more than a few locals, who appreciate the large quantities of food and the good fried rice (made in front of you, of course). We particularly like the scallops, which we've always had perfectly cooked. The steak is a good cut, especially when we upgrade to the filet. The opakapaka (Hawaiian pink snapper) is tender and takes well to the super hot grill. Keep in mind that they're not using the very best oils or brandies, and set your expectations accordingly. We skip dessert and head to **Ululani's Shave Ice** or **Ono Gelato** for an after dinner treat. If you're not into teppanyaki, you can get sushi at their sushi bar, which is decent. Reservations are recommended.

If you've got kids – or, ahem, a guy who's a kid at heart – we recommend *Kobe*.

Address: 136 Dickenson St., Lahaina, West Maui
Meals: Dinner, Late-Night
Hours: Daily 5:30pm-10pm; Sushi Bar until 11:00pm
Parking: Lot, Street
Phone: 808-667-5555
Website: www.kobemaui.com

Koiso Sushi Bar *(Sushi)*

The secret is out about *Koiso Sushi Bar.* After several years of singing Sushi Master Hiro-san's praises we find we can't get in if we just show up. We have to call and make reservations. That's OK with us – he's worth the extra planning, and we can't begrudge sushi lovers such an excellent experience, or Hiro-san the business.

Hiro-san's domain is in the back of Dolphin Plaza in Kihei, and frankly, it's tiny and doesn't look very inviting from the outside. The two glass walls are plastered with posters of fish, a crowded bulletin board features hundreds of snapshots of his loved ones, and the back wall is littered with various hand-lettered signs detailing the day's fish. There are maybe a dozen seats at his L-shaped sushi bar and one table for four. He doesn't like to seat regulars at the table, perhaps because he knows that watching him work is part of what makes this place magical.

Yes, we said magical. If you've seen a Harry Potter movie, you'll recognize the phenomena we encounter at *Koiso*. Despite the fact it's like he opened his restaurant in his living room, once we sit and look over the fresh fish, something shifts. Just as the brick wall in the train station disappears when a wizard runs into it, when we sit and ask Hiro-san to feed us, the brick wall of everyday life – all the problems, worries, and stress – drops away and reveals a magical place where time seems to stand still and even the most independent-minded diners can't help but smile at each other and strike up a conversation.

It's the impeccably fresh fish, of course. Some is local, and some is from Japan – the fishermen call him in the wee hours to let him know what they've got. If he likes the sound of it, they put it on a plane and it arrives on Maui in time for him to pick it up at the airport, tote it back to Kihei, and prepare it for that evening. With fish this delicious, you cannot help but revel – and since everyone else is reveling, you have instant friends on either side.

The magic isn't all in the fish – some of it comes from Hiro-San himself. The last time we ate at *Koiso* we watched him preparing uni (sea urchin) and noticed that he was moving his entire body as he worked. All movements seemed to come from his abdomen, not his shoulders. He was anchored to the floor, but light on his feet. Every movement was precise, and every movement counted. His long knife flashed as he sliced and flipped

OVERALL:

4

out of 5 stars

$ $

continued on next page

and scooped, and often our eyes couldn't follow the blade because it was blurry with speed.

We realized that a Sushi Master – someone like Hiro-san who swept floors for years before touching a knife – is close to a martial artist. As he flipped the soft, caramel colored pieces of uni on to squared-off loaves of his perfectly seasoned sushi rice, the look on his face was one of concentration, relaxation, and peace.

We like to sit down and ask Hiro-san to feed us. He picks the best of what he has and prepares a lovely plate. This is not the place for fancy rolls; this is straight up classic sushi. If the Molokai shrimp is fresh, we like to supplement with those plump shellfish, and he will bake the heads until they're crisp and crunchy between our teeth. The miso soup is perfectly seasoned, hearty from the earthy mushrooms that fill the bowl, yet still light and clear in the broth. Sake and beer are both available and the waitress keeps the water glasses filled and the drinks coming.

This is not a restaurant for big parties or sushi newbies – if you need beginner chopsticks you're probably better off at **Sansei** or **Hakone** – but if you have respect and admiration for sushi and want to spend an hour with a Master, call **Koiso** and see if they'll take your reservation.

Keep in mind that **Koiso** is a tiny place, and Hiro-san likes to populate it with people who really appreciate his food. We've heard from several people that he didn't give them a reservation over the phone, and we suspect it may be because he likes to keep his counter full of sushi lovers (we nicknamed him the Sushi Nazi a few years ago, after the Soup Nazi on Seinfeld – but he's not mean, just selective). If you suspect you are getting the cold shoulder, and you really want to visit **Koiso**, we suggest another tack.

Show up a little later in the evening – maybe around 8pm – and quietly step just inside his door. Wait for him to acknowledge you and then bow a little and hold up your fingers with the number of people who would like to eat. If he likes the look of you – if you look respectful and knowledgeable – he'll either remove one of the "reserved" signs from in front of an empty chair or tell you about how long the wait will be. We've seen it happen several times.

And no matter how long that wait is, once you get your sake, listen to a few minutes of the music (usually a female vocalist singing "The Girl from Ipanema"), and start watching Hiro-san work, your own brick wall will fall, and you will join us and all of Hiro-san's other fans in joyful communion.

Address: 2395 S. Kihei Rd., Kihei, South Maui
Location: Dolphin Plaza across from Kamaole Beach Park I
Meals: Dinner
Hours: M-Sa 6pm-10:30pm
Parking: Lot
Phone: 808-875-8258

Kula Lodge Restaurant *(American)*

Kula Lodge sits high up on Haleakala and features tumbling (as in hold on to something or you'll fall over at the beauty) views of Maui's central valley, the West Maui Mountains, and both sides of the hourglass shaped island. "Sweeping" does not do this scene justice.

The inn's fireplace and dated, wood-paneled interior make for cozy meals. The food is average at best, and costs more than it warrants, but the view helps take the edge off, as does the fact that if you're this high up on the mountain, you likely are hungry and limited in your dining options. We recommend it for breakfast over other meals, and also recommend that you leave time to take a walk around the beautiful grounds to digest both your meal and the incredible, nowhere-else-on-Maui scenery.

Address: 15200 Haleakala Hwy, Kula, Upcountry
Meals: Breakfast, Lunch, Dinner
Hours: Daily 7am–9pm
Parking: Lot
Phone: 808-878-1535
Website: www.kulalodge.com

OVERALL:
3.4
out of 5 stars

L&L Hawaiian Barbecue *(Local/Plate Lunch)*

L&L is a Hawaii-based chain that serves plate lunch up as fast food: they scoop two scoops of rice and a mountain of macaroni salad onto a plate, and then you tell them what meats you want. We like the barbecue chicken and the beef short ribs with spicy and sweet sauce. The katsu chicken can be dry. You can't argue with the prices ($4.95 for a combo platter), and if you insist on it, you can get a "mini" plate with only one serving of rice. *L&L* has expanded outside of the islands, but if you don't have one in your hometown, you might want to check it out for decent, inexpensive local food.

Note: fast food on Maui doesn't meat the lines move fast. As the bumper sticker says, *Slow down, this ain't the mainland.*

Address: 270 Dairy Rd., Kahului, Central Maui
Location: Maui Marketplace
Meals: Lunch, Dinner
Hours: Daily 9:30am–9pm
Parking: Lot
Phone: 808-873-0323
Website: www.hawaiianbarbecue.com

Address: 1221 Honoapiilani Rd., Lahaina, West Maui
Location: Lahaina Cannery
Meals: Lunch, Dinner
Hours: M-Sa 9am–9pm; Su 9am–7pm
Parking: Lot
Phone: 808-661-9888

OVERALL:
2.8
out of 5 stars

continued on next page

L&L Hawaiian Barbecue *(continued)*

Address: 247 Pi'ikea Ave., Kihei, South Maui
Location: Pi'ilani Village Center
Meals: Breakfast, Lunch, Dinner
Hours: Daily 4:30am–9pm
Parking: Lot
Phone: 808-875-8898

Address: 790 Eha St., Wailuku, Central Maui
Location: Wailuku Town Center
Meals: Breakfast, Lunch, Dinner
Hours: M–F 9am–9pm; Sa–Su 8am–9pm
Parking: Lot
Phone: 808-242-1380

OVERALL:
3.2
out of 5 stars

$ $

CASH

La Provence *(French)*

La Provence has excellent pastries (croissants, palmiers, etc.) in a breathtakingly beautiful location. Get there early (before 9am) to get the best selection to take with you. If you stay for breakfast, which we recommend, get the lovely eggs benedict, a crepe, or perfectly prepared eggs with tender breakfast potatoes that are crisp on the outside. The coffee is excellent. The service is very friendly, but incredibly slow, even when they're not busy. The views tend to make up for it for most of us.

La Provence serves dinners depending upon the season, but their slow service becomes less charming and more grating the darker the view becomes, something to keep in mind.

Address: 3158 Lower Kula Rd., Kula, Upcountry
Meals: Breakfast, Lunch
Hours: W–Su 7am–2pm
Parking: Lot
Phone: 808-878-1313
Website: www.laprovencekula.com

OVERALL:
3.2
out of 5 stars

Lahaina Coolers *(American)*

Lahaina Coolers is a pleasant, open-air restaurant with an active bar, big menu, and plenty of sports on the television. Service is quick and friendly.

Breakfasts are very good with big portions and speedy delivery (don't you hate waiting for breakfast?). Try the French toast, perfectly doused with cinnamon. If you're an eggs-in-the-morning type, we like the Surfer, an egg burrito with Portuguese sausages, peppers, onions, and salsa on the side, as well as rice and well-seasoned beans.

Lunch is good, with sandwiches, burgers, and pretty good pizzas. We like the pork tacos, which feature a smoky pulled pig that's roasted in-house. The ingredients are fresh and the recipes creative. We usually recommend moving on for dinner, or sticking to a drink and an appetizer.

Address: 180 Dickenson St., Lahaina, West Maui
Meals: Breakfast, Lunch, Dinner, Late-Night
Hours: Daily 8am-12am; bar until 1am
Parking: Street
Phone: 808-661-7082
Website: www.lahainacoolers.com

Lahaina Grill

Lahaina Grill is a workhorse of a restaurant that consistently creates very good to great meals with some of the best service on the island. David Paul Johnson first opened this restaurant in 1990 (he sold the restaurant nearly a decade ago, and they dropped his name in late 2007), and Chef/Owner Jurg Munch – is there a better name for a Chef? – continued many of his signature flavor combinations. This is a restaurant where every dish is designed to make you say "Wow!" from its presentation to its flavor profile to its exuberant use of high-end ingredients.

The European/Asian fusion cuisine crosses all sorts of boundaries, like the kalua duck quesadilla (sweet) bursting with roasted Maui onions and spiked with poblano peppers (heat). We like the plate of three separate seafood appetizers called the Cake Walk, because it lets you sample several standouts. The crab cake combines Kona lobster, scallops, crabs and panko. Sometimes it's a little too heavy on the panko – uh oh – but the flavors are excellent, especially in the spicy mustard sauce. The sweet Louisiana rock shrimp cake has a similar binding problem (sometimes) but the seared ahi cake – just a darling slice of ahi over a disc of sticky rice – is perfect. The accompanying wasabi sauce is light, simple, and clean-flavored; an excellent example of how swinging for a homerun often results in one.

The Kona coffee lamb is a perennial favorite: a majestic, perfectly frenched rack of lamb daintily laced with an excellent cabernet demi-glace rendered even more dark and spicy by Kona coffee.

If you've not had ahi yet, the sesame crusted seared version here is extraordinarily popular. We understand why – the flavors are excellent and the dish a powerful example of Hawaiian Fusion – but we still have to argue with the overuse of Maui onions in the crust, which are too overpoweringly sweet when combined with the bed of vanilla bean rice. We love, however, the apple-cider-and-soy-butter vinaigrette used here, because it sharpens the flavors and balances out the sweet a little. Another popular dish is the mahi-mahi, which comes with a delicious beurre blanc sauce; we ask for a lighter hand with the gorgonzola to keep the delicate fish flavor coming through.

One of the best dishes is the shrimp – pillowy and tender – with a smooth, strongly flavored, tangy tequila butter sauce. It comes with spicy "firecrack-

continued on next page

OVERALL:

4.2
out of 5 stars

Lahaina Grill *(continued)*

er" rice that perfectly balances out the sweet shrimp. We can't decide how we feel about the fact that this dish – which David Paul created and occasionally cooks at his new *David Paul's Island Grill* – is still on the menu here. As advocates for diners, we suppose we're glad we can order it at both places.

If you're a vegetarian, you're in luck, as several items are designed to give you a full, satisfying meal. We like the entrée featuring a tall "stack" of goat cheese, fresh tomatoes, grilled eggplant, marinated Portobello mushrooms, and roasted red bell peppers, all finished with a sweet Maui onion sauce. Plenty of well-prepared sides are also vegetarian.

Their lovely dessert menu is really worth saving room for. Try the Road to Hana, Maui: a concoction that secrets away chocolate cake, chocolate mousse, and a delicious macadamia nut caramel under a coating of chocolate ganache. An S-curved crisp – representing the S curves on the famous road – balances on top.

The excellent wine list (heavy on California) and the genuine and efficient service make for a lovely dinner for two or ten. There may be too much bustle for a truly intimate meal, but sometimes a little noise screens out other diners and lets you focus on yourselves … and the food.

There is no view, but the giant paintings from local artist (and fan) Jan Kasprzycki illustrate the dining experience perfectly. The giant florals are so exuberantly colored, they look like they're rejoicing at the prospect of your meal. This has often been voted the best restaurant on Maui, and we understand why. While the food doesn't always completely live up to the ambiance and service, it's a pleasure to dine here. Sometimes, if we haven't made reservations (recommended), we just sit at the bar, where the full menu is available.

Note: if you celebrate a special occasion here, this is one of the few Maui restaurants who follow up with you later with birthday and anniversary cards that include price promotions.

Address: 127 Lahainaluna Rd., Lahaina, West Maui
Location: Just off Front St. near Cheeseburger in Paradise.
Meals: Dinner
Hours: Daily 6pm–10pm
Parking: Street
Phone: 808-667-5117
Website: www.lahainagrill.com

Leilani's *(Pacific Rim)*

Leilani's is a T S Restaurant (like sister restaurants **Hula Grill** and **Kimo's**) with – of course – one of the best locations on the beach walk in Ka'anapali. Lava rock walls and wood beams soar through the two story restaurant, and the food is exactly what you might expect from a place with such a great view: only as good as it needs to be.

T S Restaurants tend to deliver on views and service but not so much on creative dishes. This works for us when we're looking at breakfast places (which is why we'll likely enjoy the new **Duke's** when it opens in Honua Kai), or burgers for lunch, but not so much for fresh fish at dinner. If you stick with the beachside grill (downstairs), the prices go down and the value proposition goes up.

Ka'anapali is designed for tourists, and it has more than its fair share of expensive restaurants serving average food to people who did not rent a car. This is certainly one of those restaurants.

Address: 2435 Ka'anapali Pkwy., Lahaina, West Maui
Location: Whaler's Village
Meals: Lunch, Dinner
Hours: Daily 11am–11pm
Parking: Lot
Phone: 808-661-4495
Website: www.leilanis.com

Longhi's *(Italian)*

Longhi's is a Maui institution that's a good choice for big group meals. Most dishes are served family style and many tables and booths are big enough for eight (or more). The restaurants are "clinky" – which is our word for the pleasant sound a restaurant makes when it's busy and people are eating a lot.

The menu is Italian, and everything is made in-house. Pastas are not listed on the regular menu because they want you to order exactly what you like. They can do just about any shape and any traditional sauce competently, but nothing blows our socks off. The steaks are good and sometimes excellent, but keep in mind that the a la carte menu means that when you ask for a steak you'll get a steak – no sides unless you order them. We recommend the asparagus or French fries.

The shrimp dishes are well made, including the signature Shrimp Longhi, a platter of pillowy shrimp perched on garlic toast points and ladled with a buttery white wine sauce. We recommend getting fish at another restaurant.

Salads are fresh, although the dressings aren't always exciting. The exception is the Endive salad, which is a real treat. Slightly bitter, long leaves of Belgian endive are laid out like little canoes, then filled with gorgonzola cheese crumbles and candied macadamia nuts. Delicious, fresh-tasting honey vinaigrette brightened with mint and spiked with scallions tops the dish.

continued on next page

Longhi's *(continued)*

Two pizza breads are served with your water, and we like the one topped with mellow tomato over the sweet roasted jalapeno version (although we eat both).

Breakfasts are nice, with actual fresh-squeezed orange juice (a rarity on Maui) and excellent coffee made with French press. This is not the cheapest breakfast menu on Maui, but they make their baked goods in house, and we like it. Lunchtime offers a menu with many of the dinner items with smaller portions (and a lower price tag), plus a very good burger.

Service is inconsistent. We've had terrific, attentive waiters, and bumbling, oblivious ones. The Wailea location is large, open-air, and has a much better atmosphere than the Lahaina location, where the view of the harbor doesn't make up for the noise – and sometimes the exhaust fumes – from Front Street.

Address: 3750 Wailea Alanui Dr., Wailea, South Maui
Location: Shops of Wailea
Meals: Breakfast, Lunch, Dinner
Hours: Daily 8am-10pm
Parking: Lot
Phone: 808-891-8883
Website: www.longhi-maui.com

Address: 888 Front St., Lahaina, West Maui
Meals: Breakfast, Lunch, Dinner
Hours: Daily 7:30am-9:30pm
Parking: Valet, Street
Phone: 808-667-2288

Lulu's *(American)*

Lulu's is a scene, and that's the main reason to go. The food is beside the point when the servers are this cute, there's a pool tournament, or a good local band is playing. Drinks are fine, but you may have to wait a while to get yours (we notice that James is more forgiving than Molly when the waitress smiles her apologies). Burgers are fine (they serve one with peanut butter that is really surprising, in a good way). Other typical sports bar items like nachos and spicy chicken wings are fine, too. The dive bar vibe is undercut during the daytime and early evening hours when lots of families with kids come.

The Kihei location draws a lot of tourists looking for a break from the heat, but also locals looking for happy hour and hanging out, too. The open-air restaurant is on the second floor and has a beautiful view. The farther back into the restaurant you go, the darker the ambiance. The brand new Lahaina location is in a fantastic, huge space (no views) that features deep booths and plenty of room to dance.

OVERALL:
2.8
out of 5 stars

$ $

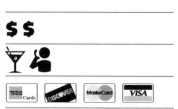

Address: 1941 S. Kihei Rd., Kihei, South Maui
Location: Second Floor, Kalama Village
Meals: Lunch, Dinner, Late-Night
Hours: Daily 11am-10pm; Bar until 1am
Parking: Lot
Phone: 808-879-9944
Website: www.lulusmaui.com

Address: 1221 Honoapiilani Hwy, Lahaina, West Maui
Location: Lahaina Cannery Mall
Meals: Breakfast, Lunch, Dinner, Late-Night
Hours: M-F 11am-2am; Sa-Su 7am-2am
Parking: Lot
Phone: 808-661-0808
Website: www.luluslahaina.com

Ma'alaea Waterfront Restaurant *(Pacific Rim)*

OVERALL:
3.2
out of 5 stars

The *Waterfront* is the one Maui restaurant mentioned most in our mail from readers. The emails usually read in one of two ways:

"I am so glad you told me about this place."

"I can't believe you recommended this restaurant."

Up until this past year we always had very good experiences here. We loved the large menu of fish preparations for the local, fresh fish and the Caesar salad made tableside. We always had great service, and the view of the harbor at sunset, especially when the whales breach in the winter, is beautiful. We've often said that if they updated their décor (the restaurant is thirty years old and we don't think it's been renovated once) and strengthened their drinks they'd be our absolute favorite fish restaurant.

Occasionally we'd get complaints from readers: burnt fish, slow and surly service, and some just could not take the almost pretentiously old-fashioned décor. We chalked the complaints up to bad days on the part of the restaurant (even the best have them), but sometimes to the diner's bad day (many Maui visitors don't realize that if you drive all the way to Hana and back in one day, you're probably not going to have the physical or emotional energy for a long, fancy, expensive meal).

But after a particularly disastrous visit of our own – we waited fifteen minutes to get our menus and the lamb was raw, not medium rare, and the soup tasted of powdered onion and we waited for twenty minutes to get the check after we asked for it – we have to throw up our hands and give up. It seems that this family-run restaurant, while an institution capable of putting out great fish, is too inconsistent to recommend without reservation. There's such a thing as being "not too touristy," but it seems they've crossed the line into "not caring enough."

If you decide to go, we recommend sticking to the fish, the salad, and being prepared to walk from the road – the parking lot is very small. (Please write to let us know what you think.)

continued on next page

Ma'alaea Waterfront Restaurant (continued)

Address: 50 Hauoli St., Ma'alaea, Central Maui
Meals: Dinner
Hours: Daily from 5pm till closing
Parking: Lot, Street
Phone: 808-244-9028
Website: www.waterfrontrestaurant.net

Mai Tai Lounge (Pacific Rim)

When we think of the **Mai Tai Lounge** we feel all soft and fuzzy.

We think it's because we usually go at around 4pm, when the view from the open-air lanai is all hazy with golden afternoon light and the little boats in the harbor line up, and the water sprays the side of the building, and we start with a mai tai, which is served in a wide, low bowl with a long straw and, when we drink it, we smile at each other and then we take another big sip and the people we are with start being really funny, like really, really funny, and then we drink some more, and have a nacho or something and then Molly realizes she's all done with her drink and maybe she has to pee and she goes to the bathroom, but sheesh these chairs are really tall and she realizes that they make very, very strong mai tais that taste very good, which is what she thinks about while she is in the bathroom, which is very clean, she notices, and when she gets back to the table hey, James ordered another mai tai for her, which she probably shouldn't have, but at this point she knows she'll have to wait much later than planned to drive home anyway, so why not have another yummy mai tai, and oh, we were planning on ordering food, too, but then maybe we don't need to order food because we just had a lot of pineapple juice and guava juice and lime juice and some nachos and isn't that enough to get us through, and maybe we should go somewhere really *great* for dinner, because after all we deserve it, a really excellent meal is so wonderful and so now it's sunset and we've been here over two hours and James wants to go and the server was soooooooooo nice so he leaves a big tip and then we take a long walk to sober up a little, and now it's like whatever, 8pm and we're still in a really good mood, but we're hungry and can't drive all the way back to the South side when we're so hungry and maybe still don't trust ourselves to drive so we decide to go to **David Paul's Island Grill** and we spend more on dinner than we meant to that night but that's OK because the food is soooooo good, and when we get out, the plumeria trees are all dropping their flowers and, even though we usually don't like Lahaina because it feels kind of like a tourist trap, tonight it just seems so **magical**.

Address: 839 Front St., Lahaina, West Maui
Meals: Lunch, Dinner, Happy Hour
Hours: Daily 11am–10pm
Parking: Street
Phone: 808-661-5288
Website: www.maitailounge.com

Main Street Bistro *(Pacific Rim)*

OVERALL:
4
out of 5 stars

$ $

MasterCard VISA

Main Street Bistro is a lunch and light dinner restaurant in Wailuku, and we recommend that you stop in on your way to or from Iao Valley. Chef Owner Tom Selman is well known on Maui and his resume includes notable spots like **David Paul's Lahaina Grill**, **Sansei**, and **Vino**. He's making straight-forward dishes – crab cakes, roast beef sandwiches, potato macaroni salad, fried chicken – with a precise hand and careful flavors.

We hear a jangle in the restaurant from the happy clinking of knives and forks and the lively chatter of locals who live and work on Main Street in Wailuku. The rather haphazard décor – big Hawaiian prints, cane chairs, lo-cal art, and the exhibition "kitchen" (read: grill) is definitely designed – or not – for those who come for the food, not the ambiance. It's clean and the tall ceilings let in a lot of natural light, so we forgive that we have to take a key attached to a large wooden spoon into the office building next door to use the bathroom.

Try the roasted beet salad. The beets are tender and sweet, the onion a little pickled from the light, refreshing pear vinaigrette, and the candied cashews add crunch. We also like the straightforward grilled steak salad, with slices of beef laid on peppery arugula and topped with bleu cheese. The fried chicken is called "southern" but we find the batter not quite as crispy as that implies. It is, however, tender, juicy, and despite the rather flat breading, better than any of the katsu we've had on the island.

If you're offered mashed potatoes with your meal, they're prepared in our favorite style: skin still on, handmade, chunky, well seasoned, tender not mushy. The crab cakes come on a toasted bun or on a salad, and they are well made and have a tangy, delicious remoulade. We love the onion rings, which are razor thin and tangle on the plate.

Service is efficient, kind, and neighborly, and you can see Chef Tom work-ing away every day of the week (the restaurant is closed after 7pm and on weekends, but sometimes stays open late for First Fridays, the town-wide art celebration on the first Friday of each month).

Address: 2051 Main St., Wailuku, Central Maui
Meals: Lunch, Dinner
Hours: M-F 11am-7pm
Parking: Street
Phone: 808-244-6816
Website: www.msbmaui.com

OVERALL:
3.4
out of 5 stars

Makawao Steak House *(Steakhouse)*

Sometimes it's fun to knowingly walk into a time warp, and when that's what we want, we eat at **Makawao Steak House**, which feels exactly like an upscale-rural steak house, circa 1975.

The cozy lounge features a big wood-burning fireplace that is necessary in the winter months. You can order the full menu here, and the service is just as good as it is in the restaurant proper (which is to say unpretentious, relatively efficient, and usually friendly).

There are no surprises on the menu — big steaks, including a sprawling, quivery prime rib that makes good sandwiches the next day. The sides are limited but acceptable, and the salad bar is one of our favorites on Maui if only because of the nostalgia (it perfectly represents the era we're revisiting). Iceberg lettuce, shaved carrots, sliced cucumbers, commercial croutons, ramekins of sunflower seeds and raisins, commercial dressings you ladle over your plate … everything you could have wanted before you found out about heirloom tomatoes. Desserts are similarly average, straightforward, and unimaginative.

The wine list is not creative, but it has a decent selection — don't expect too much guidance from the restaurant about what to eat or drink. As one waitress said to a friend of ours playing big city foodie, "your options are laid out on the menu and are self-explanatory."

Our favorite part of the meal is after dinner when we step out into the cool, crisp air on Makawao's main drag and look up at the spangly night stars. If you remember what the night skies looked like in 1975, you probably remember stars like these.

Address: 3612 Baldwin Ave., Makawao, Upcountry
Meals: Dinner
Hours: Nightly 5:30pm-9pm
Parking: Street
Phone: 808-572-8711

Makawao Sushi & Deli *(Sushi/American)*

Tucked into the back of a little storefront on Baldwin Avenue in Makawao is a tiny little sushi bar — maybe six seats and two tables — where a competent chef makes plate after plate of reasonably good, fresh sushi. We skip the miso (salty) and order a few rolls when we're upcountry and want fish. We don't go hungry, though, because while the chef is good, he's not quick.

If you're in the mood for sandwiches, the deli at the front of the store features the usual choices and makes them generous in size. The milkshakes are very good, creamy and thick and made with Roselani ice cream (local, good), which you can also get in cones. The coffee and espresso is very good, and the pastries are worth tucking into, especially the brownies.

OVERALL:
3
out of 5 stars

Address: 3647 Baldwin Ave., Makawao, Upcountry
Meals: Breakfast, Lunch, Dinner, Snacks & Treats
Hours: M–Sa 8:30am–8:30pm; Sushi Bar opens at 12pm
Parking: Street
Phone: 808-573-9044

Mala *(Pacific Rim)*

We love **Mala** for fantastic food served in a lively, casual restaurant smack dab on the water. We don't come here when we want an intimate, romantic meal – the tables are so close you're likely to find out a lot about your neighbors – but when we want to celebrate with friends, or just have a beer at sunset, this is our favorite place on the Westside.

The fabulous Maui Chef Mark Ellman – other restaurants include **Penne Pasta**, **Maui Tacos**, and the fabled (and long-closed) **Avalon** – has crafted a menu packed with a long list of small tapas-sized dishes and plenty of hearty entrees. His skill with flavors and his insistence on local, organic, and healthy ingredients makes his food both opinionated (he insists on telling you that the dark, flavorful bread is made with flax seed) and dastardly delicious.

The pale green edamame dip that comes with your water says a lot about the meal to come – nothing is going to be done exactly as expected, but everything will be done with care and attention, and all surprises will be good ones (like the spicy salsa served at the same time, which stirs up the edamame's mild flavors).

The crunchy, panko-crusted calamari is one of our favorite items on the menu (and on the island). The fish is lightly battered and just barely fried, so it stays delicate and tender. The accompanying aioli and the mojo verde (pesto made from cilantro and tomatillos) are addictive. We ration it. We also like the ahi "tartare" – chopped fish, capers, lemon, red onion on slices of crispy lavosh bread.

The burger is made with Kobe beef, applewood bacon, caramelized onions, and blue cheese, and, when cooked medium, is perfect. We love the baby back ribs mainly for the voluptuous sauce. The seared sashimi with a shiitake mushroom ginger sauce is earthy and spicy, and the Yukon gold potatoes on the side are mellow and buttery.

When in season, get the opakapaka, or pink snapper, in whatever preparation is on the menu. When they have moi, the wok-fried version is incredibly tender, and the ginger black bean sauce is as good as **Spago's**.

Lunches are less expensive and excellent, and their weekend brunch menu is wonderful (French toast fans, this one's for you). While the atmosphere is totally different, we recommend heading here over **Sea House**, and certainly **Gazebo**, if you're in the mood for a good brunch on Saturday or Sunday.

If you're here at Happy Hour, they have good drink specials and many of

continued on next page

Mala *(continued)*

the small plates are available. We've sat on the lanai many times to watch the water and the turtles – sometimes dozens of them – feed on the rocks just below the restaurant at low tide. The wine list is selective, and there is a good selection of beers on tap.

We've had great service and not-so-great service. Generally there's a too-long wait between the arrival of the water and the waiter (but the chips arrive with the water, so at least we can nibble). Attention post-order seems dependent upon how much you're spending, which is never good service.

The Wailea location has the sort of clunky hotel restaurant atmosphere that just can't be helped when you're in a Marriott. The big chairs and long tables and rather disjointed spaces—from lounge to lanai to dining room—make for a very different ambiance than the Lahaina location. The view is nice, overlooking the Marriott's pool and the beach walk below, with Molokini beyond, but the farther inside the restaurant you are, the less relevant it is, and the more aware you are of the self-conscious decor.

While the Wailea menu is the same, the execution is not. (Rubbery calamari? A sin!) The recipes are strong enough to hold up to the less-magical venue, and we wish the ***Mala*** experience were as good in Wailea as it is in Lahaina.

Address: 1307 Front St., Lahaina, West Maui
Location: Across from Lahaina Cannery Mall
Meals: Breakfast, Brunch, Lunch, Dinner
Hours: M-F 11am-9:30pm; Sa 9am-9:30pm; Su 9am-9pm
Parking: Lot, Street
Phone: 808-667-9394
Website: www.malaoceantavern.com

Address: 3700 Wailea Alanui Dr., Wailea, South Maui
Location: Wailea Beach Marriott Resort
Meals: Breakfast, Dinner
Hours: Daily 6:30am-11am; 5:30pm-9:30pm; bar 5pm-10pm
Parking: Valet, Lot
Phone: 808-879-1922

OVERALL:
4.2
out of 5 stars

Mama's Fish House *(Pacific Rim)*

Readers consistently ask us these three questions:

Should I drive the Road to Hana?

Should I go to sunrise at Haleakala?

Should I go to Mama's Fish House?

Our answer, while not particularly satisfying, is the same for all three questions: *It depends.*

The decision to go to Hana, Haleakala, or ***Mama's Fish House*** is deeply personal and requires careful examination of your true desires, expectations, and motivations. We leave the first two questions to another section of this book,

and will address **Mama's** here. While we can't offer advice to you directly, we can tell you the parameters by which we would make the decision.

Mama's is a landmark, an institution, and a well-run, profitable business that brings joy and happiness to tens of thousands of diners every year. If this were Florida, it would be Disney World or Epcot.

Just like Disney World offers its guests the best in entertainment – the best singers, dancers, rides, parades, high quality souvenirs, the most beautiful landscaping – **Mama's** offers the best in Maui restaurants. The fish is unequivocally fresh. The tropical fruit, the vegetables, the seaweed, the ferns, the roasted Macadamia nuts and everything else are of the highest quality (and the menu lists where each ingredient comes from, including the name of the fisherman). The preparations are painstakingly developed and carefully made, and delicious across the board. The strength in this food is not gourmet flourishes, but fresh fish cooked simply and garnished perfectly.

For example, one of our favorite preparations is a simple butter lemon sauce with macadamia nuts, because it is Just Done Right. Our favorite non-alcoholic drink on the island is a coconut mint concoction that blows our senses with its straightforward freshness.

When you walk through the turnstile at Disney World you enter a parallel reality, one where your total happiness is the goal. The same shift can be felt when we hand our keys to the valet at **Mama's**. Walking down to the restaurant and the grounds, we still marvel at how perfectly *Hawaiian* this place is. The restaurant sits on what is called Mama's Beach, which offers one of the most breathtakingly beautiful views available. Inside the restaurant, the gracious ceilings and wide open walls and fresh breezes create a perfect setting for the terrific meals. In this parallel reality, you go "on vacation" for the length of your meal – even if, like us, you live on Maui already.

If you've ever been to Disney, you'll remember how it's almost eerily perfect. The people who work there seem so relaxed, and they're so helpful… and there's also this feeling that behind the scenes there is an awful lot of coordinating going on.

At **Mama's**, after you check in at the hostess/souvenir/gift stand and walk through the narrow walkway to get inside, your experience begins with an almost universal "ten minute wait" for your table. This just happens to be enough time to pick up a drink at the bar – we recommend the incredible mai tai, but everything else we've had is similarly strong and delicious.

Once seated, the service is like clockwork. Servers bring menus, drinks, dishes and then clear them away with a regularity that can seem precisely timed. We suspect that it is. This is a restaurant – one of the few on the island – that can fill every table several times in one afternoon or evening – and they do not particularly want you to dawdle over dinner.

For some people, this is great; finally, a restaurant that knows how to time a meal, where the servers are on their game. *For this kind of money, I want my meal on time, darn it!*

For others, it feels artificial, rushed, and obnoxious (one reader told us they

continued on next page

Mama's Fish House *(continued)*

literally had to hold onto their plate to keep it from being cleared). *For this kind of money, I want to linger and enjoy myself, darn it!*

Knowing which kind of diner you are is one of the most important factors in choosing whether to book a table at **Mama's**.

It's also important to know who you want dining at the next table. Because **Mama's** is (rightfully) famous for its Hawaiiana décor and perfectly executed South Sea cuisine, almost everyone who visits Maui thinks they should come. That includes large families, honeymooners, retirees who travel all over the world, time share owners, and locals. You can get a great table on the rail, but so could anyone from any of those other groups. If you want an intimate dining experience, you can make one – we find it very romantic ourselves – but it won't be quiet.

If you want to take advantage of the view and cut back on the hefty prices, lunch time may be a good time for you to book a table (or walk in). The menu is reduced in size but not in quality, and the prices are definitely lower (although not inexpensive). Another strategy we suggest is to make this the meal you eat right before you get on a plane to leave Maui, especially before a red eye flight to the mainland. It may seem odd, but it makes sense: you can be sure you will enjoy your meal, that it won't last overly long due to slow service, and you're only fifteen minutes away from the airport.

The bottom line for us is that we like **Mama's** exactly for what she does: provide a lovely fresh meal with incredible views and very well-trained service. We do not expect or want her to change any more than we'd want Disney to stop doing what Disney does.

Excellent food is a critical part of **Mama's** experience, but it's not the only part. This is a business that makes money, employs a lot of local people, and is responsible for many children being able to afford four-year colleges, all the while providing thousands of people a month with a one-of-a-kind experience. You can have a wonderful meal elsewhere, yes. But only **Mama's** gives you **Mama's**.

That is our long-winded answer to **should I go to Mama's Fish House**? We hope it is helpful.

Address: 799 Poho Pl., Paia, North Shore
Meals: Lunch, Dinner
Hours: Daily 11am-10pm
Parking: Valet
Phone: 808-579-8488
Website: www.mamasfishhouse.com

Mama's Ribs & Rotisserie

Mama's Ribs is a family-run joint that sells ribs, pulled pork, pot roast, and rotisserie chickens for takeout (there are a few tables, but the strip mall location is pretty barren for a meal). Ribs are slightly dry and not juicy enough for us, but we like the tangy-sweet-sour barbecue sauce. The pulled pork is similarly prepared, but the rotisserie chicken is tender and juicy. You can get a whole chicken for $14.99 and a half chicken for $8.99. If you don't want to go to a supermarket for your chicken, this is a notch above it in quality, a couple of notches above in price. For sides, you can do the slaw or the macaroni salad and be pretty happy.

Address: 5095 Napilihau St., Napili, West Maui
Meals: Lunch, Dinner
Hours: Daily 11am–8pm
Parking:
Phone: 808-665-6262

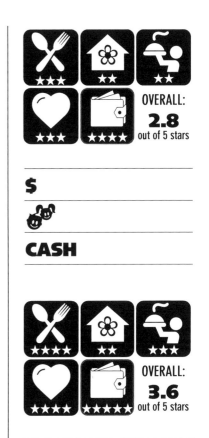

OVERALL:
2.8
out of 5 stars

$

CASH

Mana Foods *(Organic/Vegan)*

This is a very popular health food store on the island. The barely reconstructed warehouse space hosts nearly everything you could want to buy for healthy grocery items, and an amazing produce section lives here. We forgive the crowded aisles, sudden ramps in the flooring, and mismatched tiles because the prices are often lower than Safeway's.

The prepared food section is incredibly popular, and you can get good sandwiches, salads, soups, and other prepared foods. We highly recommend the dark Ukrainian sourdough bread they make in-house, and our favorite cakes are the carrot and chocolate, both vegan.

Paia is home to many surfers who come from all over the globe for the big waves, so Mana keeps a lot of gourmet and European items in stock (European butter, greek yogurt, nutella). There is a huge chocolate bar selection and plenty of natural cosmetics and supplements. We like to stop here before we drive out to Hana to stock up on road snacks.

Address: 49 Baldwin Ave., Paia, North Shore
Meals: Breakfast, Lunch, Dinner
Hours: Daily 8:30am–8:30pm
Parking: Lot, Street
Phone: 808-579-8078
Website: www.manafoodsmaui.com

OVERALL:
3.6
out of 5 stars

$

$ $

Marco's Grill & Deli *(Italian)*

Marco's is a popular restaurant with a great central location: right on the corner of Dairy Road and Hana Highway. If you are just getting on or off a plane, this is a good place to get a meal that will, as one of our best friends, a foodie from New York City who grew up in New Jersey put it, "weigh you down, but in a good way."

The owner, Marco, grew up in Philadelphia and owned a deli/diner in New Jersey, and you can tell. The tiled floors, art deco booths, and snappy service will be familiar to anyone who's ever stopped off the Turnpike looking for a bite to eat.

The sausages are ground on premises, and the pasta is made in house. All the sauces are from scratch. We like the rigatoni in the creamy, perfectly seasoned vodka sauce, which comes in half and full sizes. The ravioli stuffed with ricotta and prosciutto has been described as "pockets of love."

There are no surprises on the breakfast menu, but the food is good and the price is right and you can get it any time (just like in Jersey). Kids love the chocolate chip pancakes.

We often visit **Marco's** with modest expectations and are satisfied with the good value it offers. We recommend it if you need a filling, familiar meal in central Maui.

Address: 444 Hana Hwy., Kahului, Central Maui
Location: On the corner of Hana Highway and Dairy Road
Meals: Breakfast, Lunch, Dinner
Hours: Daily 7:30am–10pm
Parking: Lot
Phone: 808-877-4446

$ $

Market Fresh Bistro *(Pacific Rim)*

Market Fresh Bistro's mission is in its name: only the freshest local ingredients. Chef Owner Justin Pardo's goal is to cook food grown or raised within 100 miles of his small exhibition kitchen, and he's well on his way. Local farmers and growers are supplying him with all sorts of excellent ingredients, and his menu changes regularly with what's available.

We recommend **Market Fresh** for breakfast or lunch, when the (still spendy) prices are more in line with the quality of the preparations. Chef's strengths are perfectly cooked proteins: fish rendered firm and flaky, not wobbly or rubbery; beef seared well with rich, melting meat inside; pork that is tender and moist, not dried out or tough. Sides are also very well done: potato gratins stacked high on the plate, the thin slices of potato soaking up excellent cheese until starch and dairy melt together; wild rice with wheatberries and diced carrots (precise, brilliantly orange quarter-inch cubes). The tiramisu is light in texture and perfectly clean in the flavors (although we'd like those flavors a little stronger).

While we like simple food – very much so – sometimes it's a little too simple at **Market Fresh**. We admire the ethic and the effort put into the meals, but we wish for more attention paid to sauces and presentation at dinner time (the less luxurious dishes at lunch are usually successful).

An example of this is a recent meal featuring a breaded venison cutlet with a salad of greens mounded on top and a drizzle of bright red poha berry sauce surrounding, but not touching, the meat and the salad. It was very pretty and very green (the salad hid the cutlet, as salads often do at **Market Fresh Bistro**).

Upon tasting the cutlet, the meat was perfectly tender inside, but the breading was dry and had little flavor. The salad was very lightly dressed, and the overall impression was that we were eating leaves and meat. The poha berry sauce was very sour, which is to be expected if a sweetener is used sparingly. We also craved what some might call "an enrichment." Oils, fats, and butters help to spread flavor around the mouth, and are crucial to helping one taste food. Perhaps a little brown butter sauce with mushrooms and white wine and Dijon – or a reduction of port wine with cracked peppercorns and garlic – instead of the sour sauce – could have gone a long way toward helping our palate understand why we were eating a breaded venison cutlet in the first place.

We admire the ambition: creating excellent meals around the freshest ingredients (although it was strange to be told that today's watermelon gazpacho was made with "watermelons that were returned to the farmer, so we scored" – we're not sure "returned" produce is fresh produce).

But a reliance on exotic and special and local ingredients, while well in line with our own ideals, is not enough to guarantee great meals (you need great recipes, too). Great food comes from great ingredients, and all ambitious chefs know it. Certainly our favorite chefs all across the island are taking advantage of our local bounty in similar ways, even when they don't put it in their restaurant's name.

On certain nights of the month, the restaurant hosts a "farmer dinner," where a local farmer's produce is highlighted in a coursed, generously portioned, prix fixe meal.

Service is attentive, and they don't charge a corkage fee if you bring your own libations (no liquor license at this time). The kitchen can be slow, but even so weekend brunches are extremely popular with the upcountry crowd, who are enthusiastic about the mission of this restaurant. We love the location – in the courtyard behind **Makawao Steak House** – where you can sit inside at the small tables with the lace curtains blowing in the fresh breeze, or outside under the shady trees during the day.

Address: 3620 Baldwin Ave., Makawao, Upcountry
Location: in the courtyard behind Makawao Steak House
Meals: Breakfast, Brunch, Lunch, Dinner
Hours: M-W 8am-4pm; Th-Sa 8am-3pm & 5:30pm-9pm; Su 9am-3pm
Parking: Street
Phone: 808-572-4877

Matteo's Pizzeria *(Italian/Pizza)*

We go to **Matteo's** when we're in the mood for moderately priced (for Wailea) pasta and sandwiches and want to eat outside with a view. Overlooking the golf course and perched just above The Shops at Wailea, this is a good place for families looking for a break from resort prices.

If you believe in cheese, you're in luck, because everything comes with it. The lasagna has a good flavor in the sauce, but oozes so much cheese we sometimes resort to taking out a layer. The basil tomato sauce, on the other hand, is perfectly simple and made with a light hand. We also like the pink vodka sauce, which is rich without being cloying.

The sandwiches are hearty and tasty, and we note the eggplant and chicken parmesan as particularly comforting. Salads are also good choices – they're not exciting, but they're fresh and the simple oil and vinegar dressing is good.

If we're getting pizza, we ask them to lighten up on the cheese, and we choose the "thick" crust. The thin crust, while it has its fans, doesn't hold a candle to **Flatbread's**. The pizza is decent and the prices are fair.

Address: 100 Wailea Ike Dr., Wailea, South Maui
Meals: Lunch, Dinner
Hours: M–F 11:30am-9pm; Sa-Su 5pm-9pm
Parking: Lot
Phone: 808-874-1234
Website: www.matteospizzeria.com

Maui Brewing Company Brew Pub *(American)*

If you love beer, you should visit **Maui Brewing Company Brew Pub**. The Brewery makes excellent, award-winning brews, and we especially recommend the pale, clean-flavored Bikini Blonde, and the dark chocolatey CoCoNut Porter. Ordering a flight of beer lets you sample several at once. We like getting a flight when we sit at the bar, because they line up the little glasses – maybe two ounces each – on the three inch wide strip of eternally-regenerating ice that circles the bar and keeps the drinks cool.

The food menu is standard pub fare, decently made. We like their slider, a small Maui Cattle Company burger that is well made and perfect with a beer. The fish and chips platter is good. The batter is made with beer, of course, and we appreciate the well-executed traditional taste and light, fluffy, crunchy crust. The same holds true for the beer battered onion rings.

If you haven't had enough beer by the time dessert comes around, the CoCoNut Porter float – a scoop of ice cream with the porter poured over it – is an ingenious response to the root beer float. We also like the Baby Cake, a chocolate cake made with CoCoNut Porter.

[A note about CoCoNut Porter: it lends itself to both drinking and baking due to its complex, deep, dark flavors of chocolate, malt, and sometimes we taste honey. Made with toasted coconut and winner of several national and international awards, it's really something special.]

The brew pub looks like a brew pub should: concrete floors, long tables, high-ceilings. It is buzzy-sounding from the people and the televisions over the big U-shaped bar, and you shouldn't come if you're looking for a romantic meal. You should come for the beer and to get away from the palm trees, wine lists, and pretentions so easily found elsewhere. Service is best if you sit at the bar.

If you love the beer, you can get it at many grocery stores around the island. Don't bother looking for bottles, as this ecologically-friendly company chooses to can their brew so that it travels better, recycles easier, and keeps the beer fresher. Also consider stopping in to their tasting room at their brewery down the road in Lahaina.

Address: 4405 Honoapiilani Hwy, Kahana, West Maui
Location: Kahana Gateway
Meals: Lunch, Dinner, Late-Night
Hours: Daily 11am–12am
Parking: Lot
Phone: 808-669-3474
Website: www.mauibrewingco.com

Maui Coffee Roasters *(Coffeehouse)*

We like **Maui Coffee Roasters** because, in addition to serving their own roast (which you can buy, of course), they make excellent, fresh sandwiches and salads. They aren't fancy, but they're simple and straightforward and made with care. You have to wait a while for your food, but you get your coffee right away (they put it out in a coffee bar). The casual coffeehouse atmosphere attracts everyone from students to business people and lends itself to working on the laptop, chatting with companions or quietly reading a paper. This is our favorite place to hang out in Kahului when we're not running errands.

Address: 444 Hana Hwy., Kahului, Central Maui
Meals: Breakfast, Lunch, Snacks & Treats
Hours: M–F 7am-6pm; Sa 8am-5pm; Su 8am-2:30pm
Parking: Lot
Phone: 808-877-2877
Website: www.mauicoffeeroasters.com

OVERALL:
3.6
out of 5 stars

$

★★★ ★★ ★★

OVERALL:
❤ ★★★★ 💳 ★★★★★

3.2
out of 5 stars

$ $

✈ 🍸 🧍

MasterCard VISA

Maui Community College Food Court and "Class Act"

Maui Community College runs the Maui Culinary Academy, a very respectable cooking school. The students – who in just a little while will be on the line at some of the island's best restaurants – have to practice, practice, practice. One of the ways they do this is by making all of the food court offerings, which makes it one of the best lunch places in central Maui.

The dining room is a noisy cafeteria with big round tables, so if you're thinking of sitting by yourself, forget it. You'll find sandwiches, sushi, a great salad bar, hot entrees, and pastries, all at student prices (average $3-7 per person). The food court is open every weekday during the college term, and it's kind of fun to see how eager the students in their chef whites are to make sure you're happy with your meal.

If you're looking for a more upscale lunch, on Wednesdays and Fridays the students go into their exhibition kitchen and serve a four course meal to those who were smart enough to call for reservations (bar service only for walk-ins). You can watch the chefs-in-training prepare your meal, and every week it's a different cuisine. At only $25, participating in this class as a guinea pig diner is a great deal, and you don't even have to take the final. To be clear, this is a class, not a restaurant, so it's only open when class is actually in session. Call for menus, dates, and reservations.

Address: 310 W. Ka'ahumanu Ave., Pa'ina Building,
Maui Culinary Academy, Kahului, Central Maui
Meals: Lunch
Hours: (Food Court) M–F 11am-12:30pm when school is in session;
(A Class Act) when class is in session
Parking: Lot
Phone: 808-984-3280
Website: www.mauiculinary.com

★★★★ ★★ ★★★

OVERALL:
❤ ★★★★★ 💳 ★★★★★

3.8
out of 5 stars

$

🥕

MasterCard VISA

Maui Masala *(Indian)*

The owners of **Maui Masala**, which opened in August of 2009, are two Indian families who have lived on Maui for over ten years. During that time, they noted our lack of good Indian cuisine and decided to do something about it.

Their no-frills, strip mall location features a steam table and picnic tables outside (they share the space with **Taqueria Cruz**). The inexpensive, home-cook-style Indian food comes in generous portions and is flavored just right for most American palettes (mild). Newcomers to the cuisine will appreciate the lighter spicing, and if you crave more, ask and they can turn up the heat. Plate lunches with three entrees, rice, and naan run you a mere $11. The naan is quite good – soft, slightly chewy, and fragrant. It is baked in a traditional tandoor oven, and you can get it with plenty of garlic if you choose (although sometimes the garlic has been too bitter from overcooking). The menu changes daily, but always includes chicken and vegetarian choices.

We enjoy the palak paneer, which is a creamed spinach (palak) dish spiced and dotted with the mild Indian cheese (paneer) cut into cubes. We also like the dal, a lentil soup with tomatoes, garlic, ginger and masala. The chicken tikka masala is a friendly concoction of tender tandoor chicken floating in a tomato and cream sauce. The chai (black tea) is homemade, deeply spiced, and delicious.

The menu is limited to what the family cooks can do that day, and the location and décor certainly are not worth writing home about, but the price and the quality of food scratches our itch for quick Indian.

Address: 2395 S. Kihei Road, Kihei, South Maui
Location: Dolphin Plaza across from Kamaole Beach I
Meals: Lunch, Dinner
Hours: W-M 11:30am - 2pm & 5:30pm - 8pm,
Parking: Lot
Phone: 808-875-9000
Website: www.mauimasala.com

Maui Tacos *(Mexican)*

Maui Tacos is the brainchild of Mark Ellman, the superior Maui chef (*Mala, Penne Pasta*). *Maui Tacos* has become a national chain, but the Maui locations – of which there are several – are still making every dish to order and using only good, fresh ingredients.

Island foods like fish and pineapple are combined in Mexican burritos, tacos, and plate lunch dishes with beans and rice. As many Californians point out, this is not true Mexican, but it's still superlative, inexpensive, fast food. The salsa bar features homemade salsas in a range of spices and flavors, including an excellent pineapple salsa, plus pickled carrots and sweet Maui onions. If you're looking for a place to come back to several times during your visit, this is a popular choice.

Address: 840 Wainee St., Lahaina Square, Lahaina, West Maui
Meals: Lunch, Dinner
Hours: Daily 10am–8pm
Parking: Street
Phone: 808-661-8883
Website: www.mauitacos.com

Address: 275 Ka'ahumanu Ave., Kahului, Central Maui
Location: Queen Ka'ahumanu Center
Meals: Breakfast, Lunch, Dinner
Hours: Daily 9am–9pm
Parking: Lot
Phone: 808-871-7726

OVERALL:
3.2
out of 5 stars

continued on next page

Maui Tacos *(continued)*

Address: 247 Pi'ikea Ave., Kihei, South Maui
Location: Pi'ilani Village Shopping Center
Meals: Breakfast, Lunch, Dinner
Hours: Daily 9am–8pm
Parking: Lot
Phone: 808-875-9340

Address: 5095 Napilihau St., Napili, West Maui
Location: Napili Plaza
Meals: Breakfast, Lunch, Dinner
Hours: Daily 9am–8pm
Parking: Lot
Phone: 808-665-0222

Address: 2411 S. Kihei Rd., Kihei, South Maui
Location: Kamaole Beach Center
Meals: Breakfast, Lunch, Dinner
Hours: Daily 9am–8pm
Parking: Lot
Phone: 808-879-5005

Maui Thai *(Thai)*

Maui Thai is in the way back of the Rainbow Mall and serves pretty good Thai food at decent prices. We like their wide chow fun noodles with chicken or shrimp, their red pineapple curry, and their peanut-y panang curry. The atmosphere is forgettable, but the service is good.

This is a decent choice if you don't want to drive down to Kukui Mall to check out *Thailand Cuisine*. (You know, it's not *that* far.)

Address: 2439 S. Kihei Rd., Kihei, South Maui
Location: Rainbow Mall
Meals: Lunch, Dinner
Hours: M-F 11am–2:30pm; Nightly 5pm till closing
Parking: Lot
Phone: 808-874-5605
Website: www.mauithai.com

Merriman's *(Pacific Rim)*

By all rights *Merriman's* should be one of the best restaurants on the island. Chef Owner Peter Merriman is a founder of Hawaiian Regional Cuisine and famous for his eponymous restaurant on the Big Island of Hawaii. He's also played a big part in encouraging local farmers to raise delicious and organic produce. (Much of the food at his Kapalua restaurant comes from the bio-dynamic Kapalua Farms just up the hill.) Perhaps he just isn't spending enough time in this location, but unfortunately, all of the passion and quality we associate with him is just not coming through in the food or the service at this very expensive restaurant.

OVERALL:
3.2
out of 5 stars

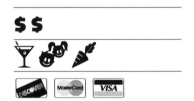

$ $

OVERALL:
2.8
out of 5 stars

The recipes all sound delicious when read off the menu, and the fish, meat and produce are all identified as local. On the plate, the recipes range from good to very good, but it can be hard to be sure, because the execution of those recipes ranges from inedible to good.

The preparations that don't require cooking fare very well. An example of one of the better dishes we've had is the Kona kampachi sashimi, which is served over a salad of calamari that's been marinated in miso and bathed in a flavorful yuzu-kombu broth. The texture of the fish – sliced thin – and the flavors of the salty-sweet-broth are an incredibly delicious combination.

On the other hand, we've had undercooked mahi-mahi not once, but twice. This fish should simply flake off on your fork, but it seems to be a standard cooking technique at **Merriman's** to minimally cook it, and we resorted to a knife to sort of tear it apart. The resulting bite was so unappealing in texture that we discreetly spit it out. We've had filet mignon (badly butchered) so salty that we scraped off the red-wine-reduction to isolate whether the problem was in the sauce, or the meat itself. It was both.

The kitchen is very slow, and the service ranges from apathetic to overly attentive (and yet still inadequate). On our first visit – about three months after they opened – we had to ask for new cutlery when our entrees came (late) because it had been cleared and not replaced. The server nodded and walked away, poured some water at another table, and then came back four minutes later (we looked at our watches) to drop a few implements on the corner of the table as she passed. The clatter was loud enough to turn heads at other tables, and we sat there with open mouths, trying to process why she treated us like an irritated mother would a bratty toddler. We didn't bother asking her for a steak knife, but flagged down a bus boy. Who gets the lion's share of the tip?

Our last visit proved to us something that we've always suspected: just because a restaurant knows a critic is in the house doesn't mean they can improve what they're doing. After all, they can't send out for good food. They can't improve training or attitude, and if the chef isn't cooking with care on a regular basis, he or she isn't likely to start when they know someone's paying attention.

On this particular visit we were "outed" by a friend, so the restaurant was expecting us. Sure, we were seated at the best table (on previous visits we were seated in the back by the kitchen), and we got there before any of the other parties who arrived ahead of us, but our experience was no better than any other. (And still just as expensive. For those readers who wonder if we were comped this meal – or any other – the answer is **no** – and if they'd offered, we would have declined.)

We were given the "best" server, a bighearted, jovial guy who knows local food and ingredients and had many entertaining stories … but we still didn't get bread for twenty minutes, and our entrees were so late that he came out to tell us "They will be out in just a minute – they're just making it perfect for you."

(As opposed to what they do for the rest of the diners, for whom they send out imperfect food?)

continued on next page

Merriman's *(continued)*

Speaking of perfect, we must mention the pastries and the baked goods, which are Absolutely Delicious. The bread, while just a simple wheat loaf, is the best we've had on Maui. The chocolate purse dessert is the deepest, darkest, most decadent we've ever had and beats out *Roy's* chocolate soufflé for flavor, texture, and certainly for creativity. The pineapple upside down cake is a similar revelation. Made with a semolina cake that reminds us of shortbread, it's lightly topped with caramel, and then generously crowned with tiny diced pineapple chunks. The pastry chef is talented and paying close attention to every detail and it comes through in the food with that ineffable flavor: Love. Unfortunately, the bread and dessert are not fabulous enough to pull up the rest of the meal.

The restaurant's huge, dark wood bar, the open walls that bring in the gentle breezes, the tiny metallic, shimmery ceiling tiles that mesmerize when we look up, the copper fire pit on the lanai below the restaurant, the bay below and the incredible views of Molokai and the horizon, the beautiful, starry skies after dark … even on our most disappointing visit, we still feel nurtured by the ambiance.

We really want to like this restaurant, and we returned many times more than we normally do before we inked this review. We're afraid that *Merriman's* has the makings of the most profitable and offensive kind of tourist trap: the intoxicating views distract the diners so much that they don't notice that the service is poor and the food is average (or worse) and the price is too dear.

If we had one wish and a magic genie lamp, we would wish for Peter Merriman's place to come up to the standards that his reputation – and those who spend hundreds of dollars on meals with his name on them – deserves.

Address: 1 Bay Drive, Kapalua, West Maui
Location: in the Bay Club
Meals: Dinner
Hours: Daily 5:00pm - 9:00pm; Bar Menu, Su- Sa 3:00pm - 8:30pm;
       Happy Hour, M- F 3:00pm - 4:30pm
Parking: Valet
Phone: 808-669-6400
Website: www.merrimanshawaii.com

OVERALL:
3.4
out of 5 stars

Milagros Food Co. *(Mexican)*

Milagros is our go-to place when we want an island-style Tex-Mex meal made with fresh ingredients accompanied by a killer margarita. The only problem is getting a table at this super-popular, super-visible corner restaurant in Paia.

Note to Texans: we know that this is not real Tex-Mex. There is no real Tex-Mex on the island. Want to move here and open a restaurant? That would be great!

What this *is*, is well-prepared, generously portioned food. We love the blackened ahi taquitos, which are spicy and tender inside their super-crispy tortilla shells. The fish sandwich comes with an excellent cut of sashimi-grade ahi, and you can get it blackened. The burgers are generous and satisfying. The salad plates are more like platters, and the baby spinach salad with seared ahi on top is the perfect light lunch with leftovers. The enchiladas are excellent, especially the spicy shrimp and seafood versions. Breakfasts are average but beautiful in the morning air.

The outdoor seating is hot in the sun (depending upon the angle, the awning doesn't shade the whole lanai), but perfectly cool at night and in the morning. The inside seating is cramped and unpleasant. The drinks are strong, and we already mentioned the margarita, but we will again, because theirs (any of theirs) are the best on Maui.

Address: 3 Baldwin Ave., Paia, North Shore
Location: Corner of Baldwin and Hana Highway
Meals: Breakfast, Lunch, Dinner
Hours: Daily 8am-10pm
Parking: Street
Phone: 808-579-8755

Moana Bakery & Café

Moana Bakery & Café is way up Baldwin past the Mana Foods parking lot, but it's worth heading up there to have a meal or at least an espresso and pastry to go.

We'll start with the pastries, which are excellent. The apple strudel is filled with more apples than anything else, and the crust flakes off under the slightest pressure from your fingers. That is a satisfying event on an island with so few pastry shops. You can also get a cherry strudel – fresh made – and a coconut empanada, which is a kind of turnover filled with a luscious coconut filling. The barista knows what she's doing.

Breakfast is wonderful here, and it's our favorite place to stop on the way down from sunrise at Haleakala crater or the way out on the Road to Hana. The burritos are hearty and filling and the eggs benedict – including several vegetarian versions – are well-made. We like the guava mimosas and the spicy bloody mary's. Prices are a little spendy, but at least the quality of the food and the portions match them.

All ingredients are as fresh and local as possible, and at dinner, the lively kitchen sends out many fresh fish dishes, an excellent rack of lamb, and many vegetarian dishes. There's live entertainment (call for the schedule) and local art on the walls. The restaurant rambles from the big front windows to a rather dark exhibition kitchen, and if you have a big party you won't feel too crowded. Service is Paia style – which means very cute, but equally (if not more so) slow.

Address: 71 Baldwin Ave., Paia, North Shore
Meals: Breakfast, Lunch, Dinner, Snacks & Treats
Hours: Daily 8am-9pm; Sushi Bar 11am - till closing; Su-M 4pm - till closing
Parking: Lot, Street
Phone: 808-579-9999

OVERALL:

3.8

out of 5 stars

Monsoon India *(Indian)*

Of all the cuisines we miss from our big city days, the one we miss most is Indian food. There is an intense joy that we feel when we dive into a spicy bowl of curry, cool it down with some yogurt-based raita (a cucumber-y sauce, kind of like Greek tzatziki) and sop it up with a flaky piece of naan (the Indian flatbread). The symphony of flavor that is Indian (whatever region it comes from) is not duplicated anywhere else. The spice blends – or masalas – often include earthy and warming cumin, the nutty citrus coriander, and/ or the cooling cardamom. Other spices are added or subtracted to provide an endless palette of flavors that can often cover all taste centers at once. The explosive feeling in the mouth – on the tongue, under the tongue, in all corners of the cheeks, at the back of the throat, even into the sinuses – can take some getting used to. But once you submit to the spices you start to crave them.

In the melting pot that is Hawaii, we just don't have that many people who hail from India. Therefore, most attempts at Indian are futile stabs in the dark or unwitting happy accidents. That's why we're very happy that a server named Hari and his Chef Bindeshor (both formerly of the ill-fated ***Shangri-La by the Sea***) figured out how to rescue the rather odd restaurant location at Menehune Shores in North Kihei and keep it Indian.

We've never seen an Indian menu that explains the cuisine as well as ***Monsoon India's*** menu does. Every dish is described in detail so that even the most timid explorer can get an idea of what they might like to try. The masala curry – tomato and cream blended with herbs and spices – is delicious with either their tandoor oven-roasted chicken or with the shrimp, which lends its rich texture to the velvety sauce. We also like the saag – finely chopped spinach with cream and spices – with lamb. Every curry can be prepared to your preferred spice level: mild, medium, or hot.

The samosas – dumplings with meat or veggie fillings – are perfectly crispy on the outside, and still moist inside. We like the mango chutney, which is just spicy enough to offset the intense sweet fruit. The naan is very good – fluffy inside, crispy around the edges. We like the garlic and the cheese versions, but we get a basket of plain to go with our meals so they don't interfere with the spices in the dishes. The rice pudding is creamy and has a hint of cardamom. The lassis – a traditional yogurt drink – are delicious. The mango is the best and most traditional, but we also like the banana.

The kitchen is slow, but they've figured out how to handle that – they take an appetizer order as soon as you sit down, and they pour your bottle of wine or beer for you without asking (bring your own, as there is no liquor license at this time). We recommend getting samosas and/or the bread basket immediately, because the main dishes are made to order and there's only one chef. The more people seated in the large, open-air restaurant, the longer the wait for the main meal, but it's worth it.

They're still working the kinks out of the service (this restaurant opened in the fall of 2009), but the food is tasty enough for us to come back and satisfy our big-city cravings. During the day, when you get the full view of the ocean and the West Maui Mountains, it's jaw-droppingly gorgeous. When the whales start breaching, well… we'll see you there.

Address: 760 S. Kihei Rd., Kihei, South Maui
Location: Menehune Shores condos in North Kihei
Meals: Lunch, Dinner
Hours: Daily 11:30am– 2:30pm, Dinner 5pm– 9pm Su Lunch Buffet 11:30am–3pm
Parking: Lot
Phone: 808–875 6666
Website: www.monsoonindiamaui.com

Moose McGillycuddy's *(American)*

The American classics at *Moose's* (burgers, sandwiches, steaks, fish) are supplemented with Americanized ethnic foods (fajitas and pastas). The purpose of this restaurant is to feed you large portions of average food while plying you with average drinks and two-for-one coupons for breakfast (look in the tourist magazines) – but also to give you a killer view and fresh breezes in your hair. The happy hour specials, late night dining, and good breakfasts are definitely bonuses. Service, unfortunately, is inconsistent, but the second story locations make for expansive and pleasant views that take the sting out of waiting for your drink.

Moose's is worth visiting if you're in the mood for a bar scene and a drink special. We also like the breakfasts at both locations (the pancakes are yummy-o) because the focus is on good food and big quantities (which is important at breakfast). This is where we take our less adventurous relatives when they come to visit, they love it.

Address: 2511 S. Kihei Rd., Kihei, South Maui
Location: Above Fred's Mexican Cafe
Meals: Breakfast, Lunch, Dinner, Late-Night
Hours: Daily 7:30am-1am
Parking: Lot, Street
Phone: 808–891–8600
Website: www.mooserestaurantgroup.com

Address: 844 Front St., Lahaina, West Maui
Meals: Breakfast, Lunch, Dinner, Happy Hour, Late-Night
Hours: Daily 7:30am-1:30am
Parking: Street
Phone: 808–667–7758

OVERALL:
3.2
out of 5 stars

OVERALL:
2.8
out of 5 stars

Mulligan's at the Wharf / Mulligan's on the Blue *(American)*

Mulligan's on the Blue has a beautiful view. It's halfway up the rolling green golf course, and the sunset is sweeping and nurtures the soul. There's a lot of live music and plenty of famous musicians hang out here (and one or two have thought of buying it for themselves). The menu lists typical pub fare like shepherd's pie (no), and burgers (yes), but the food is beside the point. Drinking a pint of tapped Guinness counts as a meal, right?

"Right," say our Irish friends back home, unless they insist on drinking Murphy's instead. At Mulligan's, both are on tap (because we're in Hawaii, not Boston, so we don't have to choose sides in the stout controversy).

Service is not good, especially during concerts when the music is loud and the waitresses are overwhelmed by the number of diners and drinkers. We recommend if you order a few appetizers to go with your beer, you order everything up front and plan on going back to the bar to get your refills from the source.

As many televisions as there are (we counted eight at last visit) there are games showing, and the bar opens at 8am on the weekends so sports fans can have their oatmeal while they watch their favorite team.

The Lahaina location, ***Mulligan's at the Wharf***, is at the back of the Wharf Center. No morning sports, but there is live entertainment, and this a good place to get a pint in Lahaina.

Address: 658 Front St., Lahaina, West Maui
Location: at the Wharf Cinema Center
Meals: Lunch, Dinner, Late-Night
Hours: Daily 11am–2am
Parking: Lot, Street
Phone: 808-661-8881

Address: 100 Kaukahi St., Wailea, South Maui
Location: on the Wailea Blue Course
Meals: Breakfast, Lunch, Dinner, Late-Night
Hours: M–F 10am–1am; Sa–Su 8am–1am
Parking: Lot
Phone: 808-874-1131
Website: www.mulligansontheblue.com

Nick's Fishmarket *(Pacific Rim)*

The last time we sat down at ***Nick's***, three servers collided over one water glass as they rushed to be the first to fill it. The resulting frenzy of tipping, righting, and mopping was a preview of the night to come. We wouldn't mention it if it weren't such a perfect illustration of our general experience of Nick's over the years: the overeager service and romantic, delightful

OVERALL:
2.8
out of 5 stars

ambiance will never, ever make up for the unforgivably expensive, mostly bland food.

The food sounds promising – especially the signature dishes, like the tempura ahi rolls and the wasabi-beurre blanc laced fish of the day. But the ahi in the ahi roll is gray around the edges and has lost most of that pleasant red-pink of fresh sushi, and three hours later we're still finding gummy bits of tempura in our teeth. (Did they make the roll, flash-fry it, refrigerate it, and then serve it hours later? We don't know, but we can't imagine how else crispy tempura gets so mushy.)

The scallops are only seared on one side (why?) and the sauce is their standard beurre blanc, which usually begins to separate by the time it gets to the table.

There are often one or two too many ingredients in the recipes, leaving them overly complex and confusing. Their "classic" ahi dish is the perfect example of this: edamame (chili-flavored, good), wasabi beurre blanc (good, but competes with the chili), and avocado (texture is mushy, which doesn't go well with the mushy texture of the seared ahi). Each plate is designed to appeal to the eye with elaborate flourishes and a rainbow of colors, but ultimately these are beautiful but empty promises.

The dessert is often better – get the flaming strawberries, as trite as it may sound – and we really like their Kona coffee. We appreciate the excellent wine list, but this, like everything else, is overpriced.

The servers are exceptionally friendly, although so hurried we've seen chairs knocked into and drinks slopping over the lips of glasses as they stop short. They have also picked up the excruciatingly bad habit of asking "how does everything taste" during dinner.

The setting could not be in a more perfect location. The koi pond at the Fairmont Kea Lani is our favorite place in any Maui resort, and passing by it to get to the restaurant is a pleasure. The interior of the restaurant is like a dream of upscale luxury, and the sunset views of the pools, grounds, and sea are fairytale romantic. They're just not enough.

Address: 4100 Wailea Alanui Dr., Wailea, South Maui
Location: Fairmont Kea Lani
Meals: Dinner
Hours: Daily 5:30pm–9:30pm
Parking: Valet, Lot
Phone: 808-879-7224
Website: www.fairmont.com

OVERALL:

3.6

out of 5 stars

$

Nikki's Pizza *(Pizza)*

Nikki's Pizza is one of the few places in Ka'anapali with good food priced proportionally. Pizzas are made to order (you can also get slices), there are enormous sandwiches and heroes, and pretty good shave ice (a little icy, but the best option if you're not driving down to Lahaina to try ***Ululani's***). ***Nikki's*** has carried us through several forgot-it's-lunchtime blood sugar crises. We like the Greek salad, which is fresh and crisp, and we like the calzones and the wraps.

In the interest of full disclosure, the owner hired James as a marketing consultant many years ago (several years before we started writing ***Top Maui Restaurants***), but what impresses us today is that he has continued to maintain the quality of the food through the years.

The food court location is less than glamorous, but it is air conditioned. You can also sit outside, or, of course, get your food to go and eat it at your condo or on the beach.

Address: 2435 Ka'anapali Pkwy, Ka'anapali, West Maui
Location: Whaler's Village
Meals: Lunch, Dinner, Snacks & Treats
Hours: Daily 10:30am–9pm
Parking: Lot
Phone: 808-667-0333

Ocean's Beach Bar & Grill *(American)*

Ocean's is a big sports bar in South Kihei that serves average food at average prices and opens up their big windows to let in plenty of light and air. It's as pleasant a sports bar as you'll find on Maui, with friendly (if inconsistent) service and good happy hour specials. Stop in if you want a brew and some company.

Address: 1819 S. Kihei Rd., Kihei, South Maui
Location: Kukui Mall
Meals: Lunch, Dinner
Hours: Daily 11am–10pm
Parking: Lot
Phone: 808-891-2414

OVERALL:

3

out of 5 stars

$ $

Old Lahaina Lu'au (Lu'au)

OVERALL:
3.8
out of 5 stars

If you want to do a "real" lu'au – well, as real a lu'au as you'll get without moving to Hawaii, making friends with a Hawaiian family, and getting *invited* to a *real lu'au* – *Old Lahaina Lu'au* is your best bet.

Once you get through the long registration line, you're greeted by an army of scantily clad men and women who drape you with leis and offer strong mai tais before showing you to your seat. The tables are long, packed together, and you sit with several other parties. Most tables have regular chairs, but some prefer to sit in the "front" row on cushions at low tables. Seats are assigned when you make your reservation, so if it matters to you, ask for your preferred table. We like the second row best, and as close to the center of the stage as possible so we can see the show well.

After the ritual of removing the pig from the imu (the traditional Hawaiian barbecue oven/pit), there are plenty of photo ops along the beach for sunset. This is one of the most beautiful spots in Lahaina, and we recommend taking a semi-private moment to enjoy the view.

The buffet begins almost immediately, although you may not get there right away, depending upon when your table gets to eat (the server will let you know when it's your table's turn at the buffet).

All of the traditional lu'au foods are represented. The kalua pig you just saw lifted from the ground, for example, is sweet, spicy, smoky, and tangy from the barbecue sauce they mix in. There is tray after tray of lomi lomi salmon (salted salmon), hui chicken (glazed with soy sauce), barbecued chicken, steak, pork, and fish dishes. Hawaiian food doesn't generally include a lot of vegetables, but there are salads featuring pohole fern (tender, fresh, and tasty, kind of like fiddlehead ferns) and the obligatory big green salad. Nothing is totally delicious, and nothing is terrible. If you haven't had poi, the traditional Hawaiian starch, this is a good place to try it – they usually station someone near the bowl of poi to tell you about it and how to eat it.

Servers visit regularly with trays of tropical cocktails that are sugary and sometimes strong, but you can also visit the open bar (all drinks are included in the ticket price). The show features good music, great hula, and a little bit of the history of the islands from the Tahitian migration through the middle of the last century. It's well-choreographed and the dancers are talented and – of course – delicious to watch.

When we have visitors who really want to go to a lu'au, we steer them away from their hotel's offering and toward *Old Lahaina Lu'au*. Is it touristy? Oh, my, yes. Will kids like it? Yup. Is it good food? Well, it's as good as buffet Hawaiian food can be, which is average. Is it worth it? Depends. The most sophisticated of our friends have loved *Old Lahaina Lu'au* for its exuberant, tightly executed, theatrical approach to Hawaiian culture.

Address: 1251 Front Street, Lahaina, West Maui
Location: Across from Lahaina Cannery Mall
Meals: Dinner
Hours: Daily 5:30pm-8:30pm
Parking: Lot
Phone: 808-667-1998
Website: www.oldlahainaluau.com

Ono Gelato *(Gelato / Ice Cream)*

Gelato, or Italian ice cream, is a most virtuous choice for a frozen treat. We will now prove this to you:

Most ice creams have air mixed into the final product to get it "lighter" and therefore "lower in calories" – but the reality is you're buying and eating air. Super premium brands have less air, which accounts for their richer, more dense texture and flavor (and higher price tag).

Gelato follows this logical process and leaves as much air out of the cream as possible. However, there is much less fat in gelato than in ice cream, and that's because – despite the dense, creamy texture – gelato is made with more milk (and less cream) and therefore has less fat.

The dense product creates dense flavors. Because the flavors are so strong, it's a very satisfying dessert, and we find we can barely finish anything larger than a small cup (automatic portion control).

There, that's our proof. You're welcome.

If you get the fruit flavored gelatos at our favorite dessert place, **Ono Gelato**, you'll be doing even more good for your body. Made with filtered water (so they're dairy-free) and local, organic, sustainable fruit, the flavors are intense and hard to find anywhere else. Try the tangerine in season (Molly loves it with vanilla or sour cream to make a creamsicle flavor), or the lilikoi (passionfruit), both of which are only made from local, organic fruit. The Kula strawberry is similarly luscious and usually available year round. We've seen dragonfruit, mango, lemon, lime, and raspberry, along with countless other tropical flavors. We never miss the dairy.

The dairy flavors use organic milk as a base, and with the exception of a few traditional Italian flavors that are imported from Italy (hazelnut, etc.) these are made from local ingredients. Try the sultry vanilla, the sour cream (tastes like cheesecake!), and pistachio (James's favorite). The Quark is another delicious choice. It's made with Surfing Goat Dairy cheese blended with lilikoi, for a lilikoi cheesecake flavor. We love the dulce de leche and the mint. If you want to combine flavors, they can pack two or three into even the smallest cups or cones, but of course they also have big waffle cones to fill up (if you can handle them). They are generous with samples.

The gelato maker is also an owner, and he's the third generation in his family to make gelato. The shops are bright, clean, and well stocked with plenty of pre-packed pints, gelato cakes (what a way to celebrate a birthday) and non-gelato items. In addition to the loose leaf teas, handmade local jelly beans, coffee, and t-shirts, the Lahaina location also serves homemade sandwiches, salads, and cupcakes. We rarely pass up an opportunity to visit **Ono Gelato**.

Address: 115D Hana Hwy, Paia, North Shore
Meals: Snacks & Treats
Hours: Daily 11am - 10pm
Parking: Street
Phone: 808-579-9201
Website: www.onogelatocompany.com

Address: 815 Front St., Lahaina, West Maui
Meals: Snacks & Treats
Hours: Daily 8am - 10pm
Parking: Street
Phone: 808-495-0203

Pacific'O *(Pacific Rim)*

Sitting on the rail at **Pacific'O** at happy hour makes us very, very … happy.

There's a beautiful view of the beach and the harbor, and the sunset views are fantastic. If we're lucky we get to see a fresh-caught tuna carried from the beach landing where the fishermen sell their day's catch and up through the restaurant and past our table. Add this "just caught" freshness to the rest of the menu, the vast majority of which is made with food grown on Chef Owner James McDonald's O'O Farm in Kula, and our foodie souls relax and reach for another sip of lava flow.

Thankfully, the recipes do justice to the quality of the ingredients. This is Pacific Rim at its best: local ingredients meet European and Asian flavors to fuse into plate after plate of food love (when the chefs are on their game, which is usually).

The appetizers and small dishes really shine. For example, we love the diver scallops roll. Scallops are seared golden brown and rolled up with arugula pesto, and then coconut rice, sliced, and bathed in a sauce made with citrusy yuzu and limes: perfect acidity to counter the sweetness.

Of all the tomato salads on the island, the tomato "stack" at **Pacific'O** is our favorite. Ripe tomato slices alternate with slabs of tangy buttermilk cheese and fresh basil leaves. They rise a few inches with artichoke hearts slipping in between a couple of layers. A carefully balanced vinaigrette made with roasted red peppers and curry is what really brings the flavors together – perfectly seasoning the sweet and tangy in the cheese and tomatoes.

The peanut sauce creamed up with coconut is the perfect background to the tropical fruit salsa that tops the coconut macadamia nut fish preparation. Mahi-mahi is good, but trust the server to steer you toward another fish if something special has come in. The Bling Bling dinner is a lovely Pacific Rim version of surf and turf: petite filet mignon paired with a poached lobster with a ginger butter sauce. The tempura asparagus that's served with this is crispy and light.

The Hapa/Hapa Tempura is our favorite. The chef takes the two best fish of the day's catch, cuts them for sashimi (two big blocks of fish – hapa means half), wraps them in seaweed, flash fries them in tempura batter, and plates them next to each other on the same plate with a ying-yang of sauces. The white miso sauce is very good, but the lime basil sauce on the other side makes us lick our fingers.

The food is exuberant, fresh, and delicious, and if you haven't had Pacific

continued on next page

Pacific'O *(continued)*

Rim yet, this is a great place to try it. While we love the food at dinner, the ambiance can suffer if you like quiet with your meal. Between the nearby *Feast at Lele* lu'au and the nightclub upstairs, timing your meal for romance can get tricksy. We do not come when we want quiet, we come when we want this food. If you want a more sedate experience, we highly recommend *Pacific'O* for either Happy Hour or lunch, when the menu is less complicated and also less expensive. We take a table on the rail to get a higher view and stay out of the sun (but then again, we live here).

Overall the service – while some individual servers are very good – can be lacking. We've seen hostesses flustered by walk-ins when the restaurant is empty and servers who size up guests who ask a lot of questions about the menu, as if dining is a foodie competition. (To be fair, we know plenty of foodies who like to catch a server in a mistake – if you're reading this, you know who you are. Stop it, relax, and enjoy your meal.)

Address: 505 Front St., Lahaina, West Maui
Meals: Lunch, Dinner
Hours: Daily 11am–4pm & 5:30–10pm
Parking: Lot, Street
Phone: 808-667-4341
Website: www.pacificomaui.com

OVERALL:
3.8
out of 5 stars

$

Paia Fish Market *(American)*

When we get off a plane and want to "re-ground" ourselves in Maui, we head for *Paia Fish Market* for a quick meal. This is also the first place we take guests for local fish that doesn't cost an arm and a leg.

It doesn't look like it'll be quick when you see the line for the order counter or the packed tables, but it's speedier than it seems. Somehow the size of the long, communal tables and the length of the line perfectly correspond. By the time you finish placing your order – or at least once your number is called and you get your food – seats will open up for you.

The menu is on the blackboard, and consists of sandwiches and fish burgers. You can get any fish you like, but we heartily recommend ono, which is a tender, white fish named for what it is – ono means "delicious." A piece of grilled fish – perfectly cooked – is placed on a bun with homemade slaw (good), shredded cheese (commercial), and a tomato slice. No matter how many times we have this burger, we enjoy it well enough to stop talking for a few minutes so we can concentrate.

The shoestring fries are ordered separately and you can get a single portion with your burger or order a basket to share. They're nicely seasoned with spices and salt.

This is one of our favorite places for an inexpensive lunch or dinner on the island.

Address: 100 Hana Hwy., Paia, North Shore
Location: Corner of Baldwin and Hana Highway
Meals: Lunch, Dinner
Hours: Daily 11am–9:30pm
Parking: Street
Phone: 808-579-8030
Website: www.paiafishmarket.com

Penguini Gelato *(Coffeehouse / Gelato)*

Penguini Gelato is a cute little gelato place tucked into the side of the charming Paia Inn. The gelato is made by the owner by hand, and she uses all local and organic ingredients, from the homemade base (not commercial) to the spices (the vanilla is grown upcountry).

The consistency is not always as luxurious as we like it, but the flavors are dead on. We like the Mexican chocolate and any of the tropical fruit flavors. The vanilla is intense and dark. Flavors change on a nearly daily basis, as each batch is made small enough to sell within a day. You can get packed pints as well as cups and cones to go.

The baked items are excellent, and what we really love to buy from **Penguini**. Selections vary by day and are made based on what's fresh and inspiring to the owner. If you like macaroons stop by and see if she has any for sale. Mounds of freshly shaved and pan-toasted coconut are mixed with local honey and baked until fluffy, chewy, and outrageously flavorful. We also love the cupcakes which sprout from their stand like small miracles; fluffy crowns of frosting perfuming the air with their sugary cream. We like the chocolate cake with chocolate mint frosting, but the buttermilk cake with orange buttercream frosting makes any day our fifth birthday party.

You order through the window and sit on the benches (or keep strolling and window shopping). This is a lovely place to stop for a mid-afternoon pick-me-up.

Address: 93 Hana Hwy, Paia, North Shore
Meals: Snacks & Treats
Hours: Tu-Su 12:30pm – 8:30pm; Closed Mondays
Parking: Street
Phone: 808-214-4608

Penne Pasta *(Italian)*

Penne Pasta is a good choice for no-frills, no surprises, well-priced Italian food. Well-known Maui chef Mark Ellman (**Mala, Maui Tacos**) cooks authentic Italian – and some Italian-American – dishes for $15 or less. (In Lahaina? Yes. In Lahaina.)

The pastas are cooked al dente, and the sauces are homemade and taste that

continued on next page

OVERALL:
3.8
out of 5 stars

$

CASH

OVERALL:
3.6
out of 5 stars

Penne Pasta (continued)

way (good). If you're from the East Coast and have a fondness for baked penne, the version here is cheesy and has good flavors (not completely bland like so many are). We like the bolognese sauce with its tender meat, and the slightly spicy meatballs. The house salad is very good and comes with an excellent piece of homemade crostini. Pizzas are thin crusted and good. The oven-roasted squash is sweet and flavored with plenty of butter, sage, and almonds.

The daily specials are worth ordering. The regulars include a tender and succulent roast chicken, a spicy and hearty sausage with pasta, and Ellman's grandmother's own lamb osso bucco – tender and meaty. Each special comes with a small salad.

You order at the counter and take a number back to your table (inside or outside), so your server can find you when your food is ready. Beer and wine are available and we always find something simple to go with the meal. The clean, well-lit restaurant features blond tables with aluminum legs and lightweight chairs (some folding), and you'll see that most of the cost of the meal goes into the ingredients, not the dishes or the ambiance. In a town where everything is overpriced, this can is a relief.

Address: 180 Dickenson St., Lahaina, West Maui
Meals: Lunch, Dinner
Hours: M-F 11am-9:30pm; Sa-Su 5pm-9:30pm
Parking: Lot, Street
Phone: 808-661-6633
Website: www.pennepastacafe.com

OVERALL:
3.8
out of 5 stars

Pineapple Grill (Pacific Rim)

We like **Pineapple Grill** for its creative Pacific Rim cuisine and for the way Chef Ryan Luckey works so hard for every bite. We have no doubt he is spending most nights in his kitchen, and it shows. Chef Ryan was born on Maui – one of the few great island chefs who can make that claim – and his love for his home is baked right into the food. The overall ethic is fine dining in a casual atmosphere, and he focuses on using locally raised vegetables, fresh and sustainable fish, and island-bred beef.

We like to order a mai tai, because – although pricey, as everything else is on the menu – they're so darn good. We put them up against **Mai Tai Lounge's** version or the one sold at **Mama's Fish House**. We also like to come a little early and sit at the big square bar to drink it, because looking at that ceiling – painted to look like you're underwater – is just very cool.

Must-orders include steamed Manila clams that come plumped up in a black bean butter broth enriched with truffle oil and studded with shiitake mushrooms. The fragrance as we lean over the bowl is overwhelmingly rich, and we save rolls for sopping up every delicious, savory drop. We also like the crispy duck spring rolls, sweet and tangy inside with a sour-sweet relish on the side. And partly because it's just so unusual for Maui, we love the cheese plate (sometimes we save it for dessert), which comes with several cow, sheep, and goat selections, including the delicious local Surfing Goat Dairy chevre.

We don't often order salmon, because it is a cold water fish and not local to Maui. However, it is tangy-sweet here in a miso preparation, seared, and served with cold soba noodles, vegetables, and a citrus-y ponzu sauce. Another favorite is the ahi encrusted with pistachio and wasabi. These flavors – familiar to those who know Pacific Rim fusion – are outstanding together. The sweet, nutty, pale green pistachios love to dance with the sinus-singing wasabi, and the ahi's firm, dramatically pink flesh stands up to them in both texture and flavor. This comes as both an appetizer and an entrée, so we suggest you order one or the other.

Our very favorite entrée is the rack of lamb with a veal cabernet reduction on the plate. The strong, sweet and dark flavor of the glaze strengthened by a hint of molasses is the perfect complement to the delicate but robust lamb. It comes with a beautiful serving of mashed purple sweet potatoes from Molokai. It is so easy to get these potatoes wrong – they are not particularly flavorful – but Chef Ryan knows to beat them until they are almost like candy.

The Maui Gold pineapple upside down cake is made with the sweetest pineapples on the planet. The rum caramel sauce is dessert on its own, and the perfect topping for the macadamia nut ice cream they serve ala mode. This is a rich and sweet dessert, so make sure you have room before you order (it's hard not to finish once you start).

The wine list is excellent, and they carefully pair wines to food (the restaurant is heavily involved in the Kapalua Wine and Food Festival each year). There are also plenty of wines by the glass. The after dinner drinks are worth looking at, too, especially the martini made with a shot of espresso.

There can be a tension in the service that is palpable and not conducive to a relaxed meal. We wish the staff were a little bit less intense when we're spending plenty of money, and a little more attentive when we're not.

With every course worth your dollars, and the wine and drink list, too, this can turn out to be an expensive meal, and we don't recommend coming when you're on a budget. Many are fooled by the casual atmosphere of the bar area when they enter. It can look like this restaurant-on-a-golf-course is more affordable than it really is. The large tables and comfortable rattan chairs definitely look like an afternoon with the boys after a few rounds is in order, perhaps not a four star meal. We wish the views – Molokai and the ocean is rather eclipsed by the brightly lit tennis courts – matched the menu (this food at **Merriman's** location would be incredible).

Address: 200 Kapalua Dr., Kapalua, HI 96761
Meals: Lunch, Dinner
Hours: Daily 11am–9pm
Parking: Lot
Phone: 808-669-9600
Website: www.pineapplekapalua.com

OVERALL:
4
out of 5 stars

$

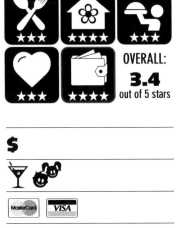

Pita Paradise *(Mediterranean)*

This little restaurant tucked in the back of Kalama Village serves wonderful Mediterranean food at very reasonable prices, and is one of our favorite places for a quick and delicious lunch.

At lunch, you order at the counter and sit down either inside or out on their shaded deck, where the server brings your food. The wind can pick up outside, so if there are tablecloth anchors on, don't remove them, and hold on to your napkins.

The gyros are excellent and feature flavorful free-range New Zealand lamb that is grilled perfectly. The pitas are fresh and warm and the tzatziki sauce is tangy and cool with cucumber flavors, while the shredded lettuce and the tomato slices bulk up the sandwich and lighten the heavier lamb. The hummus is good, and our vegetarian friends love the veggie wraps and pitas. Beer and wine are available and the servers are friendly.

Address: 1913 S. Kihei Rd., Kihei, South Maui
Location: Kalama Village
Meals: Lunch, Dinner
Hours: Daily 11am-9:30pm
Parking: Lot
Phone: 808-875-7679

Pizza Madness *(Pizza)*

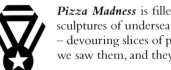

Pizza Madness is filled with huge bronzed wall and ceiling sculptures of undersea creatures – turtles, squid, a huge shark – devouring slices of pizza. They made us laugh the first time we saw them, and they still delight our inner children.

The exceptionally dark wooden paneling on the walls, the huge slabs of tables anchored to the walls, the long benches, the televisions, and the plate glass windows that let in plenty of light, make this a great place for large groups to eat. The bar and the many smaller tables for two and four make it acceptable for couples looking for a quick meal. While the art is perhaps the source of the "mad" in the name, the pizza is all East Coast middle-of-the-road 'zza.

If a junior high student imagined the perfect pie, this would be close. The crust isn't thick, or thin, there's plenty of cheese (we ask them to lighten up), and the choice of toppings is exactly what you expect: sausage, meatballs, pepperoni, and plenty of veggies. (You can also get pineapple and jalapenos.) The sauce is made in house and not spicy enough, but they're not trying to make great pizza, they're trying to make American pizza. It's good, and we like the homemade sausage and the fact that we can get an individual size for less than $7.

Sandwiches are reasonably priced, and the homemade meatballs with green peppers on a grinder are a very good representation of this classic comfort food.

Pasta is best eaten elsewhere.

The salads are little more than iceberg lettuce with tomato wedges and cheese, but we're not here for the salads. On the other hand, the full bar sells pitchers of beer (unheard of on Maui) and pitchers of soda, too (another first). The servers are speedy and very friendly.

While this is not the best food on Maui, it serves that comforting middle ground that few other restaurants here do: decent food at decent prices with good service and a fun, clean, good atmosphere.

Address: 1455 S. Kihei Rd., Kihei, South Maui
Location: Near Maui Dive Shop
Meals: Lunch, Dinner
Hours: Daily 11am–10pm
Parking: Lot
Phone: 808-270-9888

The Plantation House Restaurant *(Pacific Rim)*

 The view from **Plantation House** is unlike any other on the island. The restaurant sits high above sea level in the middle of the Kapalua golf course, which rolls down to the ocean with sky-high, ramrod-straight ironwood trees marching down the volcano beside it. You can see Molokai's dramatic shape rising out of the Pacific, and often dramatic shafts of light piercing dramatically dark clouds, and even a dramatic rainbow or two. It's very … *dramatic*, and best seen from a table close to the front of the restaurant, preferably at a window. (Ladies, bring a wrap, it can be chilly in the breeze.)

We wish the food always matched the views, but we'd stay away from most of the "from the land" entrees and focus on the fish. Our favorite preparation is the Mediterranean. The fish of the day is coated with a crust of sweet Maui onions and spicy, hearty mustard, served over more Maui onions that have been roasted until the sugar is completely caramelized, and a light and fluffy couscous. To cut this joyful sweetness, a fried caper sauce is ladled over the top. The spicy, peppery sauce pulls out the flavors of the fish – which otherwise would be smothered in this crust – and the fried capers give a satisfying crisp texture.

We also like the pistachio-crusted preparation with spinach, but we feel the **Roy's** or **Pineapple Grill's** version is better. The wine list is very good, and the drinks are well-prepared if a tad unimaginative (don't forget, this is the golf course's restaurant).

We like the breakfasts, which are reasonably priced given the million dollar views. Good options include the eggs benedict and the spinach and cheese omelet, and the sweet French toast is also satisfying. Service can be all over the place and has ranged from barely there to totally engaged and friendly. Overall, we like **Plantation House** for group meals (wedding rehearsal dinners, family celebrations) where the large menu can please many at once. We also like it for dinner when we're in the mood for overwhelming beauty and can get over to the west side for sunset.

continued on next page

OVERALL:
3.6
out of 5 stars

$ $ $

The Plantation House Restaurant *(continued)*

Address: 2000 Plantation Club Dr., Lahaina, West Maui
Meals: Breakfast, Lunch, Dinner
Hours: Daily 8am–9pm
Parking: Lot
Phone: 808-669-6299
Website: www.theplantationhouse.com

Polli's Mexican Restaurant *(Mexican)*

OVERALL:
3
out of 5 stars

Polli's is decent Mexican food at generally reasonable prices, although more so when you take advantage of their daily specials. The salsas are very good, the guacamole, as well, and we are surprised at how much we like the tender pork with chili verde. The burritos are generous and the cheese sauce is not too overpowering. The margarita is nothing to write home about, but if you must have one and can't drive down to *Milagros*, *Polli's* will just have to do.

Address: 1202 Makawao Ave., Makawao, Upcountry
Meals: Lunch, Dinner
Hours: Daily 11am–10pm
Parking: Street, Lot
Phone: 808-572-7808

Roy's Bar & Grill *(Pacific Rim)*

Roy's – owned by Roy Yamaguchi, one of the founders of Hawaiian Regional Cuisine – is now an international chain, and they've got their system down. The service is attentive, the food consistently well-made, and the menu – which changes on a regular basis – is created by chefs who know his vision and can execute against it.

We often order a selection of appetizers rather than focusing on the entrées. We especially like the Szechuan flavored baby back ribs and the potstickers, but an excellent thing to do is order their "boat" of the best appetizers of the day. It serves two easily for a light meal, especially when you add a spicy tuna roll, hot melting chocolate soufflé, and one of their strong rum cocktails – our favorite, so far, being a lovely lilikoi colada made on the spot by a friendly and creative bartender (standard disclaimer: lilikoi may not be in season when you go, etc., etc., etc.).

Our favorite entrees on *Roy's* "Classics" menu – dishes which are usually available – include the misoyaki butterfish which is sweet, falling-apart tender, and rich, and the roasted macadamia nut mahi-mahi lavished with sweet, buttery lobster sauce. We also loooooooove the pistachio and wasabi crust on the ahi, finely chopped and beautifully seared to the pink fish, and the avocado mousse served on the side is surprising (still, after all these years) and perfectly creamy.

The tenderloin is perfect. The shrimp and butternut squash risotto – usually available in the fall – is plush, perfectly made, and comforting. When dessert comes around, order one for each of you. We've never been able to share the melting hot chocolate soufflé – even with each other. The raspberry coulis and the simple vanilla ice cream sets off the dark chocolate perfectly. We also love the banana crisp, which has an excellent pudding texture that contrasts nicely with the gingery, nutty topping.

The wine list is excellent and the servers are helpful at picking something that will go with these intense flavors, but we often choose to drink a lighter, Asian beer with our meal so that it doesn't compete with the food.

Our friends with children love **Roy's** for nice dinners out because the children's menu is coursed so they don't get bored, and there are crayons available for picture books. There's a joyful, playful energy to this restaurant that has always promised a great meal, and we've never felt let down.

Note: **Roy's** Kihei location closed in late summer of 2009.

Address: 4405 Honoapiilani Hwy., Kahana, West Maui
Location: Kahana Gateway Center
Meals: Dinner
Hours: Nightly 5:30-10pm
Parking: Lot
Phone: 808-669-6999
Website: www.RoysRestaurant.com

Ruby's

This is the go-to place for kids of all ages. The big burgers wrapped in paper so they don't spill, the thick milkshakes, the reasonably good fries and onion rings, and the clean, red-boothed restaurant bring in crowds from open to close. If it's your birthday, don't tell them unless you're ready for a crew to come out and sing to you their own special song. (You will also get a free sundae.)

Other items on the menu include pretty good dinners like fish and chips and a turkey dinner that features fresh-roasted turkey (not pressed or processed). The sauces and salsas and gravies are made in house. Salads are commercial, but crisp, and the appetizers are large and can serve as entrees.

The servers are efficient and attentive, and **Ruby's** is a good, inexpensive choice for a quick meal at any time of day.

Address: 275 W. Ka'ahumanu Ave., Kahului, Central Maui
Location: Queen Ka'ahumanu Center
Meals: Breakfast, Lunch, Dinner
Hours: M–Th 7am-9pm; F–Su 7am-10pm
Parking: Lot
Phone: 808-248-7829
Website: www.rubys.com

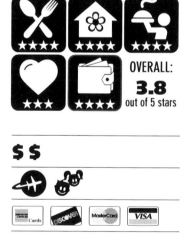

OVERALL:
3.8
out of 5 stars

$ $

OVERALL:

4

out of 5 stars

Ruth's Chris Steak House *(American)*

Ruth's Chris, a national chain of steakhouses with two locations on Maui, has started to forgo importing so much food from their mainland suppliers, and instead is using fresher, local produce – and the taste results are excellent.

The salads are fresh and assembled from local Kula greens and other vegetables grown on Haleakala (not in California). The dressings are perfectly balanced. The steakhouse salad – iceberg, micro greens, carrots, tomatoes – is generous and delicious with the traditional blue cheese dressing. The Caesar is garlicky and has an excellent anchovy flavor without the chunks of fish that can distress some diners. The mashed potatoes are perfectly seasoned and buttery, with a creamy texture. The creamed spinach is silky and the greens are so perfectly integrated with the cream that it becomes almost spinach *butter*. All of the sides are plenty big enough to pass family style.

A good steak is one of our favorite ways to get protein, iron, B vitamins, and zinc into our diet. We're not sure that we *need* the sizzling butter sauce that dances around the steaks at **Ruth's Chris** – which are served on exceedingly hot plates dotted with parsley – but it sure makes all that nutritious beef easier to swallow. The filet is tender enough to cut with a butter knife, and the ribeye is our favorite cut. The sustainable foodies in us wish the beef were local, but we admit, grudgingly, that local beef is just not as lovely in texture and consistent in quality as the beef from Omaha is.

The wine list is very good, and we like that they have several half bottles. The service at **Ruth's Chris** is excellent. They show up on time, check back often without interrupting, and clear and clean without being intrusive. They know the menu and exude genuine hospitality. The Wailea location is dark-paneled and intimate, and so is the Lahaina location, which also has a lovely view of the ocean. The tables are large and can accommodate big parties, but there are also plenty of half round booths, perfect for cozy steak dinners.

Address: 3750 Wailea Alanui Dr., Wailea, South Maui
Location: Shops of Wailea
Meals: Dinner
Hours: Nightly 5pm–10pm
Parking: Lot
Phone: 808-874-8880
Website: www.ruthschris.com

Address: 900 Front St., Lahaina, HI 96761
Meals: Dinner
Hours: Nightly 5pm–10pm
Parking: Lot (validated), Street
Phone: 808-661-8815
Website: ww.ruthschris.com

Sansei Seafood Restaurant & Sushi Bar *(Sushi / Pacific Rim)*

OVERALL:

4.2
out of 5 stars

$ $ $

 The last time we visited **Sansei** someone at the next table asked us what the name of the restaurant meant. We didn't know, but as a group speculated it could mean "circus" because of **Sansei's** slightly rowdy, cheerful, bustling approach to Pacific Rim and sushi.

[We looked it up later, and *sansei* actually means "The U.S.-born grandchild of Japanese immigrants to America." Ahhhh. We take a moment now to honor Chef Owner D.K. Kodama's Japanese grandparents who immigrated to America and gifted us his hurly burly, exuberant approach to Japanese cuisine.]

The menu at **Sansei** is several pages long and features chicken, beef, fresh fish, and even a few pasta dishes, but most diners go for the outrageous and flamboyant sushi.

The sushi is visually stunning. For example, the caterpillar rolls slinks across the plate with brilliant green avocado slice scales. Under the avocado are layers of ahi and salmon, which are wrapped around seaweed, around rice, around eel. Ah, it's an eel roll!

Most of the rolls are like this, with garnishes and tricks and treats hidden in the layers. When we want simple, we order sashimi, especially a couple of the more elegant presentations, like the Kenny G, which is delicate slips of kampachi layered with ponzu sauce.

The miso butterfish and the rock shrimp dynamite are must-orders. The butterfish – so named for the rich and velvety texture and taste – is cooked and beautifully glazed with a salty-savory-sweet brown sauce. The rock shrimp dynamite is a dish piled with teensy popcorn shrimp flash-fried in panko batter and bathed in spicy mayonnaise.

If you have sushi newbies in your party, **Sansei** is an excellent place to bring them to try out a few pieces. It's fresh, it's delicious, and the servers have plenty of beginner chopsticks to hand out. Best of all, if they really don't want sushi, the wide-ranging menu won't make them feel left out (and the chicken teriyaki is better than we've had anywhere else).

If you don't mind eating off a fish carcass, ask the waiter if the sushi chefs have a "hama kama" left. The phrase refers to the cheek (kama) of the hamachi (hama). This tender, fatty, delectable part of the fish is virtually useless in sushi preparation, but absolutely delicious baked and served with a dipping sauce and salad. Since they butcher at least one hamachi per day, they usually have cheeks available. Since it's not on the menu, you have to know to order it. Be aware that you will be served a big fish jaw – including bones and fins – but this is the perfect dish to work over with chopsticks.

Service is generally efficient, and dishes come out as soon as they are ready, so we never sit hungry for long. The wine and beer list are very good, and the restaurants are large and rather noisy. (This is not the place to come for a quiet, intimate meal.)

Even when tables are available in the busy restaurant, we like to sit at the

Sansei Seafood Restaurant & Sushi Bar *(continued)*

sushi bar or the cocktail bar, so we can watch the show. Watching a sushi chef work is just plain fun. At *Sansei*, it is fun to watch the bartenders, too, because they throw glasses and spin drinks and if you tell them what you want a drink to taste like, they'll invent a cocktail for you on the spot. (The full menu is available at both the sushi and cocktail bar.)

Both locations feature sushi price promotions. Their most popular is the Sunday and Monday early bird: 50% off food (with a few exceptions). This discount applies to all comers in the Kihei location, but only to locals with a Hawaii State ID in Kapalua. If you decide to go for this super-good deal, call to find out when the promotion starts, and then plan on showing up at least thirty minutes before the restaurant opens, because the lines form early (bring a beach chair and a book).

The late-night half-off sushi specials are particularly fun if you like Kara-oke—get in early to put your name in. Call the restaurant for details on price promotions because they can change with the seasons and the night of the week.

Address: 1881 S. Kihei Rd., Kihei, South Maui
Location: Kihei Town Center near Foodland
Meals: Dinner, Late-Night
Hours: Nightly 5:30pm-10pm; Th-Sa 10pm-1am
Parking: Lot
Phone: 808-879-0004
Website: www.sanseihawaii.com

Address: 600 Office Rd., Kapalua, HI 96761
Location: At the Kapalua Resort
Meals: Dinner, Late-Night
Hours: Nightly 5:30pm-10:30pm; Th-F 10pm-1am
Parking: Lot
Phone: 808-669-6286

Sarento's on the Beach *(Italian)*

As mentioned in the Introduction, *Sarento's* inspired us to write this book in the first place. The Italian menu is focused on providing important sounding and expensive ingredients in flamboyant preparations that don't always work as well as they should (especially at these prices). One example is the filet mignon meatballs, which if you think about it, are tricky to make well. Meatballs should be full of flavor and moist, moist, moist. The primary quality of filet mignon, on the other hand, is that it is very tender and lean. Of *course* it will make dry, nearly tasteless **balls of meat** if overcooked (which it often is).

There are some items that are better prepared, including a cioppino with lobster, scallops, crabs, and fish that satisfies anyone's cravings *di mare*. We've had good steaks with competent sauces, and the salads are generous and generally fresh. They're just all so expensive, and we're not sure the gorgeous view is enough to justify the price tag.

OVERALL:
3
out of 5 stars

The restaurant is very proud of its service, or "hospitality". According to Webster's, *hospitality* is defined as the "friendly reception and treatment of guests or strangers." We're afraid that **Sarento's** staff exhibits less hospitality – which is genuine, unforced, and relaxed – and more of what Miss Manners calls "fits of hospitality." A fit of hospitality is entertaining people who do not want to be entertained; or entertaining when you can't genuinely put your heart in it. The feeling that we're entering a place where we will be entertained with at-your-elbow-service, whether we like it or not (and we don't) – is a serious problem at **Sarento's**.

We know some people who love the doting service, who think it's wonderful that they take a sip of water and someone immediately tops off the glass, who love the clasped hands and practiced smiles. We're just saying that for this kind of money you can have a glorious Italian meal at **Capische?** or **Ferraro's**. You may not be hovered over, but you might also enjoy your food more. (And no one will offer to take your photograph "to be purchased at the end of the meal." They will, however, happily photograph you with your own camera, for free, just like Miss Manners would recommend a good host do.)

Address: 2980 S. Kihei Rd., Kihei, South Maui
Location: Next to the Mana Kai
Meals: Dinner
Features:
Hours: Nightly 5:30pm–10pm; Bar until 12am
Parking: Valet
Phone: 808-875-7555
Website: www.tristarrestaurants.com

Sea House Restaurant *(American / Pacific Rim)*

If the thought of the breakfast line at **The Gazebo** drives you crazy, take comfort in knowing that we think your best bet for breakfast in Napili is actually their neighbor, **Sea House**.

Sea House is the main restaurant at the Napili Kai, a resort that oozes the relaxed Aloha spirit Maui is famous for. The service is friendly and efficient, and the food is wonderful. A hearty breakfast panini, giant baked egg frittatas, friendly scrambles, and one of our very favorite breakfast items: the Dutch Baby pancake.

They call it a Crater Pancake, but it's a Dutch Baby. Essentially a giant custard, it comes topped with lemon juice and powdered sugar, and it's perfect. Creamy textured. Delicious. The Haleakala Pancake is the same confection, but topped with cinnamon, sugar, apples, and pineapples. Too sweet, in our opinion, but there are plenty who disagree.

Lunches and dinners are not as consistently wonderful, so we recommend elsewhere. But we drive from South Maui to have breakfast meetings here rather than at our own kitchen table … if that doesn't sound like a big deal, ask a local what would taste good enough for *them* to drive one hour before eating breakfast.

continued on next page

Sea House Restaurant *(continued)*

Note: our ratings are for breakfast only.

Address: 5900 Lower Honoapiilani Rd, Napili, West Maui
Location: Napili Kai Beach Resort
Meals: Breakfast, Lunch, Dinner
Hours: Daily 7am–9pm; Bar until 10pm
Parking: Lot
Phone: 808-669-1500
Website: www.napilikai.com

OVERALL:
3.4
out of 5 stars

Seascape at Ma'alaea *(American)*

One of our favorite places on Maui is the aquarium, Ma'alaea Ocean Center. We love the sharks, the turtles, the thousands of tropical fish, and the walk-through saltwater fish tank. We always learn something, and we think the gift shop is the best place to buy gifts on the island. If we're here at lunchtime, we stop in for a little something at *Seascape*, the little lunch café.

The sandwiches are large and satisfying. We especially like the fresh ahi sandwich, which has a good char and provides a lovely, clean base for the sweet-spicy pineapple salsa. The French fries on the side are average, but the substitute salad is fresh and local. The fish tacos feature mahi-mahi and are fresh and well seasoned.

There are plenty of tropical cocktails and fun drinks for the little ones. We recommend *Seascape* if you get the munchies while submerging yourself in the educational fun to be had at the Ocean Center. (If you just want to eat at *Seascape*, there is no need to buy admission to the Ocean Center.)

Address: 192 Ma'alaea Rd., Ma'alaea, Central Maui
Location: inside the Maui Ocean Center
Meals: Lunch, Snacks & Treats
Hours: Daily 11am–3:30pm
Parking: Lot
Phone: 808-270-7043
Website: www.mauioceancenter.com

Seawatch *(American)*

We have always relied on *Seawatch* less for dinner (it was overpriced and average) and more for reasonably priced, good breakfasts and lunches. It's a million-dollar view from the 200 feet elevation, and we loooooooove watching whales breach in season from way up high while indulging in a great eggs benedict: *Kihei Caffe* prices with Wailea views.

Bev Gannon, Chef Owner of *Hali'imaile General Store* and *Joe's* in Wailea, took over *Seawatch* very recently, and at press time the restaurant is undergoing massive renovations and a possible name change as well as several menu modifications. So far, we like the addition of several of her comfort food specialties to the menu, and miss some of what she's dropped. While we loved the ahi burger on the old lunch menu, we're glad we have her slaw on her version of a pulled pork sandwich. Service is, as it usually is at Bev's restaurants, attentive and knowledgeable.

Because things are so in flux at press time, we are not writing a full review or rating this *Seawatch*. We'll keep you up to date on our latest experiences at *Seawatch* (or whatever the restaurant is renamed) on www.MauiRestaurantsBlog.com.

Address: 100 Wailea Golf Club Dr., Wailea, South Maui
Location: On the Gold and Emerald Golf Course
Meals: Breakfast, Brunch, Lunch, Dinner
Hours: Daily 8am–10pm
Parking: Valet, Lot
Phone: 808-875-8080
Website: www.seawatchrestaurant.com

Shaka Pizza *(Pizza)*

Shaka is an East Coast-style pizzeria, and it wins lots of local awards ... but keep in mind that pizza is not indigenous to Maui. The crust is okay, but the tomato sauce is lacking the complexity we want in really good pizza, where the sauce is the star of the show. You'll do better with the white pizza—cheese, olive oil, garlic, and gourmet toppings like clam and spinach. We also like the pesto pizza.

The menu also features sandwiches, but we find everything a tad overpriced for what we're eating. The open air restaurant seats a lot of people and the pies are large, so this can be a good place to have a casual meal.

Address: 1770 S. Kihei Rd., Kihei, South Maui
Location: Across from Kukui Mall
Meals: Lunch, Dinner
Hours: Su-Th 10:30am–9pm; F-Sa 10:30am–10pm
Parking: Lot
Phone: 808-874-0331
Website: www.shakapizza.com

OVERALL:
3
out of 5 stars

Son'z at Swan Court *(Pacific Rim)*

There's a restaurant proverb that (like all proverbs) is almost always true: **the better the view, the worse the food.** The proverb holds at *Son'z*, the fine restaurant at the Hyatt. A sweeping staircase brings you down to one of the most romantic places on Maui: a waterfall-fed pond dotted with elegant white swans. Protected by the pond from the beach walk-gawkers and by the waterfalls from other restaurants, this is a beautiful spot for an intimate evening.

If we could eat the view, we would, happily, and it would be delicious.

OVERALL:
3
out of 5 stars

continued on next page

Son'z at Swan Court *(continued)*

Unfortunately, we can't. We must rely on what's coming out of the kitchen.

The menu is nearly identical to that of sister restaurants **Sarento's on the Beach** and **Nick's Fishmarket**, including the strained descriptions, overly friendly handwriting font, and extremely high dollar amounts next to each item. The overly complicated recipes result in plates that always look very colorful (all of the primary and many of the secondary colors are represented), but never blow us away with taste (strange, how so many ingredients result in so little flavor).

Our overwrought imaginations come up with all sorts of scenarios to explain why the service, which is *very* attentive, strikes us as panicked. Is there someone in the kitchen holding a gun to their heads? Do they all have nails sticking up through the soles of their shoes? We have a bias against service that is obtrusive. Don't refill our glass of water between each sip, and don't ask us more than once how we like the "flavors." (Especially when we don't.) And if you can't make an honest recommendation, find a way to guide us besides repeating what's listed on the menu.

The restaurant claims a wine cellar that holds three thousand bottles; the largest around, with a value reported to be over $250,000. Every bottle and glass on their wine list reflects that valuation.

If you are staying in Ka'anapali and want to eat a romantic dinner without driving into Lahaina or out to Kapalua, we recommend heading upstairs to the **Cascades Grille & Sushi Bar** or to the pool for **'Umalu**.

Address: 200 Nohea Kai Dr., Ka'anapali, West Maui
Location: at The Maui Hyatt hotel near the swan pond
Meals: Dinner
Hours: Su-Th 5pm-10pm; Fr-Sa 5pm-10:30pm; Bar until 12am
Parking: Valet
Phone: 808-667-4506
Website: maui.hyatt.com

OVERALL:
3.4
out of 5 stars

South Shore Tiki Lounge *(American)*

We can't help but like **Tiki Lounge**, the open-air, thatch-roofed bar in Kalama Village. The food (sandwiches, hot dogs, nachos) is average, but the drinks are generally good, and it's got a fun, relaxed vibe that just works, and has for a while. Live music, a big screen with surfing videos playing ... it's a nice little joint for a drink and an appetizer.

Address: 1913 S. Kihei Rd., Kihei, South Maui
Location: Kalama Village across from the whale
Meals: Lunch, Dinner, Late-Night
Hours: Daily 11am-2am
Parking: Lot
Phone: 808-874-6444
Website: www.southshoretikilounge.com

Spago *(Pacific Rim)*

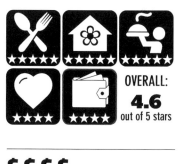

Our single favorite item served in any Maui restaurant – ironically – was created by Wolfgang Puck of California Cuisine fame and is served in his high-end-chain restaurant, ***Spago***. His incredible appetizer, the spicy ahi tuna poke in sesame-miso cones, has set our benchmark very high.

To make these little handfuls of love, the chef chops fresh ahi –maybe half-pureed – and mixes it thoroughly with chili aioli, the full-flavored Tosa soy sauce, plenty of green onions, pickled ginger, and the crunchy, brilliant orange tobikko (flying fish roe). Meanwhile, black and white sesame seeds are combined with a little flour, butter, corn syrup and miso paste, rolled into circles, baked, and carefully formed into little cones (one person does the cones, all night long). The Ahi mix is carefully spooned into the cones, garnished, and slid into wooden cone carriers. The small portion is three, and the large is five. Both sizes are incredibly expensive, and end up leaving you wanting more. When ***Spago*** has a booth at upscale foodie events like The Taste of Wailea or the Kapalua Wine and Food Festival, we admit to taking more than one for ourselves.

(We're spending a lot of time on this appetizer because it is emblematic of what you will find at ***Spago***: layers of flavors carefully thought through and then enthusiastically assembled by people who know what works and how to execute night after night.)

When you bite into a cone, it does not crumble (the corn syrup, we think, lets it bend rather than snap), and you get at least two or three full bites out of each one. The spicy poke (which means "chopped fish") dissolves on your tongue, sending spicy heat to the back of your throat and filling your entire mouth with flavor. While the fish brings the spice, the cone brings a crunchy/chewy texture and sweet, mellow cool flavor. It's like candy sushi.

So you see, we think you should order this appetizer.

Other items we particularly like include the wok-fried moi (when it's available; you might want to call ahead and ask). The fish, which at one time was only eaten by Hawaiian royalty, is small, exquisitely tender, white, and flaky. The preparation preserves all the moistness and keeps out the oil. Served over jasmine rice, shiitake mushrooms and hearts of palm, garnished with kaffir lime and Thai basil, it's a great example of Thai flavors fusing with Hawaiian fish. The server will debone the fish for you tableside. There is nothing more special, in our opinion, than a properly prepared moi at ***Spago***.

Neither of these dishes are budget items, but ***Spago*** is not a place to visit when you feel strapped for cash. However, we will point out that even the most inexpensive item on the entrée list, the pan-fried chicken, is ridiculously tasty. The chicken is delicate, moist, tender, and laid over a healthy helping of delicious, creamy mashed potatoes laced with local goat cheese and oyster mushrooms from upcountry Maui. Yum.

Other entrees include grilled lamb chops (perfectly done every time we've had them), and diver scallops sautéed until tender and an interesting contrast to the spicy eggplant puree underneath. If you are a meat eater, we also like the simply prepared prime rib and the Japanese ribeye.

continued on next page

Spago *(continued)*

Salads are fresh, local, and well-dressed. Desserts are generally good due to Wolfgang Puck's Austrian background, but we often skip them (too many Ahi cones). The wine list is extensive and the guidance from servers and the sommelier is both professional and friendly. Service is excellent, but be prepared for a leisurely pace to your evening. You will likely be at table for at least two hours, and you will not be rushed out the door. During that time, however, service will be attentive and well-paced.

The beautifully designed, open air restaurant has wonderful sunset views, but can be a little breezy in the evenings, so if you get chilled and have a table on the rail, bring something to cover up. A three course keiki (children's) menu will please most small fine diners with its cheese pizza appetizer, chicken fingers, steak, fish, pasta, and ice cream sandwich dessert.

Spago is one of our favorite special occasion restaurants on Maui and we recommend dining here.

Address: 3900 Wailea Alanui Dr., Wailea, South Maui
Location: Four Seasons Resort
Meals: Dinner
Hours: Nightly 6pm–9pm, bar open until 11pm
Parking: Valet
Phone: 808-874-8000
Website: www.fourseasons.com

OVERALL:
3
out of 5 stars

$ $ $

Stella Blues Café *(American)*

Stella Blues is serving American comfort food with Southern twists and plenty of vegetarian options to keep the local vegans happy. The large, noisy rooms, outdoor seating, pool tables, and commodious concrete bar keep its fans coming back, and back, and back.

Sadly, the heart seems to have gone out of this formerly fabulous, friendly restaurant. We used to look forward to coconut shrimp that were perfectly prepared (crunchy and sweet outside, tender inside). We loved their baby back ribs with a fruity barbecue sauce. The roasted chicken with mashed potatoes, creamed corn, and wilted spinach was one of our favorite meals. We even liked their tofu stir fries and curries.

Sometimes the magic is still there, but a lassitude has crept into the kitchen that makes the food inconsistent. One visit will be wonderful, the next awful. The service is still efficient and unobtrusive and friendly, but there's something off for us and the high prices (which have crept up over the years) are now off-putting compared to what's on the plate, no matter how big the portions remain.

All that said, breakfast seems a little perkier, and might be worth a stop in. We do hope that *Stella Blues* – named after the Grateful Dead tune – will start rocking again.

Address: 1279 S. Kihei Rd., Kihei, South Maui
Location: Azeka Mauka Marketplace
Meals: Breakfast, Brunch, Lunch, Dinner
Hours: Daily 7:30am-10pm
Parking: Lot
Phone: 808-874-3779
Website: www.stellablues.com

Stillwell's Bakery & Café *(American/Bakery)*

We skip the sandwiches, soup, and salads here, and go straight for the pastries. The best are their cream horns, which are rolled sheets of flakey pastry dough filled with a rich, vanilla cream. One end is dipped in chocolate that hardens into a decadent shell. Try the bread pudding, banana cream pie, and the generously portioned caramel chocolate brownie, which is studded with almonds, a layer of caramel, and a chocolate mousse on top. Whipped cream, chocolate shavings, very nice.

Address: 1740 Ka'ahumanu Ave., Wailuku, Central Maui
Location: On the way to Wailuku, just past the high school, on the right.
Meals: Breakfast, Lunch, Snacks & Treats
Hours: Bakery: M-Fr 6am-4pm; Deli: M-F 9:30am-3pm
Parking: Lot
Phone: 808-243-2243

Sunrise Café *(American)*

We would call this hole-in-the-wall family-run business quaint if they served excellent – or even just good – food. Instead, we call it something unprintable because of the bad coffee, bad service (we've waited thirty minutes to get that bad coffee), and mediocre, commercial ingredients prepared with very little love or attention to … taste.

The prices are low, especially for Front Street, but this is truly one of those places where you get exactly what you pay for. It's tempting to try this place for breakfast (the sign is just so darned cute), but go to Moose's instead.

Address: 693 Front St., Lahaina, West Maui
Location: Next to the library, tucked behind the activities booth and
        Lappert's
Meals: Breakfast, Lunch, Snacks & Treats
Hours: Daily 6am-4:30pm
Parking: Street
Phone: 808-661-8558

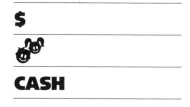

OVERALL:
3.4
out of 5 stars

Sushi Paradise *(Sushi)*

If there isn't room at **Koiso** and our sushi craving will not go away, we head to **Sushi Paradise** for fresh, no-frills sushi. The owner is as picky about his fish as Hiro-san is, and puts out a great plate.

With several tables in addition to the sushi bar, the wait can get long because the owner is the only sushi chef, and, unless you're sitting at the bar where the action is, the quiet room can be very … quiet. On the other hand, if a big group of fans comes in, it can get rowdy quickly.

Service is kind, but slow, the prices are similar to other sushi places, and we don't get that same magic feeling we get from Hiro-san... but if it's sushi you must have, this is a good option in South Maui.

Address: 1215 S. Kihei Rd., Kihei, South Maui
Location: in the Long's Shopping Center
Meals: Dinner
Hours: Tu-Su 6pm-10pm
Parking: Lot
Phone: 808-879-3751

OVERALL:
3.2
out of 5 stars

CASH

T. Komoda Store and Bakery *(Bakery)*

It looks like it's been boarded up or condemned, but Komoda isn't closed permanently … just sold out for the day. If the storefront is open, there's probably a line. Get here early for delicious malasadas, the Portuguese donut with a crisp sugary coating. While you can get them plain, the guava filling is sweet (some say too sweet), and the red bean paste filling is truly unique. You can also get stick donuts (ummm, glazed donuts with a stick stuck in them, so your fingers don't get too sticky), decent cream puffs, and fluffy butter rolls.

If you're a donut fan, this is worth the trip up to Makawao and the pastries generally still taste good the following morning. If you order ahead, they won't run out of whatever you're interested in. Note: closed on Wednesdays, which somehow is when we get motivated to visit.

Address: 3674 Baldwin Ave., Makawao, Upcountry
Location: Just down from the corner of Makawao and Baldwin, the building looks closed up
Meals: Breakfast, Lunch, Snacks & Treats
Hours: M-Tu and Th-F 7am-5pm; Sa 7am-2pm
Parking: Street
Phone: 808-572-7261

Taqueria Cruz (Mexican)

Taqueria Cruz makes decent Mexican food by hand and to order. (We know it's made to order, because it takes an intolerably long time for it to come out of the kitchen.) Their blackened fish taco makes the most flavorful choice; most other items are blander than they should be. The seating is outside in the courtyard also serving *Maui Masala*, and local musicians like to set up and play for tips in the evenings (we don't always like what we hear, though, and the amplifier is often turned up to 11).

We recommend *Taqueria Cruz* for those with a low spice tolerance who like the flavor profile of Mexican food. The ingredients are fresh and the prices moderate.

Address: 2395 S. Kihei Rd., Kihei
Location: in Dolphin Plaza across from Kamaole Beach Park I
Meals: Lunch, Dinner
Hours: M–Sa 11am–8pm
Parking: Lot
Phone: 808-875-2910

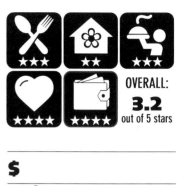

OVERALL:
3.2
out of 5 stars

Tasaka Guri Guri (Guri Guri)

Guri-Guri is a local frozen treat that is something like ice cream, something like sherbet, but not really either one. The story is that it was made for Japanese plantation workers and sold as "goodie-goodie" (which they pronounced guri-guri).

This third-generation family store is a Hawaiian institution and people on other islands make a point to stop in and get a tiny Dixie cup filled with little scoops of this treat. There are two flavors - strawberry and pineapple - and you can combine them if you like. Two scoops (the size of a melon ball) cost you $1.

Made with (as far as we can taste; the exact recipe is a closely guarded secret) strawberry guava or pineapple juice, 7 UP, sweetened condensed milk, and one other "mystery ingredient," you won't be surprised to hear that the flavor is more sweet than fruity, but very refreshing. A recipe you can make at home in your ice cream maker (or without) is on our blog, just search for "guri-guri" at www.MauiRestaurantsBlog.com. Kids of all ages back home will love you for it.

Address: 70 E. Ka'ahumanu Ave., Kahului, Central Maui
Location: in the Maui Mall
Meals: Snacks & Treats
Hours: M–Th & Sa 9am–6pm; F 9am–8pm; Su 10am–4pm
Parking: Lot
Phone: 808-871-4513

OVERALL:
3.6
out of 5 stars

$

CASH

★★ ★★ ★★

★ ★★★★★

OVERALL:
2.4
out of 5 stars

$

CASH

★★★★★ ★★★★ ★★★★

★★★★ ★★★★★

OVERALL:
4.4
out of 5 stars

$ $

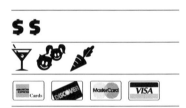

Tasty Crust *(Local/Plate Lunch)*

You probably have a version of *Tasty Crust* in your own hometown. Picture the diner that's been open since the fifties (or earlier), hasn't updated (or cleaned) since the seventies, serves cheap food and lots of it, and brings in business mainly because old habits die hard and food eaten in childhood automatically attains a nostalgic pleasure. While this is a "landmark" and an "institution," we wouldn't choose to eat here unless it was our job – and the staff and owners probably don't care either way. Sticky tables, surly (at best) service, and stiff pancakes … it compares about the same to our greasy spoons back home, but without our personal nostalgic ties.

Address: 1770 Mill St., Wailuku, Central Maui
Meals: Breakfast, Lunch, Dinner
Hours: Tu–F 6am–10pm; Sa–Su 6am–11pm; M 6am–3pm
Parking: Lot, Street
Phone: 808-244-0845
Website: www.tastycrust.com

Thailand Cuisine *(Thai)*

Thailand Cuisine is one of our favorite restaurants on the island, and its one of our "comfort" places. If we've had an exhausting day, feel a little cold coming on, or just feel too tired to cook, we walk in, sit in the first booth they put us in, and put ourselves in their soothing, capable hands.

If you already like Thai food, you can be sure that you will get good eats here. The usual suspects – pad thai, soups, curries – are freshly made and well spiced (we like it "hot" or "Thai hot", but even the milder versions are flavorful). We love the tom ka gai, the spicy coconut soup studded with big, fresh mushrooms, slices of ginger, basil leaves, and your choice of chicken and/or shrimp. The tom yum is another comforting brew, this one spicy and sour (from the kaffir lime) rather than spicy and sweet.

The green papaya salad is perfectly sour-spicy, and studded with finely chopped peanuts. It wakes up our palate for whatever main course we're ordering. The yum nuer, or beef salad, comes with marinated sour beef on top of a delicious medley of vegetables. We love the spice and the sour together, and often order this cold dish if we're in the mood for a light entrée.

The crispy chicken is a generous mound of deep fried chicken that comes with a complex, spicy red dipping sauce. We also like the Evil Prince curry with tofu, a blend of lemongrass, basil, chilies, and coconut milk. The pad pet is one of our favorites – a savory brown sauce with choice of protein (we prefer pork for this one). Dishes are served family style, and you can get sticky or brown rice on the side. We honestly have never ordered anything that we did not enjoy.

The ingredients are fresh and local, with many coming from the owner's garden. If they can't get an ingredient on Maui, they import it, which is why this is such authentic Thai. Beer and wine are limited, but they always have the Thai beer Singha on hand, which is, of course, perfect. For dessert, we often order the coconut milk tapioca pudding or the mango over sticky rice.

Their combination dinners (for two, for three, for four) include some of the best items on the menu, and we recommend them for their value. Vegetarians love this restaurant, where they can order any dish vegetarian and know it will be both delicious and satisfying as a main course.

Both locations are consistent and offer both dine in and take out. The dining rooms are wood paneled and have plenty of statuary and traditional décor, but also comfortable booths and real cloth napkins. The moderate prices, excellent service, and delicious food make us very happy.

In fact, now that we have finished writing this, it will be difficult for us to go to dinner anywhere else this evening.

Address: 70 E. Ka'ahumanu Ave., Kahului, Central Maui
Location: in the Maui Mall
Meals: Lunch, Dinner
Hours: Daily 10:30am–3:30pm; Su–Th 5–9:30pm; F–Sa 5–10:30pm
Parking: Lot
Phone: 808-873-0225
Website: www.thailandcuisinemaui.com

Address: 1819 S. Kihei Rd., Kihei, South Maui
Location: in the Kukui Mall
Meals: Lunch, Dinner
Hours: M–Sa 11am–2:30pm; Nightly 5–10pm
Parking: Lot
Phone: 808-875-0839

Tommy Bahama's Tropical Café *(American)*

Tommy Bahama's menu is filled with hyperbole (every item reads like the most extravagant, to-die-for dish you could ever eat) and high dollar signs. But the food that's presented is consistently fresh, well-prepared, and delicious. Despite our resistance to the hype, we always end up having a great time, and *Tommy's* is one of our favorite Happy Hour places in South Maui.

OVERALL:
3.8
out of 5 stars

We love the appetizers, especially the loki-loki tuna poke, a simple, fresh, delicious representation of the Hawaiian-style sashimi. The ahi tuna is uniformly chopped small, mixed with creamy mayonnaise and plenty of spices, then layered with a super fresh guacamole to smooth out the flavors. Served over crispy flatbread and tortilla chips, it is one of our favorite ways to celebrate. The scallop sliders are lighter takes on the beef slider – replace the red meat with the tender seared scallop and you get a fresh burst of sweet fish that perfectly sets off the spicy slaw on top. The simple, macadamia-nut-encrusted goat cheese served with mango salsa is also a favorite. Texture and flavor are well-balanced in all of their appetizers.

We like the buttery crab bisque, the crab cakes, and the coconut shrimp, which are usually well prepared and not overcooked. The cheeseburger has

continued on next page

Tommy Bahama's Tropical Café *(continued)*

a good sear and sweet and melty honey roasted onions. The pork sandwich with the blackberry brandy sauce continues to be one of our favorite items; savory and sweet and generously sized. The chopped salad with chicken is chunked up with apples, nuts, bacon, and corn, and completely satisfying as a light main entrée. Ribs fall off the bone (and we always take some home). The steaks are good cuts and prepared well. They often have good specials, and sometimes excellent deals on three course fixed price menus (the portions are often smaller, but we still leave plenty full).

Desserts are excellent at *Tommy's*, and we often come here late just for a little something sweet. We were skeptical when a reader (who is now a friend) told us last year that the butterscotch pudding was "the best dessert on Maui," but we were converted upon the first taste. Made from scratch and spiked with plenty of whiskey, the creamy, beautifully browned pudding comes in a giant (*giant*) goblet coated on the inside with a hard chocolate shell and topped with homemade whipped cream. While we like the brownie and the key lime pie, this pudding is what we talk about later. (And you will, too.)

The service is usually very good, there's live music at night, and the open-air restaurant features wide, comfortable booths and large tables. The central bar is a big square and excellent for hanging out at happy hour or any other time.

Address: 3750 Wailea Alanui Dr., Wailea, South Maui
Location: at the Shops at Wailea
Meals: Lunch, Dinner
Hours: Daily 11am–10pm
Parking: Lot
Phone: 808-875-9983
Website: www.TommyBahama.com

OVERALL:
3.4
out of 5 stars

Tropica *(Pacific Rim / American)*

Tropica, the beachfront dinner restaurant at The Westin in Ka'anapali, features giant thatched umbrellas, a central koi pond, and a beautiful "wall of water" fountain at the back of the open-air restaurant. If the Hawaiiana theme, slightly too loud (but good) live music, and vacationers passing close to your table don't bother you, we recommend *Tropica's* menu for fresh, local ingredients prepared with care. The prices are high, yes, but Ka'anapali is overpriced in general, and this is one of the better options in the resort area.

The wide-ranging menu features many very good appetizers, thin crust pizzas, several salads, and hearty fish dishes, steaks, and meats. Wine suggestions are listed with every item. We like to share several appetizers (portions are smaller than they should be) and add a salad or pizza to make a full meal. The ahi roll with panko crust is perfectly seared, and the presentation is elaborate and beautiful. We also like the New Caledonia Prawns – the sweet, tender protein is respected and not overcooked, and the uni butter that surrounds them adds a briny flavor with a decadent texture.

If you want to stay in Ka'anapali and don't want to go to **Cascades** for a nice dinner, this could be a good option.

Address: 2365 Ka'anapali Pkwy., Ka'anapali, West Maui
Location: Westin Ka'anapali
Meals: Dinner
Hours: W-Su 4:30pm-9:30pm
Parking: Valet
Phone: 808-667-2525
Website: www.westinmaui.com

Ululani's Hawaiian Shave Ice (Shave Ice)

OVERALL:
4.4
out of 5 stars

$

CASH

We have never bothered to recommend a shave ice place before, because we've never been impressed with the shave ice on Maui. Shave ice (not shaved ice), will remind you of a snow cone, but keep in mind that its legacy is east, not west – it came to Hawaii from Japan. The texture is flakier and lighter than an Italian ice or snow cone on the mainland. That said we still find most of the shops on Maui serve crinkly ice studded with chunks. Because they're often using inferior syrups, the dominant taste is "sweet," no matter what flavor you choose. Not exactly good eats.

Until a few months ago, we would not have heartily recommended any shave ice place on Maui for "the real thing." And now we're happy to recommend – make that strongly recommend – that you make at least one stop at **Ululani's Hawaiian Shave Ice** in Lahaina.

Tucked back behind an activities booth right near **Cheeseburger in Paradise, Ululani's** is making shave ice as good as any of the best places on Oahu. The texture of the ice – delicate flakes that nearly float down off the blade – is exactly like the fluffy, large-crystal snow that falls when winter sets in earnestly in colder climates. The ice melts instantly when it hits your tongue, sweeping the flavors you've chosen throughout your mouth. The pure water combined with the delicious homemade syrups make for a refreshing "sip" in every "bite."

The syrups are made by hand and tested until the recipe is just right, and they are beautiful. When we watch the Guava poured on the ice, for instance, we can see the fruit puree. The syrups taste like what they are, because they are made from what they are. For example, lilikoi (passionfruit) is made from lilikoi. Coconut is made from coconut. Maui cane sugar is the sweetener (no corn syrup), and that makes a huge difference in the **flavor** of the sweetness.

After watching them make shave ice, we have realized that making good shave ice is a lot like making good espresso. Every step of the process represents an opportunity to refine technique. The amount of pressure exerted on the ice, the speed of the blade as it shaves off the paper-thin slices, the way the ice is mounted in the cup, the subtle hand pressure used to form

continued on next page

Ululani's Hawaiian Shave Ice *(continued)*

the perfectly round ball of ice, the careful pouring of syrups so they don't mix, but meet exactly … it's just like watching an experienced, talented barista.

In addition to just ice and syrup, try a base of ice cream to give a different texture as you drill through layers of ice to the creamy layer below. Toppings include a drizzle of evaporated milk, which hits a nice smooth note right off the top. There are at least 30 flavors to choose from, but you can have many in combination on a single ice. The strongest seller – and with good reason – is a combination of coconut and dulce de leche that is decadent and unforgettable.

Co-owners Ululani and her husband, David, share a lovely story about growing up loving shave ice on Oahu, moving to the mainland, and missing it terribly. They opened their first place in Seattle with some retirement funds, and in 2008 moved back to Hawaii to open up their Lahaina shop. We're so glad they brought their icy Aloha home to all of us. If you are looking for a taste of pure Hawaii that also is a delicious food on its own, *Ululani's* is a must stop.

Address: 819 Front Street, Lahaina, West Maui
Location: In the Old Poi Factory next to
Meals: Snacks & Treats
Hours: Daily 11am–10pm
Parking: Street
Phone: 360-609-5678
Website: www.ululanisshaveice.com

OVERALL:
3.4
out of 5 stars

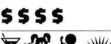

'Umalu *(Pacific Rim / American)*

The poolside restaurant at the Hyatt is above average hotel cuisine at average (read: exorbitant) Ka'anapali hotel prices. The wide-ranging menu, however, is likely to have something for even the pickiest of eaters, and we think vegetarians will be particularly happy with the varied and tasty preparations.

Appetizers are sized big enough to share or use as an entrée. We especially like the Snake River Farm kobe sliders. The American kobe beef is used to create a tray of three burgers topped with rich gorgonzola, caramelized sweet Maui onions, and a delicious aioli. With a poi (taro) bun, this is a really decadent, tender, sweet burger. Another good choice is the large platter of ahi nachos. Taro chips and sweet potato chips line the bottom, topped with a very good, balanced ahi poke, goat cheese, and guacamole made from edamame beans. The soft textures of the guacamole and the cheese meet the firmer fish, and contrast with the crisp chips. We like the unusual chips for the nachos.

Sandwiches and pizzas are available, as well as several really generous dinner-sized salads. The ingredients are fresh and local, and there is some care put into the recipes and the execution.

Service is fine, but harried when busy. The pools at the Hyatt are spectacular. If we wanted to have lunch in Ka'anapali, we would likely choose **'Umalu** for its choice of indoor or outdoor seating, pretty views, and relatively good value for the resort area.

Address: 200 Nohea Kai Dr., Ka'anapali, West Maui
Location: Hyatt Regency, right on the beach walk
Meals: Lunch, Dinner
Hours: Daily 11am - 9:30pm
Parking: Valet
Phone: 808-661-1234

Upcountry Fresh Tamales
& Mixed Plate *(Mexican / Local / Plate Lunch)*

Upcountry Fresh Tamales & Mixed Plate lives up to its name as a great place for a quick and cheap meal. Daily specials like chipotle pork or chicken mole and are not to be missed. The service is efficient, the food is authentic, and the prices are reasonable. We recommend it for a stop if you're exploring upcountry and enjoy Mexican.

Address: 55 Pukalani St., Pukalani, Upcountry
Location: In the Pukalani Terrace Center
Meals: Breakfast, Lunch
Hours: M-F 6am-4pm; Sa 6am-2pm
Parking: Lot
Phone: 808-572-8258

Vietnamese Cuisine *(Vietnamese)*

This sister restaurant to Wailuku's **A Saigon Café** is a little bigger, a little brighter, and a little cleaner. However, they're missing the funny-guy servers, and the food ranges from average to above average. If you're in South Kihei and really craving Vietnamese, you may like their *pho*, their noodle dishes, and their lemonade. They feature big portions at decent prices.

Address: 1280 S. Kihei Rd., Kihei, South Maui
Location: Azeka Makai Marketplace
Meals: Lunch, Dinner
Hours: Daily 10am-9:30pm
Parking: Lot
Phone: 808-875-2088
Website: www.mauivietnameserestaurant.com

OVERALL:
3.6
out of 5 stars

$

CASH

OVERALL:
3
out of 5 stars

$ $

OVERALL:
3.8
out of 5 stars

$

Who Cut the Cheese? *(American)*

Who Cut the Cheese? is a cutesy name for a pretty serious cheese and wine shop. If you want a little picnic lunch for the beach, we like to stop in for one of their paninis. They take a while to cut your cheese and grill it on a baguette, but it's lovely once they're finished. For $10 you get the sandwich, a little container of Greek olives, and bottled water or green tea.

Of course, you may want to visit for the many foreign and domestic cheeses. This is one of the few places on Maui where you can get cheese cut to order for you, and the people who work here are worth consulting. The wine selection is good, and they have several half bottles for your picnics, as well as cured meats and some local delicacies. Every month the shop holds a well-attended cheese and wine tasting; the schedule is on their website.

Address: 1279 S. Kihei Rd., Kihei, South Maui
Location: Azeka Mauka Marketplace
Meals: Lunch, Snacks & Treats
Hours: M–Sa 10am–6pm; Su 10am–5pm
Parking: Lot
Phone: 808-874-3930
Website: www.whocutthecheese.net

OVERALL:
3.8
out of 5 stars

$ $

Wok Star *(Asian)*

This little noodle stand on the side of the road in Kihei features decently priced, big bowls of homemade Pan-Asian noodles, as well as *jaffels*, more commonly called *paninis* or pressed sandwiches. (What jaffels have to do with noodles we don't quite understand.)

The ingredients are fresh, and there is a great love shown for the food by both the kitchen staff and the servers (you order at the counter, and they bring the food out for you). The problem is – and it's a big one – the recipes are not particularly inspired, and most often bland. Even when we ask them to kick the spice up for us, we still taste mostly noodle.

With such a brilliant palate of flavors – Indonesian, Chinese, Thai, and Japanese – we expect more punch and wow. The two dishes we like are the Indonesian peanut stir fry with broccoli, carrots, peppers, and spinach, served with egg noodles in a not-so-spicy peanut sauce (despite the two chili peppers next to the name), and the kung pow, a traditional Chinese preparation made with chilies, water chestnuts, peanuts, and peppers. You can add protein (chicken, tofu, beef, pork, mahi-mahi or shrimp) to any noodle bowl.

It's a cute name with a cute logo that's ready to license … but complex and heady flavors are important in these dishes, and ***Wok Star*** is not delivering in that department.

Address: 1913 S. Kihei Rd., Kihei, South Maui
Location: Kalama Village across from the Whale
Meals: Breakfast, Lunch, Dinner, Late Night
Hours: Daily 9am–12am
Parking: Lot
Phone: 808-495-0066
Website: www.wokstarcafe.com

Top Maui Tips

We write this guide with you in mind – literally. We like to start a writing day with a quick flip through emails from readers. This helps us to remember who you are: smart, interesting people who chose our little corner of paradise to spend your hard-earned vacation dollars. You're also someone who is interested enough in what you put in your body to purchase a guide to the food here.

We write this book as we would write a letter to a good friend who trusts our opinion. We think that's what we would want if we went to, say, Paris, and picked up a book like this one.

(Hey, writerly types – and we know you're reading this – if you live in another city, eat out a lot, and think "I could write a book like this," let us know and we'll see if we can help you out. The city we most often get requests for is New York, with Paris a close second. Come on New Yorkers, there's a market for you!)

Perhaps because of our friendly writing style, readers seem to think we know the answers to *all* questions about Maui – whether they're about what kind of fish to order or about where the sun sets or about which snorkel trip is best. We always try to help out with complete and useful answers.

But answering the same question five times in one week is not only time-consuming, it's inefficient – which is why we're dedicating this section of the guide to our **Top Maui Tips**. These are the answers to the **Most Important Frequently Asked Questions about Maui** that we get from readers like you.

We hope you find these Tips useful. Keep in mind that this is not an exhaustive list. If we save you a little time and frustration, then we've done our job. And if you have any questions that aren't answered here, feel free to send them to editor@TopMauiRestaurants.com and we'll do our best to answer you or point you in the right direction.

Where should I go for a really special night?

Whether you're planning a romantic dinner for two or a party for twelve to forty, there are certain restaurants that do parties very well. Some of these are expensive, some are moderate, but all are candidates for parties, depending upon what you're looking for.

Please refer to the full reviews for our overall impressions and contact information.

Bistro Casanova has a small dining area that has French doors, so the space is separate from the rest of the restaurant. There is no view, but it's a pretty restaurant and we enjoy the food and the busy atmosphere.

Café O'Lei in Kihei has a semi-private room, and the Dunes at Maui Lani location has a large banquet room.

Capische? defines elegance for us and has the best view. If you have eight in your party and can do *Il Teatro*, we recommend it. They also are willing to close down the restaurant to the public for private parties.

Cuatro Restaurant is one of our favorite new restaurants on Maui. A very small place with no view, we'd host a birthday or wedding rehearsal dinner there in a heartbeat. They will close the restaurant down for you.

David Paul's Island Grill has a beautiful private room at the rear of the restaurant that is very private and lovingly appointed. There is no view from back there, but the restaurant is classy and elegant.

Flatbread Pizza Company has a private room that is perfect for very casual gatherings. Acoustics can be a little loud, but the food pleases most everyone.

Gerard's Restaurant has such lovely personal attention and such good food that we'd go to any special event held here.

Hali'imaile General Store has a big back room that is perfect for large parties.

Mama's Fish House is excellent for romantic couples who want to celebrate a special occasion. They can also handle large parties.

Pineapple Grill has several very large tables that seat many people, which is nice when you have a small wedding party.

Plantation House has a large fireplace that is on a slightly elevated level. This area is often used for large parties.

Seawatch is now Bev Gannon's, which means you get her food in one of the most popular event spaces on Maui (they do about three weddings a day).

Spago can handle many special occasions and you get that killer view and the excellent service.

What kind of fish should I order?

Many visitors come eager to have the fresh fish Maui is famous for. But the Hawaiian names sound exotic and confusing, so they end up ordering mahi-mahi, which is nearly ubiquitous now. (Not that we have any problem with mahi-mahi.)

Here's a little guide to the fish you'll likely find at Maui restaurants.

`ahi (pronounce it ah' hee)

Ahi is the Hawaiian word for yellowfin, or big eye, tuna. It's excellent served raw as sashimi, or in poke (see below), but you'll also find it cooked. Usually this fish is served seared but still very pink inside, which is good; because once it is cooked it tastes like canned tuna.

aku (pronounce it ah' koo)

Aku is the Hawaiian word for skipjack tuna, also called bonito. This fish is similar to ahi in its deep red color, but it tastes more strongly of tuna. It's often served as sashimi, made into poke, or cooked similarly to ahi.

a`u (pronounce it ah' oo)

A`u is blue marlin, the common Pacific billfish. It's also known as kajiki in Japan. When eaten raw – try it in poke if you see it – it is similar to ahi in taste. If cooked, it is more like a swordfish.

mahi-mahi
(pronounce it mah' hee mah' hee)

In other parts of the world this is called the dolphin fish (it's not a mammal, don't worry). This is a very popular fish because it is firm, with white, delicate flesh. Good grilled for burgers. It's also great sautéed with a macadamia nut crust, which complements the sweet taste.

moana/o
(pronounce it moh (w)ah' nah/noh)

This is a delicate fish with really firm, white meat. Lovely.

moi (pronounce it moy)

At one time you'd be killed for eating this unless you were royalty – today anyone who can afford it is a king (this is James's favorite fish). Steamed or deep-fried, this delicate white fish is "ono" ("delicious").

onaga (pronounce it oh NAH gah)

Onaga is the Hawaiian word for red snapper, and is a broad term for several varieties found in these waters. Snapper is a bottom fish, found in deep waters, and as such is prized by restaurants for its tender flesh and delicate, fresh taste.

ono (pronounce it oh' noh)

Ono is like a large mackerel and is known as wahoo in the Caribbean. It's an open ocean fish, and one of our favorites. The meat is flaky, white, and delicate. The word "ono" means "delicious" in Hawaiian. Get the picture? Great grilled as a fillet for an "ono burger." If you're new to fish, this is a good place to start.

opah (pronounce it oh' pah)

Opah is an open ocean fish, also called a moonfish. It has a lovely firm white meat, and is considered good luck.

opakapaka (pronounce it OH' pah kah pah kah

Opakapaka is so delicious, but its fishing is regulated by the state, so it is not always on the menu. This is the pink ruby snapper, or crimson snapper found only in our waters. It's delicately flavored and moist, and we love it no matter how the chef chooses to prepare it.

How can I eat local on Maui?

Sustainability is a major issue here. The better restaurants all get their produce and most of their meat and fish from local growers and producers, so the more money you spend the more likely you are to be eating local.

One issue you should definitely be aware of is where the fish you're eating comes from. If you want to learn more about sustainable fish, go to **www.seafoodwatch.org**. This amazing guide – which you can also pick up at the Ma'alaea Ocean Center – lists every fish for the region and tells you whether it is a sustainable choice, or not. The guides change every season to reflect changes in fishing practices, seasonal and environmental issues, etc. The website is fascinating, and very detailed. They also have an iPhone application, which will let you get local recommendations for Maui with up to the minute information.

Ask your server if they're serving locally grown and produced food. The more requests restaurants get, the more likely they are to make the effort – and invest the money – in getting better, fresher, more local ingredients.

Are there any fixed price dinners on Maui?

When business is slow on Maui, nearly every restaurant responds with amazing deals on fixed price dinners. We've eaten four course meals for $39 – unheard of – during the last recession. Ask your server if there are any special deals going, because there just might be. Also check the *Maui News*, *Maui Time*, or *Maui Weekly* for the latest. We also report everything we can on our blog, **www.MauiRestaurants-Blog.com**.

Where do I go for a great Sunday Brunch?

You can get a wonderful value by taking advantage of Sunday brunches. Some even feature champagne (usually these are around $50 per person). These places also all do big, beautiful holiday meals and brunches at Thanksgiving, Christmas, New Years, Easter, Mother's Day, and so forth (usually for $75 - $100 per person).

Here are our favorites, call for details and reservations:

- **Makena Golf Resort** (used to be the Maui Prince) has a great Sunday champagne brunch, 808-875-5888.

- **The Grand Wailea's** brunch is our favorite for the killer view and excellent malasadas. Champagne is included. 808-888-6100.

- **Duo at the Four Seasons** has an excellent daily breakfast and Sunday brunch buffet. 808-874-8000.

- **The Ritz Carlton in Kapalua** kills us at holidays with their over the top champagne brunches. 808-669-6200.

- **Ka'anapali Beach Hotel** runs a Sunday brunch that keeps locals very happy – the brunch with the most local food. Great waffles and the brunch includes champagne. 808-661-0011

What is "Local" food?

There is a difference between Hawaiian food – which has been on these islands for thousands of years – and Local food, which is a response to Hawaii's more recent history.

Because of its plantation history, Hawaii is a cultural melting pot. Over the years plantations imported workers from places as far flung as Brazil, the Philippines, Japan, China, and Samoa to work in the fields. As people from these cultures worked side by side, they began to get to know each other. As anyone who went to grade school can tell you, food is a universal language, and food was certainly spoken in those plantation fields.

At lunchtime, people shared their food. The Chinese brought noodle dishes, Japanese brought their teriyaki and their rice, and Filipinos brought adobo. The Koreans brought kalbi ribs, and Hawaiians contributed their kalua pig. The "mixed plate" that resulted is still represented on every Local and Mixed Plate restaurant in the state (along with two scoops of rice and a scoop of macaroni salad, heavy on the mayonnaise).

In addition to plate lunches available at restaurants like *Da Kitchen*, *Aloha Mixed Plate*, and *L&L Barbecue*, some quintessentially Hawaiian local foods you might want to try while you are here include…

Loco Moco

This is a high-carbohydrate, high-protein dish that was invented in the middle of the last century to help teenage surfers get a fast breakfast. It *does* look like a growing boy's dream meal: a mountain of steamed rice with a fried egg on top, a hamburger patty on top of that, and brown gravy smothering everything. You can get it anywhere local food is sold, at roadside stands, and even McDonald's. We have a friend who grew up on Maui who always orders this at **Lulu's**, and it's impressive to watch him systematically put it away.

Saimin (pronounce it sigh-min)

Saimin is simple, warming Hawaiian comfort food. Inexpensive and filling, it's a noodle and broth soup that can be eaten for breakfast, lunch, dinner, and any time in between. If you've had Japanese ramen noodles, you've had something similar to saimin.

Thin white noodles float in a clear broth with green onions and fish cakes (kamaboko). Sometimes char siu (pork) is added, as well as chicken, eggs, shrimp, or whatever other protein is on hand. The soup is served extraordinarily hot, so you use chopsticks to eat the ingredients, and then when the soup has cooled a little, drink the broth directly from the bowl. You can get it just about anywhere, but you can also buy packets of the mix to bring home with you and make later.

SPAM

People in Hawaii eat more SPAM than most places (the Philippines and Guam come close). The meat was introduced during WWII as part of the rations given to the local population, and it caught on wildly. We speculate that it's because salt has always been an important (and sometimes the only) flavoring for island cookery, so the salty pork product is familiar, satisfying, inexpensive, and easy to stack in the cupboard.

A few years ago SPAM's maker sponsored a contest for which the grand prize included a year's supply of SPAM – but excluded Hawaii residents from the winner's circle. Boy, was that a mistake, one which they quickly corrected.

If you have never had SPAM and are ready to try it as part of your culinary education, try SPAM musubi, which is basically nigiri made with SPAM: a finger-sized block of seasoned rice, a thin slice of SPAM on top, and the entire thing wrapped with nori seaweed. You can get it at most grocery stores and convenience stores. One of our bloggers recommends the musubi at **Kuau Mart**, on the Hana Highway between Paia and **Mama's Fish House**.

What is Hawaiian food?

Would you believe that pineapple – the most quintessential symbol of Hawaiian hospitality – is not native to the islands? They're from Brazil!!

Given that, you'll understand why genuine Hawaiian food does not generally feature pineapples. No pineapples, no burgers with pineapple slices, no pizza with pineapple slices. In fact, traditional Hawaiian food is pretty simple: starches, proteins, and vegetables.

The ancient Hawaiians fished, of course. In addition to the many saltwater fish they harvested in their nets, they also fished for shrimp, squid, limpet, crab, and other seafood. They supplemented this with hunting birds and pigs, and they ate chickens.

They were also farmers who planted taro, yams, arrowroot, and breadfruit as staples. They harvested herbs, ferns, vines, and medicinals from the forests. They ate bananas, coconuts, raspberries, strawberries, sugar cane, and a type of apple. They used seaweed and sea salt to flavor their foods, and they cured a lot of food with salt for preservation.

Where the Meso-Americans had corn, the Hawaiians had taro root, which they pounded into a sticky, starchy purple paste called Poi. This food was incredibly important, and the key to social graces. If Poi was being eaten, you put a smile on your face and forgot your upsets.

Where Local food is high in simple carbs and saturated fat, Hawaiian food is typically low in both. When you go to a lu'au, the traditional Hawaiian celebration, you may encounter some or all of the following:

Lau Lau (pronounce it lou lou, it rhymes with how how)

Lau lau is a method of cooking meat or fish. Traditionally, fish and pork were placed on taro leaves, which were folded around this filling. Then the whole thing was wrapped in ti leaves and placed in an imu (an underground oven, kind of like a barbecue pit). Hot rocks were placed on the lau lau, and then covered in broad banana leaves to support the dirt that buried the oven until the lau lau was ready, a few hours later.

Today, you'll find lau lau contains pork, chicken, or beef, and often salted butterfish to bring flavor and a rich texture. There is often a vegetable mix added, and the whole thing is wrapped in taro leaves, then in ti leaves, and steamed in a pressure cooker. When you eat the dish, you cut right through the leaves to get to the tender fillings. We often add a little salt. Don't eat the outer ti-leaves – they are inedible and only used to cook the dish. But definitely eat the taro leaves.

Kalua Pork or Pig (pronounce it kah lu ah)

This is a smoky, tender pork dish that is extremely popular. The traditional way of making it is in an imu, as described above. The smoke in the oven flavors the pork, and the meat falls off the bone and kind of shreds. It's seasoned with sea salt, and is very delicious. Many people use a sweet barbecue sauce on the pig to balance the salt and smoke flavors.

Poke (pronounce it po kay)

Poke is one of our favorite Hawaiian dishes. The ancients used to skin and gut fresh fish, slice the meat into filets, and press them with salt and seaweed. Today, we cube ahi and mix it with soy sauce, sesame oil, roasted kukui nuts, and seaweed. Delicious. It can also be dressed up with salted tako (octopus), garlic, tobikko, tomatoes, and other sashimi grade fish. You can get excellent poke at Foodland in Kihei or Lahaina. We've also had good poke at Safeway.

Lomi Lomi Salmon
(pronounce it low me)

Salmon is not native to Hawaii. It's a cold water fish, and we do not have any cold water here. However, once salmon started showing up in Hawaii markets, it was love at first taste. Salmon is diced and salted, and then mixed by hand with tomatoes, crushed ice, and green onions in a massaging, kneading motion. (Lomi means *to massage*.) Lomi Lomi Salmon is served at nearly every modern lu'au, even though it is not truly a local fish, or an ancient dish.

Poi (pronounce it poy)

To make their traditional staple, Hawaiians cook the heavy taro root by baking it or steaming it. Then they mash it until it is completely demolished. The smooth, richly gooey paste is purple and absolutely beautiful. It's an acquired taste, but worth trying, and once you get over the absolutely weird texture (if you were a paste eater in elementary school, you won't think it's so weird), the flavor can be quite delicate and subtle. Because the ancients believed that taro was literally their ancestor, they regarded poi as a sacred food. So if you're having an argument with your spouse, don't reach for the poi.

Haupia (pronounce it how pee ah)

Haupia is a coconut dessert that is called a pudding, but we think it's closer to a gelatin. It couldn't be a simpler dessert: coconut milk is heated and mixed with arrowroot until it thickens, and then is poured into a pan to firm up in the refrigerator. Many people use cornstarch as the thickener, and while we understand that choice from a cost perspective, we vastly prefer those made with arrowroot. Arrowroot is more neutral in flavor and lets the delicate, flowery coconut come through. It also makes the pudding shinier.

What is Hawaiian Regional Cuisine, or Pacific Rim?

It is probably clear to you that Hawaiian food has always featured desperately fresh ingredients … but it is also heavily salted, and the textures can be odd to visitors. Local food, on the other hand, tends toward the heavy and the greasy (and salty).

In the late eighties a group of young chefs who loved Hawaii's unique flavors, fresh fish, island produce, and melting pot ethic decided to start a revolution they called Hawaiian Regional Cuisine.

Twelve is a significant number in many cultures, and certainly in ours, and in our more romantic moments we like to call this group of chefs the Hawaiian Apostles of Food. The twelve chefs were Sam Choy, Roger Dikon, Mark Ellman (**Mala**, **Penne Pasta**, **Maui Tacos**), Amy Ferguson Ota, Beverly Gannon (**Hali'imaile General Store**, **Joe's**, **Seawatch**), Jean-Marie Josselin, George Mavrothalassitis, Peter Merriman (**Merriman's Kapalua**), Philippe Padovani, Gary Strehl, Alan Wong and Roy Yamaguchi (**Roy's Bar & Grill**).

We'd like to take a moment now to say thank you to these chefs, who moved Hawaiian food away from pineapple on pizza and frozen food warmed up to a fusion cuisine that applies European sauces and cooking techniques to local ingredients. The result is beautiful, fanciful, delicious food that has people all over the world moaning and rolling their eyes with delight.

We'd also like to say thank you to the chefs who came after them and continue to develop Hawaii as a base for world-class cuisine. There is some debate about how Hawaiian Regional Cuisine differs from Pacific Rim, which came a little later, but we're of the mind that Pacific Rim cuisine is not just about Hawaii – it's also about Asia, Indonesia, Polynesia, South America, and California (any food that comes from the rim of the Pacific Ocean).

Whatever you call it, the best food in Hawaii's restaurants crosses boundaries, plays with the senses (taste and vision and touch and smell and even, at times, sound), is colorful, surprising, and simply scrumptious. Unlike other cuisines, with their long histories and firm rules, the fusion cuisine on the islands continues to evolve and grow.

Where Should I Get Groceries, Wine, Beer, or Alcohol?

If you're staying in a condo or vacation rental during your stay on Maui, you'll want to stock the fridge. We'll share our own favorite shopping spots with you. There are many more, but these are the places we go first for the best prices and the best selection.

Be prepared for sticker shock, though. A gallon of milk can run you as high as $8, and even a tin of sardines will be $.50-$1 more than you are used to paying back home. Food prices contribute to the overall high cost of living here. You'll do best by shopping in more than one place to get the best deals.

Costco

Locals buy a lot of groceries here. Costco stocks fresh local produce in season year-round, and local coffee from Maui Coffee Roasters, too (we drink it most every morning). With a convenient location right next to the airport, we highly recommend a stop here to stock up on everything from bottled water to local salad greens. They have a good selection of wine, beer, and spirits, and a killer chocolate/macadamia nut treat section. Just remember to bring your membership card with you. *Directions from the airport: As you exit the airport, turn left at the first light onto Haleakala Highway, and then right into the Costco parking lot. 540 Haleakala Highway, Kahului.*

Foodland

Foodland locations are typically much smaller than Safeway, but they're good local grocery stores. We like their bakery line, *Tutu's*, especially for hot dog/hamburger rolls. Prepared sandwich bar, fried chicken, and sushi are all pretty good for supermarket food. We like their poke. We also think they have a pretty good wine buyer, and carry a good line of beer and spirits. *90 Kane St., Kahului; Kihei Town Ctr, Kihei; 878 Front Street, Lahaina.*

Hawaii Liquor Superstore

This big liquor store stocks everything we can think of when we think cocktails: syrups, mixes, and all the spirits, plus wine and beer; and everything at good prices. They have the largest selection of wine on the island. *Maui Marketplace, Dairy Road, Kahului*

Lahaina Farms

This is a Foodland–owned and operated full-service grocery store that focuses on natural and whole foods. They still have plenty of chips and sodas, however, and a good wine selection. Their prices are high, but we like shopping here if we're on the West Side. *In the Barnes & Noble Shopping Center, Lahaina*

Long's Drug Store

Buy your wine and beer here! Believe it or not, this we-stock-a-little-of-everything drug store has the best selection, some of the most knowledgeable buyers, and the best prices on the island outside of Costco. Also get your Maui Cattle Company steaks here. *100 E Kaahumanu Ave Kahului; 1215 South Kihei Road, Kihei; 1221 Honoapiilani Hwy., Lahaina.*

Mana Foods

We love this health food store in Paia for everything from skin care products to local produce. The owner works hard to keep prices low on everything. See the review in the restaurant section. *Baldwin Ave., Paia*

Maui Prime

Maui Prime wholesales to many of the best restaurants, but they also have a very good retail outlet. Cheese, olives, fresh local eggs, and a good meat and fish section, as well as many gourmet grocery items and a careful selection of wine. *808.661.4912, 142 Kupuohi St., Lahaina*

Maui Swap Meet

This farmer's market/crafts fair is a Saturday ritual for us. Go early for the best produce, and try all the exotic treats. Make a point of stopping at the **Ono Organic Farms** stand, with its fresh Hana produce. If you like to cook, this is a must. Plenty of souvenirs, too. *At Maui Community College, Kahului.*

Safeway

Safeway is the best all-around standard grocery store. Their weekly sales start on Wednesdays. Decent prices on beer and wine. If you have a Safeway club card, you'll get the same special deals you get at home (our sale prices aren't quite as good a deal as yours probably are). Note to Canadians: yes, your card works here. *170 E Kamehameha Ave, Kahului; 277 Pi'ikea Ave, Kihei; 1221 Honoapiilani Hway, Lahaina.*

Times Supermarket

The Times Supermarket chain of grocery stores very recently bought the Star Market that we used to love for the freshest fish you can buy in Maui groceries stores (we'll see if this changes over time). *70 E Kaahumanu Ave, Kahului; 1310 South Kihei Road, Kihei.*

Wailea Wine

Not just a very good collection of wine, also gourmet foods and pantry items, beer, liquor … and cigars. *161 Wailea Ike Place, Wailea; 808-879-0555*

Wine Corner

The Wine Corner has two locations, very knowledgeable staff, and careful selections. *149 Hana Hwy., Paia, 808-579-8904; 08 Wainee St, Lahaina, 808-667-5511*

Who Cut the Cheese

We go for the wine selection, but mostly the

cheese selection, hand–cut to your specifications. These ladies love their work. *Azeka Mauka Marketplace, South Kihei Road, Kihei*

Whole Foods Market

Whole Foods (who is a sponsor of this edition of *Top Maui Restaurants*) is opening a Maui location in early spring of 2010, after years of teasing Maui foodies with delays. We're excited because their prepared food and deli section is fabulous, as is their grocery selection, produce, meat, fish, and wine selections. As you probably know, their nickname is Whole Paycheck – but we don't mind spending ours there. *Maui Mall, Kahului*

Where Should I Buy Local, Fresh Fish?

Our real answer is this: buy local fish out of that truck you see parked on the side of the road with the sign that says "fresh fish, $5 per pound."

Most of the fresh fish goes from the boat directly to the restaurants, where the chefs are waiting eagerly to see what's come out of the water. If fishermen caught so much they can't sell it all (unlikely, but it happens), they'll sell it to you out of their truck. This happens most often along the Hana Highway, but we've seen people along South Kihei Road and out near Kapalua, too.

If you don't see these guys but still want to try cooking fish at your home, try these places:

Costco: best prices, but huge quantities. They almost always have slabs of salmon, ahi sashimi, rainbow trout, and pretty good poke, and sometimes shellfish at great prices (scallops,

King crab legs).

Times Supermarket in Kihei (used to be Star Market): unless they change their fish buyer, this is the best selection of local fish with the best prices.

Foodland in Kahului has a good fish section.

Lahaina Farms in Lahaina has a good fish section, a little pricey.

Eskimo Candy in Kihei occasionally has local fish, and always has fish from Taiwan and Alaska. Spendy prices.

Fish Market Maui in Honokowai has local fresh fish, spendy prices.

Valley Isle Seafood in Kahului wholesales to restaurants and hotels, but has a small retail operation. Good fish, a little spendy. *475 Hukilike Street, Bay D, Kahului*

Where should I buy beef or steak?

Maui Cattle Company grazes their cows on the slopes of Haleakala, so the beef is usually not frozen before you get it. It also tastes amazingly rich and complex, although the butchering leaves something to be desired. You can buy it at Long's Drug Stores.

If you prefer, Costco and Safeway have the best quality and prices on the island for beef, chicken, and other meat. The USDA Prime cuts of beef that are sold at Costco are some of the best steaks we've had in or out of restaurants. Also, Whole Foods usually has a great meat department.

Where should I go for really good produce?

Our favorite place to buy produce is the **Maui Swap Meet** at Maui Community College on Saturdays in Kahului. There are smaller farmer's markets all over the island, too.

In Central Maui, check out the Queen Ka'ahumanu Center's market in Kahului on Tuesdays, Wednesdays, and Fridays. There is also a good market at Maui Mall on Tuesdays, Wednesdays, and Fridays.

In West Maui, check out the market in Honokowai across from Honokowai Park. They sell on Mondays, Wednesdays, and Fridays.

In South Maui, there's a market on South Kihei Road, in the Suda Store parking lot on every weekday.

Upcountry, you can find a market in the morning on Saturdays at the Eddie Tam Center on Makawao Avenue in Makawao.

In Hana there's a market on Saturdays across from Hasegawa General Store, and the Hana Fresh market is open at the Hana Medical Center on Mondays, Thursdays, and Saturdays.

We also go to **Costco** for local tomatoes, local Kula greens, and papayas and mangos in season, as well as organic produce from the mainland.

Another good bet is **Mana Foods** in Paia for a consistently excellent selection of local produce at prices that usually beat Safeway's and match Costco's.

Other natural food stores with good produce sections are **Hawaiian Moons** in Kihei, and **Down to Earth** in Kahului (both are reviewed in the Guide). And of course, the new Whole Foods in Kahului will be a good bet.

I've heard there's a lot of traffic on Maui – is that true?

Well, yes, and no. We're pretty funny about traffic on Maui.

Whether we grew up here, come from big cities with lots of traffic, or small towns with one stoplight, people who live on Maui think that traffic here is Just Awful. Why, it can take us a whole thirty minutes to drive from our home in Kihei to the Home Depot in Kahului! How inconvenient! (It used to take Molly that long to cross New York City's midtown on the bus.)

We get remarkably complacent in our little corners of the island. It's entirely possible that someone who lives and works on the West Side (Lahaina, Ka'anapali, etc.) hasn't visited South Maui in over a year. When we go to dinner on the west side and servers find out we're from Kihei, they marvel that we were willing to drive *so far*.

How far is it? Maybe forty-five minutes or an hour, tops.

So when we complain about traffic, we might really be complaining about driving. The relaxed lifestyle can lead to a particular Maui-style *inertia*.

Given all of the above it's also true that there is a rush hour here on Maui. In the morning and in the evening, you will see a marked increase in the number of cars on the road. You're not likely to be terribly *slowed down* by them, but you will need to pay more attention while you drive.

Because there is generally one road to any part of the island, when an accident occurs or something happens to close the road, travel can go from slow to nonexistent.

Many visitors are so struck by the gorgeous, ever-changing scenery that they drive as if they were a little drunk, which is another reason why traffic can be slow.

And when it's whale season, *fuhgeddaboudit* (as they say in New York). Everyone's distracted when giant mammals throw themselves into the air and make gigantic splashes.

Our advice is to remind yourself that you're driving a dangerous vehicle, fasten your seat belt (both seat belts and child restraints are required by law in Hawaii), and make sure you pay attention to the speed limit, which changes quite often on our roads.

We also recommend never, ever leaving anything of value in your car, because break-ins and theft can be a problem. When we drive to Hana, we tend to keep our car messy so that it looks local, and we make sure that any maps or guidebook-looking books come with us when we leave the car. We even have friends who leave their doors unlocked so that it is easy for someone to find out there's nothing of value in the car. This mitigates the risk of a smashed window. We don't leave valuables in the trunk, either, because it's just too easy these days to get in through the backseat.

Where do you recommend I go when I get off the plane for suntan lotion?

If you're a Costco member, you're in luck, be-cause it's right outside the airport. We highly recommend stopping here for good suntan lotion. In addition to several other brands, they sell Molly's favorite, Neutrogena, which is the only one that doesn't make her skin break out. You might think that buying a package that has three tubes of lotion is excessive, but the sun is very strong here, and you should go through this stuff by the end of the week.

We also like recommending Costco for buying a couple of leis. They sell purple orchid leis, two to a box, for $8.99. If you're with your sweetheart, you can "lei" each other in your rental car and properly welcome yourselves to Maui.

If you're very hungry when you get off the plane, a Krispy Kreme is the first place you'll see outside the airport, and they're open very late in order to satisfy your craving for a little post-flight sugar. If you want something more substantial, **Marco's** is the first restaurant you'll see at the next intersection, and it's a good place to get a quick and familiar meal before you move on to your hotel.

Depending upon when you arrive, you can also stop at any of the other big box stores or fast food joints along Dairy Road in Kahului. You'll see a Kmart, McDonald's, Starbucks, Burger King, and a Wal-Mart. You'll also see **Down to Earth**, a big health food store. If you scan through the review section of the guide, you'll see a little airplane symbol next to other restaurants that are near enough to the airport to make a quick detour.

What do you recommend for food-related activities? Do any farmers give tours?

Yes! Several farms open their doors to visitors. Here are a few of our favorite ways to spend our time.

Surfing Goat Dairy (who is a sponsor of this edition of *Top Maui Restaurants*) is a working goat farm that produces delicious, award-winning cheese. We highly recommend stopping by and sampling the cheese or taking one of their tours (ever milked a goat?). The goats play on surfboards (for real) and it's a dry, dusty, but pungent and tasteful stop. **808-878-2870, www.surfinggoatdairy.com**

Ono Organic Farms grows some pretty exotic fruit, which is all organic, and all hand-picked. The farm is beautiful, and our favorite episode of Wolfgang Puck's old cooking show featured Wolfgang visiting with owner Chuck Boerner. They give thirty minute tours of the farm, but call for details. If you're driving to Hana, this is a must stop. **808-248-7779, www. onofarms.com**

Tedeschi Winery is up in Kula, in a historic building that is peaceful and lovely to visit. We like the free tour of the grounds, and if you try the wines, the pineapple sparkling wine is interesting. **877-878-6058, www.mauiwine. com**

We really like going up to Kula to **Ali'i Kula Lavender Farm**. This serene, delicious-smelling working farm grows over 45 varieties of lavender and makes several soaps, potpourri, and other lavender-themed products. You can walk through the grounds yourself, or take a tour. The view is stunning. **808-878-3004, www.aliikulalavender.com**

One of our favorite Maui chefs, James McDonald of *I'O*, *Pacific'O*, and *Feast at Lele*, established his own organic farm in Kula, **O'O Farm**, specifically to grow fresh produce for his restaurants. You can take a tour that includes a picnic lunch made from what you pick. Delicious. **808-667-4341, www.oofarm.com**

Kapalua Farms, an organic farm run by Maui Pineapple Company, offers tours of their working farm, including lunch. **808-665-5491, www.mauipineapple.com**

Local foodie Jeannie Wenger owns **Maui Culinary Tours**. She'll take you on a driving tour of local farms and then arrange a three course dinner at one of her favorite restaurants. **808-283-5924, www.mauiculinarytours.com**

Is the Road to Hana really worth it?

This is one of the hardest questions to answer. We know it's worth it for us, but we also know people who felt it was a waste of time on their vacation. If you hate long, twisty roads on the mainland, or if you get carsick, or if you just aren't that interested in a beautiful scene that changes with every mile, it may not be for you.

If, on the other hand, gorgeous waterfalls, beautiful pools, endless ocean vistas, incredibly lush rainforests, and soaring mountain peaks sound like fun, you might want to drive the Road after all. If you do go, we have some things for you to keep in mind.

Here's what it's like for the driver on The Road to Hana:

You drive a car you don't know that well for several hours (two if you don't stop) at 20 miles per hour around endless hairpin curves.

Your hands clench the wheel (whether you want them to or not) because you keep getting surprised by what's around the next bend.

Everyone else in the car ooooohs and ahhhhs and exclaims "Look at that!"

You miss whatever they saw, and are surprised by how fast that car is coming from the other direction on the one lane bridge.

There are two ways to mitigate the fatigue the driver inevitably feels after a while. You can switch driving responsibilities with someone else, so that no one gets too tired and no one misses all the beauty, or you can go on a tour and let someone else do all the driving. We recommend **Valley Isle Excursions**, 808-661-8687. (Valley Isle is a sponsor for this edition of *Top Maui Restaurants*).

If you drive yourself, of course, you get full control and can stop as often as you like. Stopping along the Road to gawk at the beauty is good, because once you get to Hana, you might wonder what the fuss is about – it's a little fishing village, and not much is happening (and they like it that way).

If you stay in Hana, you'll find that a lot happens here, but it's mostly internal. When we're here for more than twenty-four hours, something inside starts to unwind, and we relax more deeply than we do anywhere else.

Most people, however, are not staying. If you are one of those, budget at least eight hours to drive to Hana and then back. If you decide to keep going "all the way around" Haleakala – which we recommend – you are going to take at least 8 hours. This includes plenty of stopping, but a fairly measured pace. It can take as long as twelve hours to do it at a leisurely pace.

There are only a couple of places to eat in Hana, so we highly recommend packing a picnic lunch and road snacks to eat in the car. We like to pack a cooler with plenty of water and caffeinated drinks, leave very early (at around 7am), stop in Paia for breakfast, and be on the Road by 8am. This puts us at the head of the long lines of cars and gives us plenty of time to meander and stop wherever we want to.

There are several little roadside stands along the Road, and several farms. The following is a list of some of our favorite places to stop that are reliably open:

Ono Organic Farms is a must stop, as we described above. **808-248-7779, www.ono-farms.com**

Our beautiful friends Krista and Ian own a beautiful tropical flower farm in Hana. Make a point of stopping at **Hana Tropicals** to visit their orchid house, ask you're your tropical flower questions, and take a tour of the pesticide-free farm. They also have a sacred labyrinth that you can use for a walking meditation to work the kinks out from the road. They ship their flowers anywhere, and their bouquets are spectacular. Say hi from Molly and James when you stop in. **808-248-7533, www.hanatropicals.com**

The **Hana Coast Gallery** is just next to the Hotel Hana-Maui and is one of our favorite places to view art on Maui. It's a very particular collection of the absolute cream of the crop of local artists. If you love art, it's a must-do. While you're there, get a drink in the hotel's gracious lobby and look at Hana's beautiful harbor. **808–248–8636, www.hanacoast. com**

Kahanu Gardens is a National Tropical Botanical Garden located in Hana, and if they're open when you visit, we highly recommend stopping in and walking the gardens. The largest heiau in Polynesia is located here. This massive lava-rock structure is an ancient place of worship known as Pi`ilanihale. **808–248–8912 www.ntbg.org**

Is going to sunrise at Haleakala Crater worth it?

Another impossible question! If you go on a morning when the sunrise is perfect – the clouds perfectly encircle the mountain just below the crater, and the sunlight comes up through them and creates a stunning ocean of rainbows below you – it's definitely worth it.

If you go on a morning when there are no clouds, well, it's still very pretty, but not spectacular. You might think *what's the big deal?*

Of course, you can never predict nature, so if you get the intuitive feeling that yes, you should venture up the mountain, we recommend going on your first full day, or your second, when you are still on mainland time. It will be easier to wake up early enough to drive up the mountain – which can take at least two hours from our home in Kihei. We'd leave at least two and a half hours to drive there from Ka'anapali.

Sunrise does not wait for you, so make sure you are there at least thirty to forty-five minutes before the show. If sunrise is at 5:30am, we would leave Kihei by 3:00am at the latest. You can call the National Weather Service at 866-944-5025 for sunrise time and the weather forecast at the summit.

We always bring plenty of layers and gloves and scarves and hats, because it's very cold up there at 10,000 feet. We often leave the extra clothes off at first, and then add layers as we get higher in altitude. Even with our down parkas we can get cold. You might even want to take the comforter off the bed!

Bring a few snacks to tide you over before breakfast. After sunrise, you can grab breakfast at **La Provence** or **Kula Lodge** if you are starving, or wait the extra twenty minutes to get down to Paia and go to **Moana Bakery and Café**, our personal favorite for this trip.

If sunrise is just too early for you, you might consider catching a sunset, instead. It's not as dramatic, because the western cloud cover is not as likely to give that stained window effect as it does in the east. However, it's still a beautiful place to watch the sun go down. If it's a full moon (or the day before) you can watch the full moon rise in the east while the sun sets in the west – which is very, very beautiful.

Is driving the whole way around the West Maui Mountains worth it?

This road scares us way more than the Road to Hana does. It's truly one way, and built for mountain goats, not cars. But it's breathtaking, too. **Julia's Best Banana Bread** is out there, as well as our favorite artist gallery, **Turnbull Studios**.

Steve and Christine are friends of ours, and they and their uncle make up the trio of artists who live and work at the studio. In addition to their own sculpture, you can find many other local Maui artists' work for sale, and several smaller items that make precious souvenirs. This and the Hana Coast Gallery (where you can also see Christine's work) are two very special places for anyone who loves art.

And best of all, if you choose not to drive all the way around the West Maui Mountains from Kapalua, you can take the road from the other direction, Wailuku, and the studio is only twenty minutes from town. *5030 Kahekili Hwy., Wailuku,* **808–244–0101,** **www.turn-bullstudios.org**

Where can I see movies?

If you want to see movies on Maui, there are several movie theaters that show the most popular offerings: two in Lahaina, two in Kahului, and one in Kihei. You can find the listings in the *Maui News, Maui Time,* or *Maui Weekly.*

But if you like seeing art films, documentaries, and independent movies in a beautiful space, go to the **Maui Arts and Cultural Center** (MACC) and catch a movie from the **Maui Film Festival** (MFF).

Most Wednesdays during the year the MFF shows a first run film in the gorgeous, plush Castle Theater at the MACC. If you're here in December, check out their First Light Festi-

val, which shows all the films Festival Director Barrie Rivers believes will win Oscar Awards.

If you're here in June, make a point of attending the weeklong, star-studded, foodie-fabulous **Maui Film Festival**. This is James's favorite event of the year. Our favorite venue (they show films all over the island) is the Celestial Cinema, a giant outdoor movie theater with a gigantic screen and state of the art sound (honest, it's miraculous that they can make outdoor sound systems this good). There is nothing like sitting outside on a Maui summer night and watching a beautiful film.

Every evening begins with a short tour of the stars with Maui's resident philosopher-astronomer, Harriet Witt. She's a lovely soul with a cosmic passion for the skies, and her presentation is worth the price of admission.

Check out the Maui Film Festival's schedule of events at **www.mauifilmfestival.com**.

Are there any clubs on Maui?

Sometimes! The nightlife on Maui is pretty sedate, especially in contrast to Honolulu's scene. Places to dance open and close fairly rapidly, so it's best to check out the local papers for listings. The *Maui Time* is especially useful. Your concierge will also have some ideas, as well.

You will be able to see plenty of live music, however, and those listings will be in any of the newspapers and posted everywhere flyers are located.

Besides lu'aus, are there any shows we should see?

Yes, there are.

'Ulalena is amazing. (The show is a sponsor of this edition of *Top Maui Restaurants*.) We know of no better way to understand how Hawaiians feel about Hawaii than to see this show. Kids love it. Toll free number is **808-856-7958, www.ulalena.com**

We also love **Warren and Annabelle's**, the incredibly funny magic show that is harder to get into than you might think. The close up magic performed in this intimate theater is nothing short of astonishing. Be prepared to laugh, a lot. That's all we're saying – it's too fun to give away more. Over twenty-one only. **808-667-6244, www.warrenandannabelles.com**

If you like circus, you will definitely get a kick out of **Cirque Polynesia** at the Hyatt in Ka'anapali. We held our breath through a couple of death-defying acts. The stage construction is less-than-professional, but the acts are definitely the real deal. A fun evening that is great for kids as well as adults. **808-667-4540, www.cirquepolynesia.com**

The **Maui Arts and Cultural Center** in Kahului is a great place to see world-class concerts and wonderful gallery exhibitions. To find out what they're doing when you're here, check out their schedule on line or pick up their calendar at activity booths. **808-242-7469, www.mauiarts.org**

Maui Onstage at the Iao Theater in Wailuku puts on several musicals and plays every year. This is community theater at its best in a beautiful Mission style theater that was built in 1928. **808-244-8680, www.mauionstage.com**

I've heard Lanai is beautiful, but it's so expensive – is it worth it?

We chose to be married on Lanai, and yes, we think it is worth staying there. The island is beautiful in a completely different way from Maui, and there is nothing to "do" so we relax really deeply there.

But if your wallet can't spring for Four Seasons accommodations (there are two resorts and both are run by the Four Seasons) you can stay in the less expensive (but not inexpensive) Hotel Lanai, or just go over for a day.

The ferry to Lanai leaves from Lahaina several times a day. You can take a very early ferry out, hang out on the beach just a short walk from the ferry dock, have lunch at the hotel (or bring it with you), and get back on a ferry in the afternoon. Call Expeditions Ferry for ferry tickets (passenger only, no cars): **808-661-3756 or www.go-lanai.com**.

The Four Seasons resorts run a shuttle between the beachside Manele Bay resort and the pine-tree-ringed Lodge at Koele resort, with a stop in quaint Lanai City. They will let you ride this shuttle for a fee, but please call them directly for the details. **808-565-2000.**

We have especially enjoyed our meals at the formal dining room at **The Lodge at Koele**. Their afternoon tea service in the big lobby with one-story fireplaces is lovely. We also like the restaurant at the **Hotel Lanai**, which is run by Bev Gannon.

We're dreaming of moving to Maui. Any advice?

Keep dreaming, and when it's time to do it, you will know. Most people who visit Maui have the passing thought "It would be so great to live here."

But living here is not like being on vacation all the time. You're far away from friends and family, you don't have much in the way of culture or art, and the cost of living is very high (unless you're from places like New York City, in which case you won't think it's all *that* expensive).

Everyone we know who moved to Maui from somewhere else ultimately did it because they *knew* they were supposed to.

Be prepared for anyone who lives here to roll their eyes a little when you express your desire, and don't take it personally. So many people say it, and so few do it, that we on Maui take a "wait and see" approach. Until you have actually moved here, you might not find a job or a place to live, for example. It's like you have to prove that you're here before Maui opens her arms.

Now, it's a little different for retirees. And it's also different for people with special skills that are needed on the island. If you're really serious about moving to Maui, we recommend you ask plenty of locals when they got here, how they got here, and why they came. Also ask, *why do you live here*, rather than stating *it must be great to live here*. We can't argue with the fact that it is a great place to live, but why we stay is a little different for everyone.

We have a neighbor, **Lee Wheeler**, who is the hardest working realtor on Maui and a font of information for people looking to make the jump (he is also a sponsor of this edition of *Top Maui Restaurants*). We highly recommend talking to him about what the market's doing if you're considering buying a home. **808-298-3416, www.LivingMauiStyle.com**

If you have a pet and want to find out what's involved in bringing them to Maui, call our vet, **Dr. Demian Dressler**. His hospital, **South Shore Veterinary Care**, has a wonderful service that we recommend pet lover moving to Maui use. They'll coordinate every detail of your pet's move with the state's vaccination and quarantine inspectors (we don't have rabies here, so the state makes you jump through some hoops to prove that your pet isn't infected). A vet tech will even meet your pet as they leave the plane so they aren't alone while the state inspects their papers. It's a great service and helps you avoid the ninety day quarantine. **808-874-3422.**

FYI: Why We Have Sponsors

It may seem strange that we have local Maui businesses sponsoring *Top Maui Restaurants*, but it's a lot less strange than you might think. First, a little about the economics of food journalism: most dining reviews are written for magazines and newspapers, which make money by taking advertising. Bloggers make money from advertising, as do online peer-review travel websites.

You may or may not know this, but a shocking amount of travel writing is actually comped by the establishments featured – in other words, the restaurant or hotel gave the writer free meals and accommodations!

(We don't understand this. If we don't share your pain at having to pay $120 for a bad meal, how can we possibly review it? No restaurant can influence our review, because we don't take restaurant advertising in our book.)

Over the last five years that we have been writing *Top Maui Restaurants*, we have funded it completely on our own. All told, we've spent close to $107,000 on meals on Maui – most of them, unfortunately, not worth the cash. Our favorite slogan is "We eat bad food so you don't have to."

Book sales have been good, but they haven't been good enough to cover that entire tab, and we actually considered not publishing a 2010 edition. But we got so many requests from our readers that we decided to take sponsors to help underwrite our research.

This was a really hard decision to make because we know that our reputation is on the line when we endorse other businesses. To underwrite *Top Maui Restaurants*, sponsors had to offer services or products that are of superior quality and that would be relevant and useful to you. We also had to have had personal experience with the sponsor or have heard great things about them from our readers and/or our trusted friends here on Maui.

Obviously we can't take advertising from restaurants, not even from restaurants we love. It's too much of a conflict of interest, and even if we could be sure the advertising relationship wouldn't influence our review, we don't want even the *appearance* of a biased review.

Every sponsor shares a few things in common. First, they appreciate the value this book delivers. Second, they love food – whether they eat at the most expensive restaurants or the least. (It was funny how many quizzed us about our methods and our favorite restaurants – or even read the book cover to cover – before they decided we were telling the unvarnished truth about Maui restaurants.)

Third, they consider our readers the cream of the crop of Maui visitors. If you care enough about your vacation to plan your meals, and know that just relying on Internet reviews or concierge recommendations can get you into trouble, you will appreciate the high quality business they run.

Our Sponsors

As you read what we have to say about these businesses, keep in mind that we have hand-selected these for **you**, our readers. Just like we don't want you to waste your time or money at bad restaurants, we don't want you to waste it on anything else. We have had many requests over the years for advertising (mostly from restaurants), but when we finally started accepting sponsorships (with this edition) we only approached businesses worthy of your vacation dollars.

If you do choose to patronize any of our sponsors, please let them know that you found them in *Top Maui Restaurants*. And if you don't agree with our assessment that they are high quality businesses, please let us know by dropping an email to **editor@TopMauiRestaurants.com**.

This is a small island for us Maui locals, and these are not just business owners, they're our neighbors, our friends, and our community. Next time we see them at Costco

what will you create?

Experience programs that support lifelong lerning in the arts:

Art Classes, Workshops, Open Studios, Lectures, Exhibitions, Special Events, Historical House and Garden Tours, and More!

Hui No'eau Visual Arts Center
2841 Baldwin Avenue in Makawao
(808) 572.6560 | www.huinoeau.com
Open Monday - Saturday, 10 am - 4 pm

or bump into them at the movies, we'll pass on your feedback!

There's No Place Like This Home

If you love the visual arts – painting, photography, jewelry, sculpture – or if you love glimpsing times past by touring historic mansions – make a point of driving up to **Hui No'eau** (the word *hui* means community in Hawaiian, and *no'eau* means talented, clever, or wise). There is no better place to meet local artists at work or purchase one–of–a–kind gifts you literally can't get anywhere else on the island.

You cannot see the mansion easily from the road, but careful as you drive in – be prepared for a beautiful Italianate villa set upon a rolling green lawn. Every time we drive in we think *is this really on Maui?* The gracious art gallery takes up most of the first floor, and features both juried and solo exhibitions. The gallery shop offers original art created by members of the Hui on the premises. The shop changes its wares every three months, guaranteeing that what you see this time will not be back later.

Walking around the grounds gives you a chance to see the remains of an ancient sugar mill, many sculptures, and the gracious architecture that makes up this lovingly tended mansion. The Hui offers many art classes, and you are welcome to drop in whether you live here or are visiting. Children love their art classes, and we love to see what they've made.

Special events – weddings and parties of all kinds – are extra special at the Hui. If you planning a special occasion, we can't think of a better view to celebrate as it sweeps far across the sugar fields to the ocean and West Maui Mountains.

Fantasy Camp for Pro Cyclist Wannabes

If you've ever daydreamed about riding like Lance Armstrong, you have got to call **Go Cycling Maui**. A day spent with Donnie Arnoult, former pro racer, is a bike fanatic's fantasy come true.

Depending upon which route you take – the most heart-thumping is the 38 mile, 10,000 foot ascent of Haleakala – you will see luscious rainforests, pounding

waves, or soaring mountain peaks. This is a road trip experience you simply can't get anywhere else, and if you're an avid cyclist you should just book a trip now, because you will never get to go on a ride like this anywhere else.

The tour includes everything you need for the day, including a super-high-end Litespeed bike, Bell helmet, Kaenon sunglasses, and cycling shoes. You'll also get a team jersey and vest, shorts, arm warmers, and gloves – even cycling socks (bring your own pedals and shoes for the best fit). Their support vehicle follows you and your fellow riders, and they'll have plenty of water, energy bars, electrolyte replacement, and of course, repair gear. If the ride ends up too challenging, yes, you can ride in the van, and no, they won't make fun of you.

If Molly's brother, Dave – a bike mechanic since he started on a tricycle – ever visits (come on Dave, visit at least once), she is sending him on this tour. If you're not a diehard, or if you need a kinder route, call them and ask for their advice. And if you just

erally) on surfboards and the cheese-making equipment going full steam.

While kids love visiting the goats at Surfing Goat Dairy, we think that foodies of all ages must make a point of stopping in. For a mere $7 you can get a twenty minute guided walking tour of the farm, and for $12 you can register for their Evening Chores tour (which includes hand-milking a goat). We like the milking, but we also recommend the "Grand Tour" which is every few weeks and includes watching the cheese getting made (and lots of samples).

Surfing Goat Dairy is not just a "local" dairy making "good" cheese; **it's won seventeen national awards from the American Cheese Society and the American Dairy Goat Association**. On our shopping list for holiday and birthday indulgences: Rolling Green, the award-winning chevre made with fresh garlic and chives.

want to rent a bike for a little beach tour, their shop in Paia is fully equipped to help any level of rider.

Q: How Many Does Will It Take to Make Award Winning Cheese?
A: Three Bucks

Early in our relationship James took Molly to **Surfing Goat Dairy** for a piece of lilikoi quark cheesecake. Quark is a fresh cheese that makes a cake very similar to cheesecake, but lighter and a little wobblier in texture. Molly had never had it, and the combination of the tangy goat's cheese with the light, sweet-tart passionfruit (lilikoi) set her into a kind of reverie. James didn't want to disturb her pleasure by asking for a bite – he just bought another piece. They had a lovely little picnic at the farm, surrounded by the sounds of goats playing (lit-

True Love –
But Are You In Over Your Head??

Our readers love diving with **Makena Coast Dive Charters**, and if Molly were ever going to face her fear of diving deep under water, she would call Steve Hogan of Makena Coast to help her. This gentle, thoughtful, experienced Dive Master would be a reassuring presence as she makes her Introductory dive in the open water.

Not that Makena Coast only works with newbies like Molly. They also take certified divers with their own equipment, snorkelers, and even daytrippers – but never more than seven divers per leader (their thirty-five foot boat, the Makena Mele, can carry thirteen divers or twenty-one snorkelers or some combination of both). Our readers who have gone out with the crew of the Makena Mele rave about the plumb diving sites, the personal attention, and the patient, easy-going attitude.

Steve's wife, Eve, is a popular relationship columnist and author here on Maui, and is certified to conduct a SCUBA wedding if you want a really *exclusive* ceremony (bet your mother-in-law-to-be doesn't dive). Private charters are also available, and fans say they are "no ka oi" (the best).

Sexy Views, Smooth Rides, and Super Highs

There is nothing that can compare – and we mean *nothing* – to seeing Maui from a helicopter. The vast majority of the island – towering waterfalls, lush rainforests, misty valleys knifed from volcano walls, extraordinary rainbows – can only be seen from above.

If you've every wondered if you should spend the money on a helicopter tour, our advice is *yes* … it's worth the splurge.

Readers have told us that **Blue Hawaiian Helicopters** is their hands down favorite, and we concur. James used to hire a lot of helicopter pilots for his video business, and his priority was to hire the best pilots flying the best equipment. Blue Hawaiian invests a tremendous amount of money and time into both.

The pilots are handpicked by the owner and certified as tour guides by the State of Hawaii. The helicopters are incredibly smooth, quiet, and fuel efficient (and safe). There's a two-way communication system in the cabin so you and your pilot can talk to each other without shouting, and you wear Bose® aviation-grade noise-canceling headsets. This is first class, all the way (and their Eco-Star helicopters actually feature first class cabin seats).

The Aloha spirit is alive and well with Blue Hawaiian. Not

only do they take excellent care of you, they take excellent care of their employees, many of whom have worked for them for decades. A neighbor of ours went through a serious health crisis this year, and Blue Hawaiian held his job for him (he was gone for several months).

Small Boats, Big Whales

If you've never kayaked before, book a tour with **Maui Eco Tours**. And if you have, and you know how deeply satisfying it can be to dip your own oar in the water and get to the best snorkel spots under your own power, book a tour with Maui Eco Tours.

This small kayaking outfit comes highly rated by our readers. They like the careful and thorough instruction that comes before you ever get in the water (including how to get in and out of the kayak with your snorkel gear intact without flipping the boat). They like that there are tours for every level of experience – from timid newbies to swashbuckling veterans – and some adult only tours, as well. They like that the tour guides get in the water with you to point out the turtles you might have mistaken for rocks and the various tropical fish (or on the whale tour, the whales themselves).

This is a minimal impact business. We're sure they have demand for more tours, but they keep it to twenty guests, island-wide, on any given day. The choice of vehicle – canoe – is clearly low impact, but they even use blue canoes so they don't disrupt the marine environment more than they have to. This is a carefully run, thoughtful business. Our own personal experience – one of the most fun days we've had on the water after years of living on Maui – matches that of our readers.

Sixty Friends for a Three Hour Tour

There are dozens of boats that will take you on a snorkel cruise to Molokini, Coral Gardens, or one of the many "Turtle Towns" … but according to our readers, you should book with the crew of the **Lani Kai**, which is owned and run by Friendly Charters.

The powerful catamaran holds sixty-nine passengers,

We're not surprised to hear that the Lani Kai is so popular with our readers, because we chose this boat and this crew a few years ago to take us and sixty of our friends on a sunset cruise to celebrate James's fortieth birthday.

He Doesn't Do Windows... But He Knows Who Does

If you're one of the many readers who dream of moving to Maui someday, you might want to talk to our neighbor, **Lee Wheeler**. He's the hardest working realtor we know (you can't throw a stone on Maui without hitting a realtor), and we are impressed by how much attention and care he puts into his work. Lee is one of the few Maui agents who have earned the national Accredited Buyers Representative designation.

There are dozens of realtors who will sell you a place to live – be it timeshare, condo, or home – but what we like about Lee (and what his clients like) is his dedication and his matchmaking ability. He really pays attention to you, and he tells it like it is. He doesn't waste your time (whether he's selling your home for you or selling a home to you). He is completely honest and upfront with you, and he's a tough negotiator on your behalf. Lee is one of the top producing agents for his company and for all Maui realtors.

which means smaller groups and more personal attention and instruction from the crew. We've even heard a story that a crew member spent half an hour swimming with a newbie until she was perfectly comfortable snorkeling on her own. But what we really like is that if you know what you're doing, they leave you alone to enjoy yourself. They don't "narrate" the cruise too much, which we like, but are also available for questions, which we like even more.

The Lani Kai anchors at a choice spot at Molokini Crater, which means a better chance of clear water and more wildlife to see. They offer SNUBA®, which means you can dive deeper and see more. Extra bonus points for including free mai tais and beer in their coolers. Extra *extra* bonus points for the whales so often seen during season.

In short, Lee is a wealth of information about Maui real estate, and his helpfulness doesn't stop after you pick up the keys and move in. We've even seen him helping his clients get the best deals on home furnishings.

Lee is also a great cook and a real foodie – he used to run a kitchen store – and if we were to list our home, Lee is the realtor we'd call.

We Laughed, We Cried: It Was _Way_ Better Than "Cats"

We hear from many readers that – while your Maui vacation was fabulous – you wish you had learned more about Hawaiian culture while you were here. You know it's not all sandy beaches, flower leis, and big smiles. It's something much, much deeper, and it can't be fully captured at a lu'au or a visitor attraction.

Or can it? If you go to Lahaina's Maui Theatre and watch **'Ulalena** – which runs just under ninety minutes – you will get much more than a glimpse of Ha-

waii. You will get an unforgettable, visceral *experience*
of Hawaii.

'Ulalena tells the story of
the islands – myth, history,
and culture – through world-
class song, dance, chant, mu-
sical and aerial artistry. Pup-
pets, costumes, elaborate
make up, stilt walking, acro-
batics, heart-thumping live
music, incredible lighting
effects, and audience interac-
tion intermingle to literally
take your breath away (and in
some places, make you tear
up a little).

We can't really describe this
show without reducing it to
something much less than it
is. Readers who have taken
our advice and seen **'Ulalena**
inevitably thank us later. The
dinner-and-a-show pack-
age – which includes dinner
at **Ruth's Chris** – is an un-
believably great deal in both
price and quality. The fascinating question-and-answer
session with cast members
after the show is well worth
your time. And while you
may smirk at the CD and
DVD on your way in, you
won't on your way out. We
listen to the soundtrack at
least once a month. Whether

"Voted Best
Show 2007,
2008, 2009"

I am Maui
I walk in the realm between gods and men.
I gave my people more daylight by
capturing the Sun and making him
promise to move more slowly across the sky.

This is my story...

'ulalena
A story of Hawaii's people

RUTH'S CHRIS U.S. PRIME STEAK HOUSE

'Ulalena Dinner and a Show
Enjoy a Three Course Dinner at Ruth's Chris Steak House
before or after the 'Ulalena Maui Theater show.

VIP seating with after-show experience with cast and crew
FOR RESERVATIONS FOR THE DINNER PACKAGE
PLEASE CONTACT 'ULALENA MAUI THEATER
808.856.7958
www.MauiTheatre.com

this is your first time to Maui, your seventeenth time, or you live here, we cannot recommend **'Ulalena** highly enough.

Call This Guy Right After You Book Your Flight

When you get off that plane from the mainland, your body is stiff and sore, and your body clock is off by at least two hours (and often more). Molly, who is a New York State licensed massage therapist (no, she does not practice professionally anymore), always recommends that visitors get a massage as soon as they get to Maui. Not only does a massage help to smooth out the travel-worn body, it also helps you to emotionally and mentally adjust to the fact that *you are on Maui*. When you need to know you're finally on vacation, call **Marty Guer-**

riero, the talented massage therapist and owner of **Relax Therapeutic Massage**.

It may seem indulgent and unnecessary to get a massage first thing – *"Hey isn't Maui relaxing enough?"* – but the reality is that it takes most people at least two or three days to fully relax. That is, in our opinion, a big waste of time. Why not get your body "grounded" in Maui's relaxing vibe before your day at the beach or your Molokini snorkel?

Marty blends several styles of bodywork – like Swedish Massage, Hawaiian Lomi Lomi, and Deep Tissue Massage – into beautifully coordinated sessions that are totally tailored to what your individual body needs at that individual time. He can come to you or you can visit him in his home office with stunning ocean views. Whether you're like Molly, who's received thousands of massages from hundreds of therapists, or like a reader who just told us last week they had never had a massage, Marty is the guy to call.

All Things Good

A few years ago we went to Oahu for a weekend and took a little ride. We stopped at the Kahala location of **Whole Foods** for a snack – and ended up spending four hours and eating dinner. That's how much we miss having a Whole Foods in our life, and why we're so delighted to welcome the store to Maui.

Whole Foods is a big deal for people who live on Maui who are serious foodies, but also for the local vendors who get to reach a wider market, and for visitors who already know and love this grocery store.

We have sorely missed having access to not only excellent quality groceries, but wines, gourmet items, and prepared foods we can't find anywhere else on the island. Not only is the selection delicious, but we can shop in peace, knowing that the store's strict vendor regulations guarantee that what we are buying is safe, well-made, and follows organic and natural foods guidelines.

If you're a foodie looking for groceries, make a pit stop at Whole Foods. And if you're catching

a movie at the Maui Mall, don't forget their prepared food section can easily feed you a snack or a meal.

Hold on To Your Hat and Tie Down Your Wife

Whoopee!! Do we ever love riding with **Ocean Riders**. Several readers raved about this high speed excursion, so much so that we had to go ourselves.

Several boats promise that they take you all the way around the island of Lanai, but not every boat can fulfill that promise in all weather (those waves can get too tough for some of the thinner hulled boats). But because their hull is just so darn thick, Ocean Riders can always take you all the way around, with plenty of stops for snorkeling.

Opening at Maui Mall in Kahului
Spring 2010

70 E. Ka'ahumanu Ave., Kahului, HI 96732 · 808.872.3310

The boat is a rigid hull inflatable, or H.B.I. It's the same boat the Coast Guard uses for search and rescue. It positively zooms over the water and can stop on a dime. It's the race car of excursion boats – but still perfect for snorkeling. They only take eighteen people on the boat, the crew provides excellent snorkeling instructions if you need it, and they don't time the trip like they do on the bigger snorkel boats. You start early, but you get in just about what we call "mai tai time" at our house (that's about 3pm).

Riding on this boat feels like flying – and when Captain Patty – a petite, calm, confident, and skilled captain who's been working these waters for twenty years and this boat for ten – decides to give you a thrill, it's exhilarating. You'll skim so close to cliffs you'll swear you're about to crash – only to turn at the last second and carve a huge swath of water out of the bay. You'll see hidden caves, snorkel in isolated locations, and get a lot of local history and color in between the heart-thumping rides. This excursion is worth every penny, and we give the captains A+ as guides.

Leave the Driving to Them

When a friend or relative stays with us who has never been to Maui we silently prepare ourselves for our duty as hosts: to drive them on the Road to Hana, and "all the way around Haleakala." Don't get us wrong; the trip is spectacular and very special, but it's also exhausting and really, really tiresome for the driver, who has to navigate hundreds of hairpin turns, unpaved and one-way roads, and never really gets to see the sights.

When we ask our readers about their trips to Hana, we hear over and over again that **Valley Isle Excursions** is the only way to go. After taking their trip ourselves, we may never drive the Road again.

Sitting in comfortable seats high up over the road, looking out spotless windows that stretch from your waist to well above your head, getting to know ten other travelers (the van seats twelve), listening to the driver – a certified tour guide – tell us things we didn't know about our island – it was one of the most relaxing days we've ever had on Maui, and since neither one of us had to be the driver, we both got to appreciate all the beauty.

The tours are available every single day of the year. Your driver/guide picks you up early in the morning at (or very close to) your accommodations, and drops you off that evening just before dinner. Valley Isle makes a point to hire drivers who ooze Aloha, and they train their

drivers for two months before they get to drive the Road on their own. Because the trip goes all the way around Haleakala, you get to see parts of the island most visitors never, ever do, including our favorite, the windswept mountains and dramatic gorges in Kaupo.

Finicky Beans, Splendid Cup, You Must Drink This!

When *you* think Hawaiian coffee, you might think Kona, but when *we* think Hawaiian coffee, we think **MauiGrown Coffee**. Our favorite coffee bean of all time – and the one we always choose to end a *Mama's Fish House* feast – is Maui Mokka™, which is grown on a five hundred acre farm just above Ka'anapali. (You can get this bean in roasts from *Maui Coffee Roasters*, but we recommend visit-ing the MauiGrown Coffee store; see below).

Maui Mokka™ is dark and deeply flavored, with a delightful chocolate base. Depending upon how well it's brewed, we sometimes taste red wine and currants, too. It's not an easy bean to grow, because it's finicky, doesn't yield a big harvest, and is difficult to hand pick. Because of this, it's not grown commercially anywhere else on the planet. We count ourselves lucky that Kimo Falconer, the owner of MauiGrown Coffee, is as finicky about great coffee as this bean is about climate and soil, and that he has dedicated a third of his farm to its trees.

You can get a cup of Maui Mokka™ – or their other yummy varieties – at the MauiGrown Coffee Store in Lahaina, next to the smokestack. When you stop in, be sure to get a map of their farm so you can take a self-guided tour. If you get addicted to Maui Mokka™ like we are you can buy a bag to take home with you (and you can get it anytime on their website). When we send Maui Mokka™ to our coffee-freak relatives and friends, we earn many brownie points.

Straw Hat, Sarong … Aloha and Welcome to Maui!

Hilo Hattie's retail stores have been selling everything from Aloha Shirts to t-shirts to local chocolate to grass skirts and sarongs to visitors for a long time. What you may not realize is that locals shop there, too, for Hawaiian music, beautiful home décor, and, of course, sarongs and Aloha shirts.

We stop in every holiday to pick up gifts for our friends and family on the mainland who want shark tooth necklaces, calendars with beautiful photos of the islands, and Christmas ornaments. Molly still uses a straw tote she bought at Hilo Hattie's years ago, and keeps the sun off her face on the beach with one of their big-brimmed straw hats. A must stop.

Ten Meals on Maui

If we only had ten days on Maui, these are the restaurants we would most like to patronize. Restaurants are listed in alphabetical order in each category.

When Money's No Object

The Banyan Tree *(Pacific Rim)* 24
Address: 1 Ritz-Carlton Drive, Kapalua, West Maui
Phone: 808-669-6200 **$ $ $ $**

Capische? *(Italian)* 40
Address: 555 Kaukahi St., Wailea, South Maui
Phone: 808-879-2224 **$ $ $ $**

Ferraro's Bar e Ristorante *(Italian)* 66
Address: 3900 Wailea Alanui Dr., Wailea, South Maui
Phone: 808-874-8000 **$ $ $ $**

Gerard's Restaurant *(French)* 72
Address: 174 Lahainaluna Rd., Lahaina, West Maui
Phone: 808-661-8939 **$ $ $ $**

Hali'imaile General Store *(Pacific Rim)* 77
Address: 900 Hali'imaile Rd., Makawao, Upcountry
Phone: 808-572-2666 **$ $ $**

I'O *(American/Pacific Rim)* 81
Address: 505 Front St., Lahaina, West Maui
Phone: 808-661-8422 **$ $ $ $**

Lahaina Grill 93
Address: 127 Lahainaluna Rd., Lahaina, West Maui
Phone: 808-667-5117 **$ $ $ $**

Mama's Fish House *(Pacific Rim)* 102
Address: 799 Poho Pl., Paia, North Shore
Phone: 808-579-8488 **$ $ $ $**

Pineapple Grill *(Pacific Rim)* 126
Address: 200 Kapalua Dr., Kapalua, HI 96761
Phone: 808-669-9600 **$ $ $ $**

Spago *(Pacific Rim)* 139
Address: 3900 Wailea Alanui Dr., Wailea, South Maui
Phone: 808-874-8000 **$ $ $ $**

I'm Kind of on a Budget

Café O'Lei *(Pacific Rim/American)* 38
Address: 2439 S. Kihei Rd., Kihei, South Maui
Phone: 808-891-1368 **$ $**

Cuatro Restaurant *(Latin/Asian Fusion)* 52
Address: 1881 S. Kihei Rd., Kihei, South Maui
Phone: 808-879-1110 **$ $ $**

David Paul's Island Grill *(Pacific Rim)* 56
Address: 900 Front St., Lahaina, West Maui
Phone: 808-662-3000 **$ $ $**

Flatbread Pizza Company *(Pizza)* 68
Address: 89 Hana Hwy., Paia, North Shore
Phone: 808-579-8989 **$ $**

Joe's Bar & Grill *(American)* 84
Address: 131 Wailea Ike Place, Wailea, South Maui
Phone: 808-875-7767 **$ $**

Koiso Sushi Bar *(Sushi)* 89
Address: 2395 S. Kihei Rd., Kihei, South Maui
Phone: 808-875-8258 **$ $**

Mala *(Pacific Rim)* 101
Address: 1307 Front St., Lahaina, West Maui
Phone: 808-667-9394

Roy's Bar & Grill *(Pacific Rim)* 130
Address: 4405 Honoapiilani Hwy., Kahana, West Maui
Phone: 808-669-6999 **$ $ $**

Sansei Seafood Restaurant & Sushi Bar
(Sushi/Pacific Rim) 133
Address: 1881 S. Kihei Rd., Kihei, South Maui
Phone: 808-879-0004

Address: 600 Office Rd., Kapalua, HI 96761
Phone: 808-669-6286 **$ $ $**

Thailand Cuisine *(Thai)* 144
Address: 70 E. Ka'ahumanu Ave., Kahului, Central Maui
Phone: 808-873-0225

Address: 1819 S. Kihei Rd., Kihei, South Maui
Phone: 808-875-0839 **$ $**

Recommended Restaurants by Food Craving

Baked Goods and Pastries

Colleen's *(American/Pacific Rim)* 50
Address: 810 Haiku Rd., Haiku, Upcountry
Phone: 808-575-9211 $$

Dad's Donut Shop *(Bakery)* 55
Address: 1910 E. Vineyard St., Wailuku, Central Maui
Phone: 808-244-3303 $

Green Banana Café *(Coffeehouse)* 75
Address: 137 Hana Hwy., Paia, North Shore
Phone: 808-579-9130 $

Julia's Best Banana Bread *(Banana Bread)* 85
Address: Honoapiilani Highway, Kahakuloa, West Maui
$

La Provence *(French)* 92
Address: 3158 Lower Kula Rd., Kula, Upcountry
Phone: 808-878-1313 $$

Mana Foods *(Organic/Vegan)* 105
Address: 49 Baldwin Ave., Paia, North Shore
Phone: 808-579-8078 $

Moana Bakery & Café 115
Address: 71 Baldwin Ave., Paia, North Shore
Phone: 808-579-9999 $$

Ono Gelato *(Gelato/Ice Cream)* 122
Address: 115D Hana Hwy, Paia, North Shore
Phone: 808-579-9201

Address: 815 Front St., Lahaina, West Maui
Phone: 808-495-0203 $

Penguini Gelato *(Coffeehouse/Gelato)* 125
Address: 93 Hana Hwy, Paia, North Shore
Phone: 808-214-4608 $

T. Komoda Store and Bakery *(Bakery)* 142
Address: 3674 Baldwin Ave., Makawao, Upcountry
Phone: 808-572-7261 $

Barbecue

Beach Bums Bar & Grill *(American/Barbecue)* 25
Address: 300 Ma'alaea Rd., Ma'alaea, Central Maui
Phone: 808-243-2286 $$

Fat Daddy's Smokehouse *(American/Barbecue)* 64
Address: 1913 S. Kihei Rd., Kihei, South Maui
Phone: 808-879-8711 $

Hali'imaile General Store *(Pacific Rim)* 77
Address: 900 Hali'imaile Rd., Makawao, Upcountry
Phone: 808-572-2666 $$$

Honolua Store *(American/Local/Plate Lunch)* 79
Address: 900 Office Rd., Kapalua, West Maui
Phone: 808-665-9105 $

Isana Restaurant *(Korean/Sushi)* 82
Address: 515 S. Kihei Rd., Kihei, South Maui
Phone: 808-874-5700 $$$

Joe's Bar & Grill *(American)* 84
Address: 131 Wailea Ike Place, Wailea, South Maui
Phone: 808-875-7767 $$

Kai Wailea *(Sushi)* 86
Address: 3750 Wailea Alanui Dr., Wailea, South Maui
Phone: 808-875-1955 $$$

L&L Hawaiian Barbecue *(Local/Plate Lunch)* 91
Address: 270 Dairy Rd., Kahului, Central Maui
Phone: 808-873-0323

Address: 1221 Honoapiilani Rd., Lahaina, West Maui
Phone: 808-661-9888

Address: 247 Pi'ikea Ave., Kihei, South Maui
Phone: 808-875-8898

Address: 790 Eha St., Wailuku, Central Maui
Phone: 808-242-1380 $

Boxed/Picnic Lunch

Café Mambo and Picnics *(Mediterranean)* 35
Address: 30 Baldwin Ave., Paia, North Shore
Phone: 808–579–8021 **$ $**

CJ's Deli & Diner *(American)* 49
Address: 2580 Keka'a Dr., Ka'anapali, West Maui
Phone: 808–667–0968 **$**

Da Kitchen *(Local/Plate Lunch)* 54
Address: 425 Koloa St, Kahului, Central Maui
Phone: 808–871–7782

Address: 2439 S. Kihei Rd, Kihei, South Maui
Phone 808–875–7782

Address: 658 Front St., Lahaina, West Maui
Phone: 808–661–4900 **$**

Who Cut the Cheese? *(American)* 150
Address: 1279 S. Kihei Rd., Kihei, South Maui
Phone: 808–874–3930 **$**

Breakfast

Big Wave Café *(Pacific Rim/American)* 27
Address: 1215 S. Kihei Rd, Kihei, South Maui
Phone: 808–891–8688 **$ $ $**

Café Des Amis *(Mediterranean/Indian)* 34
Address: 42 Baldwin Ave., Paia, North Shore
Phone: 808–579–6323 **$**

Café @ La Plage *(American)* 35
Address: 2395 S. Kihei Rd., Kihei, South Maui
Phone: 808–875–7668 **$**

Café Kapalua *(American)* 35
Address: 2000 Village Rd., Kapalua, West Maui
Phone: 808–665–4386 **$ $**

Café Mambo and Picnics *(Mediterranean)* 35
Address: 30 Baldwin Ave., Paia, North Shore
Phone: 808–579–8021 **$ $**

CJ's Deli & Diner *(American)* 49
Address: 2580 Keka'a Dr., Ka'anapali, West Maui
Phone: 808–667–0968 **$**

Colleen's *(American/Pacific Rim)* 50
Address: 810 Haiku Rd., Haiku, Upcountry
Phone: 808–575–9211 **$ $**

Duo *(American)* 60
Address: 3900 Wailea Alanui, Wailea, South Maui
Phone: 808–874–8000 **$ $ $ $**

Five Palms Restaurant *(American/Pacific Rim)* 67
Address: 2960 S. Kihei Rd., Kihei, South Maui
Phone: 808–879–2607 **$ $ $**

Fred's Mexican Café *(Mexican)* 70
Address: 2511 S. Kihei Rd., Kihei, South Maui
Phone: 808–891–8600 **$ $**

Gazebo Restaurant *(American)* 71
Address: 5315 Lower Honoapiilani Rd., Napili, West
   Maui
Phone: 808–669–5621 **$ $**

Honolua Store *(American/Local/Plate Lunch)* 79
Address: 900 Office Rd., Kapalua, West Maui
Phone: 808–665–9105 **$ $**

Kihei Caffe *(American)* 87
Address: 1945 S. Kihei Rd., Kihei, South Maui
Phone: 808–879–2230 **$**

La Provence *(French)* 92
Address: 3158 Lower Kula Rd., Kula, Upcountry
Phone: 808–878–1313 **$ $**

Lahaina Coolers *(American)* 92
Address: 180 Dickenson St., Lahaina, West Maui
Phone: 808–661–7082 **$ $**

Longhi's *(Italian)* 95
Address: 3750 Wailea Alanui Dr., Wailea, South Maui
Phone: 808–891–8883

Address: 888 Front St., Lahaina, West Maui
Phone: 808–667–2288 **$ $ $**

Mala *(Pacific Rim)* 101
Address: 1307 Front St., Lahaina, West Maui
Phone: 808-667-9394 **$ $ $**

Marco's Grill & Deli *(Italian)*.................................. 106
Address: 444 Hana Hwy., Kahului, Central Maui
Phone: 808-877-4446 **$ $**

Market Fresh Bistro *(Pacific Rim)* 106
Address: 3620 Baldwin Ave., Makawao, Upcountry
Phone: 808-572-4877 **$ $**

Maui Coffee Roasters *(Coffeehouse)* 109
Address: 444 Hana Hwy., Kahului, Central Maui
Phone: 808-877-2877 **$**

Milagros Food Co. *(Mexican)*.................................. 114
Address: 3 Baldwin Ave., Paia, North Shore
Phone: 808-579-8755 **$ $**

Moana Bakery & Café 115
Address: 71 Baldwin Ave., Paia, North Shore
Phone: 808-579-9999 **$ $**

Moose McGillycuddy's *(American)* 117
Address: 2511 S. Kihei Rd., Kihei, South Maui
Phone: 808-891-8600

Address: 844 Front St., Lahaina, West Maui
Phone: 808-667-7758 **$ $**

The Plantation House Restaurant *(Pacific Rim)* 129
Address: 2000 Plantation Club Dr., Lahaina, West Maui
Phone: 808-669-6299 **$ $ $**

Ruby's 131
Address: 275 W. Ka'ahumanu Ave., Kahului, Central Maui
Phone: 808-248-7829 **$ $**

Sea House Restaurant *(American/Pacific Rim)* 135
Address: 5900 Lower Honoapiilani Rd, Napili, West Maui
Phone: 808-669-1500 **$ $ $**

Seawatch *(American)* 136
Address: 100 Wailea Golf Club Dr., Wailea, South Maui
Phone: 808-875-8080 **$ $ $**

Stella Blues Café *(American)* 140
Address: 1279 S. Kihei Rd., Kihei, South Maui
Phone: 808-874-3779 **$ $ $**

Burgers

Bistro Molokini *(American)* 29
Address: 3850 Wailea Alanui Dr., Wailea, South Maui
Phone: 808-875-1234 **$ $**

Café Mambo and Picnics *(Mediterranean)* 35
Address: 30 Baldwin Ave., Paia, North Shore
Phone: 808-579-8021 **$ $**

Café O'Lei *(Pacific Rim/American)*............................ 38
Address: 2439 S. Kihei Rd., Kihei, South Maui
Phone: 808-891-1368

Address: 62 N. Market St., Wailuku, Central Maui
Phone: 808-986-0044

Address 1333 Maui Lani Parkway, Kahului, Central Maui
Phone: 808-877-0073 **$ $**

CJ's Deli & Diner *(American)* 49
Address: 2580 Keka'a Dr., Ka'anapali, West Maui
Phone: 808-667-0968 **$**

Colleen's *(American/Pacific Rim)* 50
Address: 810 Haiku Rd., Haiku, Upcountry
Phone: 808-575-9211 **$ $**

Cool Cat Café *(American)* 51
Address: 658 Front St., Lahaina, West Maui
Phone: 808-667-0908 **$ $**

Five Palms Restaurant *(American/Pacific Rim)* 67
Address: 2960 S. Kihei Rd., Kihei, South Maui
Phone: 808-879-2607 **$ $ $**

Honolua Store *(American/Local/Plate Lunch)* 79
Address: 900 Office Rd., Kapalua, West Maui
Phone: 808-665-9105 **$**

Hula Grill *(Pacific Rim)*.. 80
Address: 2435 Ka'anapali Parkway, Ka'anapali, West Maui
Phone: 808-667-6636 **$ $**

Longhi's *(Italian)* 95
Address: 3750 Wailea Alanui Dr., Wailea, South Maui
Phone: 808-891-8883

Address: 888 Front St., Lahaina, West Maui
Phone: 808-667-2288 **$ $ $**

Lulu's *(American)* 96
Address: 1941 S. Kihei Rd., Kihei, South Maui
Phone: 808-879-9944

Address: 1221 Honoapiilani Hwy, Lahaina, West Maui
Phone: 808-661-0808 **$ $**

Main Street Bistro *(Pacific Rim)* 99
Address: 2051 Main St., Wailuku, Central Maui
Phone: 808-244-6816 **$ $**

Mala *(Pacific Rim)* 101
Address: 1307 Front St., Lahaina, West Maui
Phone: 808-667-9394 **$ $ $ $**

Maui Brewing Company Brew Pub *(American)* 108
Address: 4405 Honoapiilani Hwy, Kahana, West Maui
Phone: 808-669-3474 **$ $**

Milagros Food Co. *(Mexican)* 114
Address: 3 Baldwin Ave., Paia, North Shore
Phone: 808-579-8755 **$ $**

Moose McGillycuddy's *(American)* 117
Address: 2511 S. Kihei Rd., Kihei, South Maui
Phone: 808-891-8600

Address: 844 Front St., Lahaina, West Maui
Phone: 808-667-7758 **$ $**

Mulligan's at the Wharf / Mulligan's on the Blue
(American) 118
Address: 658 Front St., Lahaina, West Maui
Phone: 808-661-8881

Address: 100 Kaukahi St., Wailea, South Maui
Phone: 808-874-1131 **$ $**

The Plantation House Restaurant *(Pacific Rim)* 129
Address: 2000 Plantation Club Dr., Lahaina, West Maui
Phone: 808-669-6299 **$ $ $**

Ruby's 131
Address: 275 W. Ka'ahumanu Ave., Kahului, Central Maui
Phone: 808-248-7829 **$ $**

Seawatch *(American)* 136
Address: 100 Wailea Golf Club Dr., Wailea, South Maui
Phone: 808-875-8080 **$ $ $**

Tommy Bahama's Tropical Café *(American)* 145
Address: 3750 Wailea Alanui Dr., Wailea, South Maui
Phone: 808-875-9983 **$ $ $**

'Umalu *(Pacific Rim/American)* 148
Address: 200 Nohea Kai Dr., Ka'anapali, West Maui
Phone: 808-661-1234 **$ $ $ $**

Cheese

Café Marc Aurel *(American)* 37
Address: 28 N. Market St., Wailuku, HI 96793
Phone: 808-244-0852 **$ $**

Who Cut the Cheese? *(American)* 150
Address: 1279 S. Kihei Rd., Kihei, South Maui
Phone: 808-874-3930 **$**

Chinese

Dragon Dragon Chinese Restaurant *(Chinese)* 59
Address: 70 E. Kaahumanu Ave., Kahului, Central Maui
Phone: 808-893-1628 **$ $**

East Ocean *(Chinese)* 62
Address: 2463 S. Kihei Rd., Kihei, South Maui
Phone: 808-879-1988 **$ $**

Coffee/Espresso

Café Des Amis *(Mediterranean/Indian)* 34
Address: 42 Baldwin Ave., Paia, North Shore
Phone: 808-579-6323 **$**

Café @ La Plage *(American)* 35
Address: 2395 S. Kihei Rd., Kihei, South Maui
Phone: 808-875-7668 **$**

Café Kapalua *(American)* 35
Address: 2000 Village Rd., Kapalua, West Maui
Phone: 808-665-4386 **$$**

Café Mambo and Picnics *(Mediterranean)* 35
Address: 30 Baldwin Ave., Paia, North Shore
Phone: 808-579-8021 **$$**

Café Marc Aurel *(American)* 37
Address: 28 N. Market St., Wailuku, HI 96793
Phone: 808-244-0852 **$$**

Colleen's *(American/Pacific Rim)* 50
Address: 810 Haiku Rd., Haiku, Upcountry
Phone: 808-575-9211 **$$**

Grandma's Coffeehouse *(Coffeehouse)* 75
Address: 153 Kula Hwy, Kula, Upcountry
Phone: 808-375-7853 **$**

Green Banana Café *(Coffeehouse)* 75
Address: 137 Hana Hwy., Paia, North Shore
Phone: 808-579-9130 **$**

La Provence *(French)* 92
Address: 3158 Lower Kula Rd., Kula, Upcountry
Phone: 808-878-1313 **$$**

Maui Coffee Roasters *(Coffeehouse)* 109
Address: 444 Hana Hwy., Kahului, Central Maui
Phone: 808-877-2877 **$**

Moana Bakery & Café 115
Address: 71 Baldwin Ave., Paia, North Shore
Phone: 808-579-9999 **$$**

Ono Gelato *(Gelato/Ice Cream)* 122
Address: 115D Hana Hwy, Paia, North Shore
Phone: 808-579-9201

Address: 815 Front St., Lahaina, West Maui
Phone: 808-495-0203 **$**

Penguini Gelato *(Coffeehouse/Gelato)* 125
Address: 93 Hana Hwy, Paia, North Shore
Phone: 808-214-4608 **$**

Crepes

Bistro Casanova *(Mediterranean/Italian)* 28
Address: 33 Lono Ave, Kahului, HI 96732
Phone: 808-873-3650 **$$$**

Café Des Amis *(Mediterranean/Indian)* 34
Address: 42 Baldwin Ave., Paia, North Shore
Phone: 808-579-6323 **$**

Early Bird Specials

Big Wave Café *(Pacific Rim/American)* 27
Address: 1215 S. Kihei Rd, Kihei, South Maui
Phone: 808-891-8688 **$$$**

Cuatro Restaurant *(Latin/Asian Fusion)* 52
Address: 1881 S. Kihei Rd., Kihei, South Maui
Phone: 808-879-1110 **$$$**

Sansei Seafood Restaurant & Sushi Bar
(Sushi/Pacific Rim) 133
Address: 1881 S. Kihei Rd., Kihei, South Maui
Phone: 808-879-0004

Address: 600 Office Rd., Kapalua, HI 96761
Phone: 808-669-6286 **$$$**

Fajitas

Café Mambo and Picnics *(Mediterranean)* 35
Address: 30 Baldwin Ave., Paia, North Shore
Phone: 808-579-8021 **$$**

Fred's Mexican Café *(Mexican)* 70
Address: 2511 S. Kihei Rd., Kihei, South Maui
Phone: 808-891-8600 **$ $**

French/Bistro

Bistro Casanova *(Mediterranean/Italian)* 28
Address: 33 Lono Ave, Kahului, HI 96732
Phone: 808-873-3650 **$ $ $**

Gerard's Restaurant *(French)* 72
Address: 174 Lahainaluna Rd., Lahaina, West Maui
Phone: 808-661-8939 **$ $ $ $**

La Provence *(French)* 92
Address: 3158 Lower Kula Rd., Kula, Upcountry
Phone: 808-878-1313 **$ $**

Market Fresh Bistro *(Pacific Rim)* 106
Address: 3620 Baldwin Ave., Makawao, Upcountry
Phone: 808-572-4877 **$ $**

Gelato

Ono Gelato *(Gelato/Ice Cream)* 122
Address: 115D Hana Hwy, Paia, North Shore
Phone: 808-579-9201

Address: 815 Front St., Lahaina, West Maui
Phone: 808-495-0203 **$**

Penguini Gelato *(Coffeehouse/Gelato)* 125
Address: 93 Hana Hwy, Paia, North Shore
Phone: 808-214-4608 **$**

German

Brigit & Bernard's Garden Café *(German)* 32
Address: 335 Hoohana St., Kahului, Central Maui
Phone: 808-877-6000 **$ $**

Happy Hour

Beach Bums Bar & Grill *(American/Barbecue)* 25
Address: 300 Ma'alaea Rd., Ma'alaea, Central Maui
Phone: 808-243-2286 **$ $**

Bistro Casanova *(Mediterranean/Italian)* 28
Address: 33 Lono Ave, Kahului, HI 96732
Phone: 808-873-3650 **$ $ $**

Café Mambo and Picnics *(Mediterranean)* 35
Address: 30 Baldwin Ave., Paia, North Shore
Phone: 808-579-8021 **$ $**

Dog & Duck *(Pub)* 58
Address: 1913 S. Kihei Rd., Kihei, South Maui
Phone: 808-875-9669 **$ $**

Five Palms Restaurant *(American/Pacific Rim)* 67
Address: 2960 S. Kihei Rd., Kihei, South Maui
Phone: 808-879-2607 **$ $ $**

Fred's Mexican Café *(Mexican)* 70
Address: 2511 S. Kihei Rd., Kihei, South Maui
Phone: 808-891-8600 **$ $**

Gaby's Pizzeria *(Pizza)* 71
Address: 505 Front St., Lahaina, West Maui
Phone: 808-661-8112 **$ $**

Hula Grill *(Pacific Rim)* 80
Address: 2435 Ka'anapali Parkway, Ka'anapali, West Maui
Phone: 808-667-6636 **$ $**

Lahaina Coolers *(American)* 92
Address: 180 Dickenson St., Lahaina, West Maui
Phone: 808-661-7082 **$ $**

Leilani's On the Beach *(Pacific Rim)* 95
Address: 2435 Ka'anapali Pkwy., Lahaina, West Maui
Phone: 808-661-4495 **$ $ $**

Lulu's *(American)* 96
Address: 1941 S. Kihei Rd., Kihei, South Maui
Phone: 808-879-9944

Address: 1221 Honoapiilani Hwy, Lahaina, West Maui
Phone: 808-661-0808 **$ $**

Hawaiian Regional Cuisine/Pacific Rim

Lahaina Grill. 93
Address: 127 Lahainaluna Rd., Lahaina, West Maui
Phone: 808-667-5117 **$ $ $ $**

Mala *(Pacific Rim)* 101
Address: 1307 Front St., Lahaina, West Maui
Phone: 808-667-9394 **$ $ $**

Market Fresh Bistro *(Pacific Rim)* 106
Address: 3620 Baldwin Ave., Makawao, Upcountry
Phone: 808-572-4877 **$ $**

Pacific'O *(Pacific Rim)* 123
Address: 505 Front St., Lahaina, West Maui
Phone: 808-667-4341 **$ $ $ $**

Pineapple Grill *(Pacific Rim)* 126
Address: 200 Kapalua Dr., Kapalua, HI 96761
Phone: 808-669-9600 **$ $ $ $**

The Plantation House Restaurant *(Pacific Rim)* 129
Address: 2000 Plantation Club Dr., Lahaina, West Maui
Phone: 808-669-6299 **$ $ $**

Roy's Bar & Grill *(Pacific Rim)* 130
Address: 4405 Honoapiilani Hwy., Kahana, West Maui
Phone: 808-669-6999 **$ $ $**

Sansei Seafood Restaurant & Sushi Bar
(Sushi/Pacific Rim) 133
Address: 1881 S. Kihei Rd., Kihei, South Maui
Phone: 808-879-0004

Address: 600 Office Rd., Kapalua, HI 96761
Phone: 808-669-6286 **$ $ $**

Seawatch *(American)* 136
Address: 100 Wailea Golf Club Dr., Wailea, South Maui
Phone: 808-875-8080 **$ $ $**

Spago *(Pacific Rim)* 139
Address: 3900 Wailea Alanui Dr., Wailea, South Maui
Phone: 808-874-8000 **$ $ $ $**

Tropica *(Pacific Rim/American)* 146
Address: 2365 Ka'anapali Pkwy., Ka'anapali, West Maui
Phone: 808-667-2525 **$ $ $ $**

Healthy/Organic

Alive & Well *(Organic/Vegan)* 17
Address: 340 Hana Hwy., Kahului, Central Maui
Phone: 808-877-4950 **$**

The Banyan Tree *(Pacific Rim)* 24
Address: 1 Ritz-Carlton Drive, Kapalua, West Maui
Phone: 808-669-6200 **$ $ $ $**

Café Kapalua *(American)* 35
Address: 2000 Village Rd., Kapalua, West Maui
Phone: 808-665-4386 **$ $**

Café Mambo and Picnics *(Mediterranean)* 35
Address: 30 Baldwin Ave., Paia, North Shore
Phone: 808-579-8021 **$ $**

Coconut's Fish Café *(American)* 50
Address: 1279 S. Kihei Rd., Kihei, South Maui
Phone: 808-875-9979 **$**

Down to Earth *(Health Food Store)* 59
Address: 305 Dairy Rd, Kahului, Central Maui
Phone: 808-877-2661 **$**

Feast at Lele *(Lu'au)* 65
Address: 505 Front St., Lahaina, West Maui
Phone: 808-667-5353 **$ $ $ $**

Flatbread Pizza Company *(Pizza)* 68
Address: 89 Hana Hwy., Paia, North Shore
Phone: 808-579-8989 **$ $**

Fresh Mint *(Vegan/Vietnamese)* 70
Address: 115 Baldwin Ave., Paia, North Shore
Phone: 808-579-9144 **$ $**

Hawaiian Moons Natural Foods *(Organic/Vegan)* 79
Address: 2411 S. Kihei Rd., Kihei, South Maui
Phone: 808-875-4356 **$**

I'O *(American/Pacific Rim)* 81
Address: 505 Front St., Lahaina, West Maui
Phone: 808-661-8422 **$ $ $ $**

Joy's Place *(Vegetarian/American)* 85
Address: 1993 S. Kihei Rd., Kihei, South Maui
Phone: 808-879-9258 $

Mala *(Pacific Rim)* 101
Address: 1307 Front St., Lahaina, West Maui
Phone: 808-667-9394

Mana Foods *(Organic/Vegan)* 105
Address: 49 Baldwin Ave., Paia, North Shore
Phone: 808-579-8078 $

Market Fresh Bistro *(Pacific Rim)* 106
Address: 3620 Baldwin Ave., Makawao, Upcountry
Phone: 808-572-4877 $ $

Moana Bakery & Café 115
Address: 71 Baldwin Ave., Paia, North Shore
Phone: 808-579-9999 $ $

Pacific'O *(Pacific Rim)* 123
Address: 505 Front St., Lahaina, West Maui
Phone: 808-667-4341 $ $ $ $

Pineapple Grill *(Pacific Rim)* 126
Address: 200 Kapalua Dr., Kapalua, HI 96761
Phone: 808-669-9600 $ $ $ $

Stella Blues Café *(American)* 140
Address: 1279 S. Kihei Rd., Kihei, South Maui
Phone: 808-874-3779 $ $ $

Ice Cream/Frozen Treats

Ono Gelato *(Gelato/Ice Cream)* 122
Address: 115D Hana Hwy, Paia, North Shore
Phone: 808-579-9201

Address: 815 Front St., Lahaina, West Maui
Phone: 808-495-0203 $

Penguini Gelato *(Coffeehouse/Gelato)* 125
Address: 93 Hana Hwy, Paia, North Shore
Phone: 808-214-4608 $

Tasaka Guri Guri *(Guri Guri)* 143
Address: 70 E. Ka'ahumanu Ave., Kahului, Central Maui
Phone: 808-871-4513 $

Ululani's Hawaiian Shave Ice *(Shave Ice)* 147
Address: 819 Front Street, Lahaina, West Maui
Phone: 360-609-5678 $

Indian

Café Des Amis *(Mediterranean/Indian)* 34
Address: 42 Baldwin Ave., Paia, North Shore
Phone: 808-579-6323 $

Maui Masala *(Indian)* 110
Address: 2395 S. Kihei Road, Kihei, South Maui
Phone: 808-875-9000 $

Monsoon India *(Indian)* 116
Address: 760 S. Kihei Rd., Kihei, South Maui
Phone: 808-875 6666 $ $

Italian

Antonio's *(Italian)* 21
Address: 1215 S. Kihei Rd., Kihei, South Maui
Phone: 808-875-8800 $ $

Aroma D'Italia Ristorante *(Italian)* 21
Address: 1881 S. Kihei Rd., Kihei, South Maui
Phone: 808-879-0133 $ $

Bistro Casanova *(Mediterranean/Italian)* 28
Address: 33 Lono Ave, Kahului, HI 96732
Phone: 808-873-3650 $ $ $

Capische? *(Italian)* 40
Address: 555 Kaukahi St., Wailea, South Maui
Phone: 808-879-2224 $ $ $ $

Casanova *(Italian)* 43
Address: 1188 Makawao Ave., Makawao, Upcountry
Phone: 808-572-0220 **$ $**

Ferraro's Bar e Ristorante *(Italian)* 66
Address: 3900 Wailea Alanui Dr., Wailea, South Maui
Phone: 808-874-8000 **$ $ $ $**

Longhi's *(Italian)* 95
Address: 3750 Wailea Alanui Dr., Wailea, South Maui
Phone: 808-891-8883

Address: 888 Front St., Lahaina, West Maui
Phone: 808-667-2288 **$ $ $**

Marco's Grill & Deli *(Italian)* 106
Address: 444 Hana Hwy., Kahului, Central Maui
Phone: 808-877-4446 **$ $**

Matteo's Pizzeria *(Italian/Pizza)* 108
Address: 100 Wailea Ike Dr., Wailea, South Maui
Phone: 808-874-1234 **$ $**

Penne Pasta *(Italian)* 125
Address: 180 Dickenson St., Lahaina, West Maui
Phone: 808-661-6633 **$ $**

Japanese

Cane and Taro *(Pacific Rim/Sushi)* 39
Address: 2435 Ka'anapali Pkwy, Ka'anapali, West Maui
Phone: 808-662-0668 **$ $**

Hakone *(Japanese/Sushi)* 76
Address: 5400 Makena Alanui Dr., Makena, South Maui
Phone: 808-875-5888 **$ $ $**

Kai Wailea *(Sushi)* 86
Address: 3750 Wailea Alanui Dr., Wailea, South Maui
Phone: 808-875-1955 **$ $ $**

Kobe *(Japanese Steakhouse)* 88
Address: 136 Dickenson St., Lahaina, West Maui
Phone: 808-667-5555 **$ $ $**

Sansei Seafood Restaurant & Sushi Bar
(Sushi/Pacific Rim) 133
Address: 1881 S. Kihei Rd., Kihei, South Maui
Phone: 808-879-0004

Address: 600 Office Rd., Kapalua, HI 96761
Phone: 808-669-6286 **$ $ $**

Kama'aina Specials
(For locals only, when available)

The Banyan Tree *(Pacific Rim)* 24
Address: 1 Ritz-Carlton Drive, Kapalua, West Maui
Phone: 808-669-6200 **$ $ $ $**

Duo *(American)* 60
Address: 3900 Wailea Alanui, Wailea, South Maui
Phone: 808-874-8000 **$ $ $ $**

Feast at Lele *(Lu'au)* 65
Address: 505 Front St., Lahaina, West Maui
Phone: 808-667-5353 **$ $ $ $**

Ferraro's Bar e Ristorante *(Italian)* 66
Address: 3900 Wailea Alanui Dr., Wailea, South Maui
Phone: 808-874-8000 **$ $ $ $**

Gerard's Restaurant *(French)* 72
Address: 174 Lahainaluna Rd., Lahaina, West Maui
Phone: 808-661-8939 **$ $ $ $**

Hakone *(Japanese/Sushi)* 76
Address: 5400 Makena Alanui Dr., Makena, South Maui
Phone: 808-875-5888 **$ $ $**

Hali'imaile General Store *(Pacific Rim)* 77
Address: 900 Hali'imaile Rd., Makawao, Upcountry
Phone: 808-572-2666 **$ $ $**

Humuhumunukunukuapua'a *(Pacific Rim)* 80
Address: 3850 Wailea Alanui Dr., Wailea, South Maui
Phone: 808-875-1234 **$ $ $ $**

I'O *(American/Pacific Rim)* 81
Address: 505 Front St., Lahaina, West Maui
Phone: 808-661-8422 **$ $ $ $**

Joe's Bar & Grill *(American)* 84
Address: 131 Wailea Ike Place, Wailea, South Maui
Phone: 808-875-7767 **$ $**

Kobe *(Japanese Steakhouse)* 88
Address: 136 Dickenson St., Lahaina, West Maui
Phone: 808-667-5555 **$ $ $**

Lahaina Grill 93
Address: 127 Lahainaluna Rd., Lahaina, West Maui
Phone: 808-667-5117 **$ $ $ $**

Mala *(Pacific Rim)* 101
Address: 1307 Front St., Lahaina, West Maui
Phone: 808-667-9394 **$ $**

Monsoon India *(Indian)* 116
Address: 760 S. Kihei Rd., Kihei, South Maui
Phone: 808-875 6666 **$ $**

Old Lahaina Lu'au *(Lu'au)* 121
Address: 1251 Front Street, Lahaina, West Maui
Phone: 808-667-1998 **$ $ $ $**

Pacific'O *(Pacific Rim)* 123
Address: 505 Front St., Lahaina, West Maui
Phone: 808-667-4341 **$ $ $ $**

Pineapple Grill *(Pacific Rim)* 126
Address: 200 Kapalua Dr., Kapalua, HI 96761
Phone: 808-669-9600 **$ $ $ $**

Roy's Bar & Grill *(Pacific Rim)* 130
Address: 4405 Honoapiilani Hwy., Kahana, West Maui
Phone: 808-669-6999 **$ $ $**

Ruby's 131
Address: 275 W. Ka'ahumanu Ave., Kahului, Central Maui
Phone: 808-248-7829 **$ $**

Ruth's Chris Steak House *(American)* 132
Address: 3750 Wailea Alanui Dr., Wailea, South Maui
Phone: 808-874-8880

Address: 900 Front St., Lahaina, HI 96761
Phone: 808-661-8815 **$ $ $ $**

Sansei Seafood Restaurant & Sushi Bar
(Sushi/Pacific Rim) 133
Address: 1881 S. Kihei Rd., Kihei, South Maui
Phone: 808-879-0004

Address: 600 Office Rd., Kapalua, HI 96761
Phone: 808-669-6286 **$ $ $**

Sea House Restaurant *(American/Pacific Rim)* 135
Address: 5900 Lower Honoapiilani Rd, Napili, West Maui
Phone: 808-669-1500 **$ $ $**

Seawatch *(American)* 136
Address: 100 Wailea Golf Club Dr., Wailea, South Maui
Phone: 808-875-8080 **$ $ $**

Spago *(Pacific Rim)* 139
Address: 3900 Wailea Alanui Dr., Wailea, South Maui
Phone: 808-874-8000 **$ $ $ $**

Korean

Isana Restaurant *(Korean/Sushi)* 82
Address: 515 S. Kihei Rd., Kihei, South Maui
Phone: 808-874-5700 **$ $ $**

Late Night Dining (After 9pm)

Bubba Gump Shrimp Co. *(American)* 32
Address: 889 Front St., Lahaina, West Maui
Phone: 808-661-3111 **$ $**

Cane and Taro *(Pacific Rim/Sushi)* 39
Address: 2435 Ka'anapali Pkwy, Ka'anapali, West Maui
Phone: 808-662-0668 **$ $**

Casanova *(Italian)* 43
Address: 1188 Makawao Ave., Makawao, Upcountry
Phone: 808-572-0220

Cool Cat Café *(American)* 51
Address: 658 Front St., Lahaina, West Maui
Phone: 808-667-0908 **$ $**

Cuatro Restaurant *(Latin/Asian Fusion)* 52
Address: 1881 S. Kihei Rd., Kihei, South Maui
Phone: 808-879-1110 **$ $ $**

David Paul's Island Grill *(Pacific Rim)* 56
Address: 900 Front St., Lahaina, West Maui
Phone: 808-662-3000 **$ $ $**

Dog & Duck *(Pub)* 58
Address: 1913 S. Kihei Rd., Kihei, South Maui
Phone: 808-875-9669 **$ $**

Flatbread Pizza Company *(Pizza)* 68
Address: 89 Hana Hwy., Paia, North Shore
Phone: 808-579-8989 **$ $**

Fred's Mexican Café *(Mexican)* 70
Address: 2511 S. Kihei Rd., Kihei, South Maui
Phone: 808-891-8600 **$ $**

Gaby's Pizzeria *(Pizza)* 71
Address: 505 Front St., Lahaina, West Maui
Phone: 808-661-8112 **$ $**

Hula Grill *(Pacific Rim)*...................................... 80
Address: 2435 Ka'anapali Parkway, Ka'anapali, West Maui
Phone: 808-667-6636 **$ $**

I'O *(American/Pacific Rim)* 81
Address: 505 Front St., Lahaina, West Maui
Phone: 808-661-8422 **$ $ $ $**

Isana Restaurant *(Korean/Sushi)* 82
Address: 515 S. Kihei Rd., Kihei, South Maui
Phone: 808-874-5700 **$ $ $**

Kai Wailea *(Sushi)* 86
Address: 3750 Wailea Alanui Dr., Wailea, South Maui
Phone: 808-875-1955 **$ $ $**

Kobe *(Japanese Steakhouse)* 88
Address: 136 Dickenson St., Lahaina, West Maui
Phone: 808-667-5555 **$ $ $**

Lahaina Coolers *(American)*................................ 92
Address: 180 Dickenson St., Lahaina, West Maui
Phone: 808-661-7082 **$ $**

Lahaina Grill 93
Address: 127 Lahainaluna Rd., Lahaina, West Maui
Phone: 808-667-5117 **$ $ $ $**

Leilani's On the Beach *(Pacific Rim)* 95
Address: 2435 Ka'anapali Pkwy., Lahaina, West Maui
Phone: 808-661-4495 **$ $ $**

Longhi's *(Italian)* 95
Address: 3750 Wailea Alanui Dr., Wailea, South Maui
Phone: 808-891-8883

Address: 888 Front St., Lahaina, West Maui
Phone: 808-667-2288 **$ $ $**

Lulu's *(American)* 96
Address: 1941 S. Kihei Rd., Kihei, South Maui
Phone: 808-879-9944

Address: 1221 Honoapiilani Hwy, Lahaina, West Maui
Phone: 808-661-0808 **$ $**

Mai Tai Lounge *(Pacific Rim)* 98
Address: 839 Front St., Lahaina, West Maui
Phone: 808-661-5288 **$ $**

Marco's Grill & Deli *(Italian)*............................ 106
Address: 444 Hana Hwy., Kahului, Central Maui
Phone: 808-877-4446 **$ $**

Maui Brewing Company Brew Pub *(American)*......... 108
Address: 4405 Honoapiilani Hwy, Kahana, West Maui
Phone: 808-669-3474 **$ $**

Milagros Food Co. *(Mexican)* 114
Address: 3 Baldwin Ave., Paia, North Shore
Phone: 808-579-8755 **$ $**

Moose McGillycuddy's *(American)* 117
Address: 2511 S. Kihei Rd., Kihei, South Maui
Phone: 808-891-8600

Address: 844 Front St., Lahaina, West Maui
Phone: 808-667-7758 **$ $**

Mulligan's at the Wharf / Mulligan's on the Blue
(American) 118
Address: 658 Front St., Lahaina, West Maui
Phone: 808-661-8881

Address: 100 Kaukahi St., Wailea, South Maui
Phone: 808-874-1131 **$ $**

Pacific'O *(Pacific Rim)* 123
Address: 505 Front St., Lahaina, West Maui
Phone: 808-667-4341 **$ $ $ $**

Pizza Madness *(Pizza)* 128
Address: 1455 S. Kihei Rd., Kihei, South Maui
Phone: 808-270-9888 **$**

Roy's Bar & Grill *(Pacific Rim)* 130
Address: 4405 Honoapiilani Hwy., Kahana, West Maui
Phone: 808-669-6999 **$ $ $**

Ruth's Chris Steak House *(American)* 132
Address: 3750 Wailea Alanui Dr., Wailea, South Maui
Phone: 808-874-8880

Address: 900 Front St., Lahaina, HI 96761
Phone: 808-661-8815 **$ $ $ $**

Sansei Seafood Restaurant & Sushi Bar
(Sushi/Pacific Rim) 133
Address: 1881 S. Kihei Rd., Kihei, South Maui
Phone: 808-879-0004

Address: 600 Office Rd., Kapalua, HI 96761
Phone: 808-669-6286 **$ $ $**

Seawatch *(American)* 136
Address: 100 Wailea Golf Club Dr., Wailea, South Maui
Phone: 808-875-8080 **$ $ $**

South Shore Tiki Lounge *(American)* 138
Address: 1913 S. Kihei Rd., Kihei, South Maui
Phone: 808-874-6444 **$ $**

Stella Blues Café *(American)* 140
Address: 1279 S. Kihei Rd., Kihei, South Maui
Phone: 808-874-3779 **$ $ $**

Sushi Paradise *(Sushi)* 142
Address: 1215 S. Kihei Rd., Kihei, South Maui
Phone: 808-879-3751 **$ $ $**

Thailand Cuisine *(Thai)* 144
Address: 70 E. Ka'ahumanu Ave., Kahului, Central Maui
Phone: 808-873-0225

Address: 1819 S. Kihei Rd., Kihei, South Maui
Phone: 808-875-0839 **$ $**

Tommy Bahama's Tropical Café *(American)* 145
Address: 3750 Wailea Alanui Dr., Wailea, South Maui
Phone: 808-875-9983 **$ $ $**

Ululani's Hawaiian Shave Ice *(Shave Ice)* 147
Address: 819 Front Street, Lahaina, West Maui
Phone: 360-609-5678 **$**

Latin American Fusion

Cuatro Restaurant *(Latin/Asian Fusion)* 52
Address: 1881 S. Kihei Rd., Kihei, South Maui
Phone: 808-879-1110 **$ $ $**

Local/Plate Lunch

Aloha Mixed Plate *(Local/Plate Lunch)* 18
Address: 1285 Front St., Lahaina, West Maui
Phone: 808-661-3322 **$**

Café O'Lei *(Pacific Rim/American)* 38
Address: 2439 S. Kihei Rd., Kihei, South Maui
Phone: 808-891-1368

Address: 62 N. Market St., Wailuku, Central Maui
Phone: 808-986-0044

Address 1333 Maui Lani Parkway, Kahului, Central Maui
Phone: 808-877-0073 **$ $**

Da Kitchen *(Local/Plate Lunch)* 54
Address: 425 Koloa St, Kahului, Central Maui
Phone: 808-871-7782

Address: 2439 S. Kihei Rd, Kihei, South Maui
Phone 808-875-7782

Da Kitchen *(continued)* 54
Address: 658 Front St., Lahaina, West Maui
Phone: 808-661-4900 $

Eskimo Candy *(American)* 63
Address: 2665 Wai Wai Pl, Kihei, South Maui
Phone: 808-879-5686 $

Honolua Store *(American/Local/Plate Lunch)* 79
Address: 900 Office Rd., Kapalua, West Maui
Phone: 808-665-9105 $

L&L Hawaiian Barbecue *(Local/Plate Lunch)* 91
Address: 270 Dairy Rd., Kahului, Central Maui
Phone: 808-873-0323

Address: 1221 Honoapiilani Rd., Lahaina, West Maui
Phone: 808-661-9888

Address: 247 Pi'ikea Ave., Kihei, South Maui
Phone: 808-875-8898

Address: 790 Eha St., Wailuku, Central Maui
Phone: 808-242-1380 $

**Upcountry Fresh Tamales
& Mixed Plate** *(Mexican/Local/Plate Lunch)* 149
Address: 55 Pukalani St., Pukalani, Upcountry
Phone: 808-572-8258 $

Lu'au

Feast at Lele *(Lu'au)* 65
Address: 505 Front St., Lahaina, West Maui
Phone: 808-667-5353 $ $ $ $

Old Lahaina Lu'au *(Lu'au)* 121
Address: 1251 Front Street, Lahaina, West Maui
Phone: 808-667-1998 $ $ $ $

Mexican/Tex-Mex

Amigo's *(Mexican)* 19
Address: 41 E. Lipoa St., Kihei, South Maui
Phone: 808-879-9952

Address: 333 Dairy Rd., Kahului, Central Maui
Phone: 808-872-9525

Amigo's *(continued)* 19
Address: 658 Front St., Wharf Cinema Center, Lahaina,
    West Maui
Phone: 808-661-0210 $

Cilantro *(Mexican)* 48
Address: 170 Papalaua St., Lahaina, HI 96761
Phone: 808-667-5444 $

Jawz Tacos *(Mexican)* 83
Address: 1279 S. Kihei Rd., Kihei, South Maui
Phone: 808-874-8226 $

Maui Tacos *(Mexican)* 111
Address: 840 Wainee St., Lahaina Square, Lahaina, West
    Maui
Phone: 808-661-8883

Address: 275 Ka'ahumanu Ave., Kahului, Central Maui
Phone: 808-871-7726

Address: 247 Pi'ikea Ave., Kihei, South Maui
Phone: 808-875-9340

Address: 5095 Napilihau St., Napili, West Maui
Phone: 808-665-0222

Address: 2411 S. Kihei Rd., Kihei, South Maui
Phone: 808-879-5005 $

Milagros Food Co. *(Mexican)* 114
Address: 3 Baldwin Ave., Paia, North Shore
Phone: 808-579-8755 $ $

**Upcountry Fresh Tamales
& Mixed Plate** *(Mexican/Local/Plate Lunch)* 149
Address: 55 Pukalani St., Pukalani, Upcountry
Phone: 808-572-8258 $

Mediterranean

Bistro Casanova *(Mediterranean/Italian)* 28
Address: 33 Lono Ave, Kahului, HI 96732
Phone: 808-873-3650 $ $ $

Café Des Amis *(Mediterranean/Indian)* 34
Address: 42 Baldwin Ave., Paia, North Shore
Phone: 808-579-6323 $

Café Mambo and Picnics *(Mediterranean)* 35
Address: 30 Baldwin Ave., Paia, North Shore
Phone: 808-579-8021 **$ $**

Pita Paradise *(Mediterranean)* 128
Address: 1913 S. Kihei Rd., Kihei, South Maui
Phone: 808-875-7679 **$**

Pasta

Antonio's *(Italian)* 21
Address: 1215 S. Kihei Rd., Kihei, South Maui
Phone: 808-875-8800 **$ $**

Aroma D'Italia Ristorante *(Italian)* 21
Address: 1881 S. Kihei Rd., Kihei, South Maui
Phone: 808-879-0133 **$ $**

Bistro Casanova *(Mediterranean/Italian)* 28
Address: 33 Lono Ave, Kahului, HI 96732
Phone: 808-873-3650 **$ $ $**

Casanova *(Italian)* 43
Address: 1188 Makawao Ave., Makawao, Upcountry
Phone: 808-572-0220 **$ $**

Ferraro's Bar e Ristorante *(Italian)* 66
Address: 3900 Wailea Alanui Dr., Wailea, South Maui
Phone: 808-874-8000 **$ $ $ $**

Longhi's *(Italian)* 95
Address: 3750 Wailea Alanui Dr., Wailea, South Maui
Phone: 808-891-8883

Address: 888 Front St., Lahaina, West Maui
Phone: 808-667-2288 **$ $ $**

Marco's Grill & Deli *(Italian)* 106
Address: 444 Hana Hwy., Kahului, Central Maui
Phone: 808-877-4446 **$ $**

Matteo's Pizzeria *(Italian/Pizza)* 108
Address: 100 Wailea Ike Dr., Wailea, South Maui
Phone: 808-874-1234 **$ $**

Penne Pasta *(Italian)* 125
Address: 180 Dickenson St., Lahaina, West Maui
Phone: 808-661-6633 **$ $**

Pizza

BJ's Chicago Pizzeria *(American)* 31
Address: 730 Front St., Lahaina, West Maui
Phone: 808-661-0700 **$ $**

Casanova *(Italian)* 43
Address: 1188 Makawao Ave., Makawao, Upcountry
Phone: 808-572-0220 **$ $**

Costco Food Court *(American)* 52
Address: 540 Haleakala Highway, Kahului, Central Maui
Phone: 808-877-5248 **$**

Ferraro's Bar e Ristorante *(Italian)* 66
Address: 3900 Wailea Alanui Dr., Wailea, South Maui
Phone: 808-874-8000 **$ $ $ $**

Flatbread Pizza Company *(Pizza)* 68
Address: 89 Hana Hwy., Paia, North Shore
Phone: 808-579-8989 **$ $**

Gaby's Pizzeria *(Pizza)* 71
Address: 505 Front St., Lahaina, West Maui
Phone: 808-661-8112 **$ $**

Gianotto's Pizzeria *(Pizza)* 75
Address: 2050 Main St., Wailuku, Central Maui
Phone: 808-244-8282 **$**

Matteo's Pizzeria *(Italian/Pizza)* 108
Address: 100 Wailea Ike Dr., Wailea, South Maui
Phone: 808-874-1234 **$ $**

Nikki's Pizza *(Pizza)* 120
Address: 2435 Ka'anapali Pkwy, Ka'anapali, West Maui
Phone: 808-667-0333 **$**

Pizza Madness *(Pizza)* 128
Address: 1455 S. Kihei Rd., Kihei, South Maui
Phone: 808-270-9888 **$**

Shaka Pizza *(Pizza)* 137
Address: 1770 S. Kihei Rd., Kihei, South Maui
Phone: 808-874-0331 **$**

Prepared Foods

Alive & Well *(Organic / Vegan)* 17
Address: 340 Hana Hwy., Kahului, Central Maui
Phone: 808-877-4950 **$**

Down to Earth *(Health Food Store)* 59
Address: 305 Dairy Rd, Kahului, Central Maui
Phone: 808-877-2661 **$**

Hawaiian Moons Natural Foods *(Organic / Vegan)* 79
Address: 2411 S. Kihei Rd., Kihei, South Maui
Phone: 808-875-4356 **$**

Honolua Store *(American / Local / Plate Lunch)* 79
Address: 900 Office Rd., Kapalua, West Maui
Phone: 808-665-9105 **$**

Mana Foods *(Organic / Vegan)* 105
Address: 49 Baldwin Ave., Paia, North Shore
Phone: 808-579-8078 **$**

**Maui Community College Food Court
and "Class Act"** 110

Address: 310 W. Ka'ahumanu Ave., Pa'ina Building,
         Maui Culinary Academy, Kahului, Central
         Maui
Phone: 808-984-3280 **$$**

Ono Gelato *(Gelato / Ice Cream)* 122
Address: 815 Front St., Lahaina, West Maui
Phone: 808-495-0203 **$**

Sandwiches/Panini

Ba-Le Sandwiches *(Vietnamese)* 22
Address: 1221 Honoapiilani Highway, Lahaina, West
         Maui
Phone: 808-661-5566

Address: 270 Dairy Rd., Kahului, Central Maui
Phone: 808-877-2400

Ba-Le Sandwiches *(continued)* 22
Address: 247 Pi'ikea Ave., Kihei, South Maui
Phone: 808-875-6400

Address: 1824 Oihana St., Wailuku, Central Maui
Phone: 808-249-8833

Big Wave Café *(Pacific Rim / American)* 27
Address: 1215 S. Kihei Rd, Kihei, South Maui
Phone: 808-891-8688 **$$$**

Bistro Casanova *(Mediterranean / Italian)* 28
Address: 33 Lono Ave, Kahului, HI 96732
Phone: 808-873-3650 **$$$**

Bistro Molokini *(American)* 29
Address: 3850 Wailea Alanui Dr., Wailea, South Maui
Phone: 808-875-1234 **$$**

Café @ La Plage *(American)* 35
Address: 2395 S. Kihei Rd., Kihei, South Maui
Phone: 808-875-7668 **$**

Café Kapalua *(American)* 35
Address: 2000 Village Rd., Kapalua, West Maui
Phone: 808-665-4386 **$$**

Café Mambo and Picnics *(Mediterranean)* 35
Address: 30 Baldwin Ave., Paia, North Shore
Phone: 808-579-8021 **$$**

Café Marc Aurel *(American)* 37
Address: 28 N. Market St., Wailuku, HI 96793
Phone: 808-244-0852 **$$**

Café O'Lei *(Pacific Rim / American)* 38
Address: 2439 S. Kihei Rd., Kihei, South Maui
Phone: 808-891-1368

Address: 62 N. Market St., Wailuku, Central Maui
Phone: 808-986-0044

Address 1333 Maui Lani Parkway, Kahului, Central Maui
Phone: 808-877-0073 **$$**

CJ's Deli & Diner *(American)* 49
Address: 2580 Keka'a Dr., Ka'anapali, West Maui
Phone: 808-667-0968 **$**

Seafood

Pineapple Grill *(Pacific Rim)* 126
Address: 200 Kapalua Dr., Kapalua, HI 96761
Phone: 808-669-9600 **$ $ $ $**

The Plantation House Restaurant *(Pacific Rim)* 129
Address: 2000 Plantation Club Dr., Lahaina, West Maui
Phone: 808-669-6299 **$ $ $**

Roy's Bar & Grill *(Pacific Rim)*............................... 130
Address: 4405 Honoapiilani Hwy., Kahana, West Maui
Phone: 808-669-6999 **$ $ $**

Sansei Seafood Restaurant & Sushi Bar
(Sushi/Pacific Rim) 133
Address: 1881 S. Kihei Rd., Kihei, South Maui
Phone: 808-879-0004

Address: 600 Office Rd., Kapalua, HI 96761
Phone: 808-669-6286 **$ $ $**

Spago *(Pacific Rim)*..................................... 139
Address: 3900 Wailea Alanui Dr., Wailea, South Maui
Phone: 808-874-8000 **$ $ $ $**

Tropica *(Pacific Rim/American)*................................. 146
Address: 2365 Ka'anapali Pkwy., Ka'anapali, West Maui
Phone: 808-667-2525 **$ $ $ $**

Shave Ice

Ululani's Hawaiian Shave Ice *(Shave Ice)* 147
Address: 819 Front Street, Lahaina, West Maui
Phone: 360-609-5678 **$**

Smoothies

Bistro Molokini *(American)* 29
Address: 3850 Wailea Alanui Dr., Wailea, South Maui
Phone: 808-875-1234 **$ $**

Café Mambo and Picnics *(Mediterranean)* 35
Address: 30 Baldwin Ave., Paia, North Shore
Phone: 808-579-8021 **$ $**

Colleen's *(American/Pacific Rim)* 50
Address: 810 Haiku Rd., Haiku, Upcountry
Phone: 808-575-9211 **$ $**

Green Banana Café *(Coffeehouse)* 75
Address: 137 Hana Hwy., Paia, North Shore
Phone: 808-579-9130 **$**

Hawaiian Moons Natural Foods *(Organic/Vegan)* 79
Address: 2411 S. Kihei Rd., Kihei, South Maui
Phone: 808-875-4356 **$**

Snacks & Treats

Dad's Donut Shop *(Bakery)* 55
Address: 1910 E. Vineyard St., Wailuku, Central Maui
Phone: 808-244-3303 **$**

Grandma's Coffeehouse *(Coffeehouse)* 75
Address: 153 Kula Hwy, Kula, Upcountry
Phone: 808-375-7853 **$**

Green Banana Café *(Coffeehouse)* 75
Address: 137 Hana Hwy., Paia, North Shore
Phone: 808-579-9130 **$**

Julia's Best Banana Bread *(Banana Bread)* 85
Address: Honoapiilani Highway, Kahakuloa, West Maui
$

La Provence *(French)* 92
Address: 3158 Lower Kula Rd., Kula, Upcountry
Phone: 808-878-1313 **$ $**

Moana Bakery & Café 115
Address: 71 Baldwin Ave., Paia, North Shore
Phone: 808-579-9999 **$ $**

Ono Gelato *(Gelato/Ice Cream)* 122
Address: 115D Hana Hwy, Paia, North Shore
Phone: 808-579-9201

Address: 815 Front St., Lahaina, West Maui
Phone: 808-495-0203 **$**

Penguini Gelato *(Coffeehouse / Gelato)* 125
Address: 93 Hana Hwy, Paia, North Shore
Phone: 808-214-4608 **$**

T. Komoda Store and Bakery *(Bakery)*.................... 142
Address: 3674 Baldwin Ave., Makawao, Upcountry
Phone: 808-572-7261 **$**

Tasaka Guri Guri *(Guri Guri)*................................. 143
Address: 70 E. Ka'ahumanu Ave., Kahului, Central Maui
Phone: 808-871-4513 **$**

Ululani's Hawaiian Shave Ice *(Shave Ice)* 147
Address: 819 Front Street, Lahaina, West Maui
Phone: 360-609-5678 **$**

Sports Bar

Beach Bums Bar & Grill *(American / Barbecue)* 25
Address: 300 Ma'alaea Rd., Ma'alaea, Central Maui
Phone: 808-243-2286 **$ $**

Fat Daddy's Smokehouse *(American / Barbecue)* 64
Address: 1913 S. Kihei Rd., Kihei, South Maui
Phone: 808-879-8711 **$**

Fred's Mexican Café *(Mexican)* 70
Address: 2511 S. Kihei Rd., Kihei, South Maui
Phone: 808-891-8600 **$ $**

Lahaina Coolers *(American)*....................................... 92
Address: 180 Dickenson St., Lahaina, West Maui
Phone: 808-661-7082 **$ $**

Lulu's *(American)* 96
Address: 1941 S. Kihei Rd., Kihei, South Maui
Phone: 808-879-9944

Address: 1221 Honoapiilani Hwy, Lahaina, West Maui
Phone: 808-661-0808 **$ $**

Maui Brewing Company Brew Pub *(American)*......... 108
Address: 4405 Honoapiilani Hwy, Kahana, West Maui
Phone: 808-669-3474 **$ $**

Moose McGillycuddy's *(American)* 117
Address: 2511 S. Kihei Rd., Kihei, South Maui
Phone: 808-891-8600

Address: 844 Front St., Lahaina, West Maui
Phone: 808-667-7758 **$ $**

Mulligan's at the Wharf / Mulligan's on the Blue
(American) 118
Address: 658 Front St., Lahaina, West Maui
Phone: 808-661-8881

Address: 100 Kaukahi St., Wailea, South Maui
Phone: 808-874-1131 **$ $**

Pizza Madness *(Pizza)*.. 128
Address: 1455 S. Kihei Rd., Kihei, South Maui
Phone: 808-270-9888 **$**

Steak/Beef

Big Wave Café *(Pacific Rim / American)* 27
Address: 1215 S. Kihei Rd, Kihei, South Maui
Phone: 808-891-8688 **$ $ $**

Bistro Casanova *(Mediterranean / Italian)* 28
Address: 33 Lono Ave, Kahului, HI 96732
Phone: 808-873-3650 **$ $ $**

Bistro Molokini *(American)* 29
Address: 3850 Wailea Alanui Dr., Wailea, South Maui
Phone: 808-875-1234 **$ $**

Café O'Lei *(Pacific Rim / American)* 38
Address: 2439 S. Kihei Rd., Kihei, South Maui
Phone: 808-891-1368

Address: 62 N. Market St., Wailuku, Central Maui
Phone: 808-986-0044

Address 1333 Maui Lani Parkway, Kahului, Central Maui
Phone: 808-877-0073 **$ $**

Capische? *(Italian)* 40
Address: 555 Kaukahi St., Wailea, South Maui
Phone: 808-879-2224 **$ $ $ $**

Casanova *(Italian)* 43
Address: 1188 Makawao Ave., Makawao, Upcountry
Phone: 808-572-0220 **$ $**

Cascades Grille & Sushi Bar *(Pacific Rim/Sushi)* 44
Address: 200 Nohea Kai Dr., Ka'anapali, West Maui
Phone: 808-667-4727 **$ $ $**

Colleen's *(American/Pacific Rim)* 50
Address: 810 Haiku Rd., Haiku, Upcountry
Phone: 808-575-9211 **$ $**

Cuatro Restaurant *(Latin/Asian Fusion)* 52
Address: 1881 S. Kihei Rd., Kihei, South Maui
Phone: 808-879-1110 **$ $ $**

David Paul's Island Grill *(Pacific Rim)* 56
Address: 900 Front St., Lahaina, West Maui
Phone: 808-662-3000 **$ $ $**

Duo *(American)* 60
Address: 3900 Wailea Alanui, Wailea, South Maui
Phone: 808-874-8000 **$ $ $ $**

Ferraro's Bar e Ristorante *(Italian)* 66
Address: 3900 Wailea Alanui Dr., Wailea, South Maui
Phone: 808-874-8000 **$ $ $ $**

Gerard's Restaurant *(French)* 72
Address: 174 Lahainaluna Rd., Lahaina, West Maui
Phone: 808-661-8939 **$ $ $ $**

Hali'imaile General Store *(Pacific Rim)* 77
Address: 900 Hali'imaile Rd., Makawao, Upcountry
Phone: 808-572-2666 **$ $ $**

I'O *(American/Pacific Rim)* 81
Address: 505 Front St., Lahaina, West Maui
Phone: 808-661-8422 **$ $ $ $**

Joe's Bar & Grill *(American)* 84
Address: 131 Wailea Ike Place, Wailea, South Maui
Phone: 808-875-7767 **$ $**

Lahaina Grill 93
Address: 127 Lahainaluna Rd., Lahaina, West Maui
Phone: 808-667-5117 **$ $ $ $**

Longhi's *(Italian)* 95
Address: 3750 Wailea Alanui Dr., Wailea, South Maui
Phone: 808-891-8883

Address: 888 Front St., Lahaina, West Maui
Phone: 808-667-2288 **$ $ $**

Makawao Steak House *(Steakhouse)* 100
Address: 3612 Baldwin Ave., Makawao, Upcountry
Phone: 808-572-8711 **$ $ $**

Mala *(Pacific Rim)* 101
Address: 1307 Front St., Lahaina, West Maui
Phone: 808-667-9394

Pacific'O *(Pacific Rim)* 123
Address: 505 Front St., Lahaina, West Maui
Phone: 808-667-4341 **$ $ $ $**

Pineapple Grill *(Pacific Rim)* 126
Address: 200 Kapalua Dr., Kapalua, HI 96761
Phone: 808-669-9600 **$ $ $ $**

Roy's Bar & Grill *(Pacific Rim)* 130
Address: 4405 Honoapiilani Hwy., Kahana, West Maui
Phone: 808-669-6999 **$ $ $**

Ruth's Chris Steak House *(American)* 132
Address: 3750 Wailea Alanui Dr., Wailea, South Maui
Phone: 808-874-8880

Address: 900 Front St., Lahaina, HI 96761
Phone: 808-661-8815 **$ $ $ $**

Spago *(Pacific Rim)* 139
Address: 3900 Wailea Alanui Dr., Wailea, South Maui
Phone: 808-874-8000 **$ $ $ $**

Tommy Bahama's Tropical Café *(American)* 145
Address: 3750 Wailea Alanui Dr., Wailea, South Maui
Phone: 808-875-9983 **$ $ $**

Tropica *(Pacific Rim/American)* 146
Address: 2365 Ka'anapali Pkwy., Ka'anapali, West Maui
Phone: 808-667-2525 **$ $ $ $**

Sushi

Cane and Taro *(Pacific Rim/Sushi)* 39
Address: 2435 Ka'anapali Pkwy, Ka'anapali, West Maui
Phone: 808-662-0668 **$ $**

Cascades Grille & Sushi Bar *(Pacific Rim/Sushi)* 44
Address: 200 Nohea Kai Dr., Ka'anapali, West Maui
Phone: 808-667-4727 **$ $ $**

Hakone *(Japanese/Sushi)* 76
Address: 5400 Makena Alanui Dr., Makena, South Maui
Phone: 808-875-5888 **$ $ $**

Isana Restaurant *(Korean/Sushi)* 82
Address: 515 S. Kihei Rd., Kihei, South Maui
Phone: 808-874-5700 **$ $ $**

Kai Wailea *(Sushi)* 86
Address: 3750 Wailea Alanui Dr., Wailea, South Maui
Phone: 808-875-1955 **$ $ $**

Koiso Sushi Bar *(Sushi)* 89
Address: 2395 S. Kihei Rd., Kihei, South Maui
Phone: 808-875-8258 **$ $**

Makawao Sushi & Deli *(Sushi/American)* 100
Address: 3647 Baldwin Ave., Makawao, Upcountry
Phone: 808-573-9044 **$ $**

Sansei Seafood Restaurant & Sushi Bar
(Sushi/Pacific Rim) 133
Address: 1881 S. Kihei Rd., Kihei, South Maui
Phone: 808-879-0004

Address: 600 Office Rd., Kapalua, HI 96761
Phone: 808-669-6286 **$ $ $**

Sushi Paradise *(Sushi)* 142
Address: 1215 S. Kihei Rd., Kihei, South Maui
Phone: 808-879-3751 **$ $ $**

Tapas/Small Dishes

Bistro Casanova *(Mediterranean/Italian)* 28
Address: 33 Lono Ave, Kahului, HI 96732
Phone: 808-873-3650 **$ $ $**

Cane and Taro *(Pacific Rim/Sushi)* 39
Address: 2435 Ka'anapali Pkwy, Ka'anapali, West Maui
Phone: 808-662-0668 **$ $**

Cuatro Restaurant *(Latin/Asian Fusion)* 52
Address: 1881 S. Kihei Rd., Kihei, South Maui
Phone: 808-879-1110 **$ $ $**

David Paul's Island Grill *(Pacific Rim)* 56
Address: 900 Front St., Lahaina, West Maui
Phone: 808-662-3000 **$ $ $**

I'O *(American/Pacific Rim)* 81
Address: 505 Front St., Lahaina, West Maui
Phone: 808-661-8422 **$ $ $ $**

Kai Wailea *(Sushi)* 86
Address: 3750 Wailea Alanui Dr., Wailea, South Maui
Phone: 808-875-1955 **$ $ $**

Main Street Bistro *(Pacific Rim)* 99
Address: 2051 Main St., Wailuku, Central Maui
Phone: 808-244-6816 **$ $**

Mala *(Pacific Rim)* 101
Address: 1307 Front St., Lahaina, West Maui
Phone: 808-667-9394 **$ $ $**

Maui Brewing Company Brew Pub *(American)* 108
Address: 4405 Honoapiilani Hwy, Kahana, West Maui
Phone: 808-669-3474 **$ $**

Pacific'O *(Pacific Rim)* 123
Address: 505 Front St., Lahaina, West Maui
Phone: 808-667-4341 **$ $ $ $**

Sansei Seafood Restaurant & Sushi Bar
(Sushi/Pacific Rim) 133
Address: 1881 S. Kihei Rd., Kihei, South Maui
Phone: 808-879-0004

Address: 600 Office Rd., Kapalua, HI 96761
Phone: 808-669-6286 **$ $ $**

Tommy Bahama's Tropical Café *(American)* 145
Address: 3750 Wailea Alanui Dr., Wailea, South Maui
Phone: 808-875-9983 **$ $ $**

Tropica *(Pacific Rim/American)*.................................. 146
Address: 2365 Ka'anapali Pkwy., Ka'anapali, West Maui
Phone: 808-667-2525 **$ $ $ $**

Thai

Thailand Cuisine *(Thai)*.............................. 144
Address: 70 E. Ka'ahumanu Ave., Kahului, Central Maui
Phone: 808-873-0225

Address: 1819 S. Kihei Rd., Kihei, South Maui
Phone: 808-875-0839 **$ $**

Vegetarian Dishes

A Saigon Café *(Vietnamese)* 15
Address: 1792 Main St, Wailuku, Central Maui
Phone: 808-243-9560 **$ $**

Alive & Well *(Organic/Vegan)* 17
Address: 340 Hana Hwy., Kahului, Central Maui
Phone: 808-877-4950 **$**

Antonio's *(Italian)* 21
Address: 1215 S. Kihei Rd., Kihei, South Maui
Phone: 808-875-8800 **$ $**

Ba-Le Sandwiches *(Vietnamese)* 22
Address: 1221 Honoapiilani Highway, Lahaina, West
          Maui
Phone: 808-661-5566

Address: 270 Dairy Rd., Kahului, Central Maui
Phone: 808-877-2400

Address: 247 Pi'ikea Ave., Kihei, South Maui
Phone: 808-875-6400

Address: 1824 Oihana St., Wailuku, Central Maui
Phone: 808-249-8833 **$**

The Banyan Tree *(Pacific Rim)* 24
Address: 1 Ritz-Carlton Drive, Kapalua, West Maui
Phone: 808-669-6200 **$ $ $ $**

Bistro Casanova *(Mediterranean/Italian)* 28
Address: 33 Lono Ave, Kahului, HI 96732
Phone: 808-873-3650 **$ $ $**

Café Des Amis *(Mediterranean/Indian)* 34
Address: 42 Baldwin Ave., Paia, North Shore
Phone: 808-579-6323 **$**

Café Mambo and Picnics *(Mediterranean)* 35
Address: 30 Baldwin Ave., Paia, North Shore
Phone: 808-579-8021 **$ $**

Down to Earth *(Health Food Store)* 59
Address: 305 Dairy Rd, Kahului, Central Maui
Phone: 808-877-2661 **$**

Dragon Dragon Chinese Restaurant *(Chinese)* 59
Address: 70 E. Kaahumanu Ave., Kahului, Central Maui
Phone: 808-893-1628 **$ $**

East Ocean *(Chinese)* 62
Address: 2463 S. Kihei Rd., Kihei, South Maui
Phone: 808-879-1988 **$ $**

Flatbread Pizza Company *(Pizza)* 68
Address: 89 Hana Hwy., Paia, North Shore
Phone: 808-579-8989 **$ $**

Fresh Mint *(Vegan/Vietnamese)* 70
Address: 115 Baldwin Ave., Paia, North Shore
Phone: 808-579-9144 **$ $**

Hakone *(Japanese/Sushi)* 76
Address: 5400 Makena Alanui Dr., Makena, South Maui
Phone: 808-875-5888 **$ $ $**

Hawaiian Moons Natural Foods *(Organic/Vegan)* 79
Address: 2411 S. Kihei Rd., Kihei, South Maui
Phone: 808-875-4356 **$**

Humuhumunukunukuapua'a *(Pacific Rim)* 80
Address: 3850 Wailea Alanui Dr., Wailea, South Maui
Phone: 808-875-1234 **$ $ $ $**

I'O *(American/Pacific Rim)* 81
Address: 505 Front St., Lahaina, West Maui
Phone: 808-661-8422 **$ $ $ $**

Joy's Place *(Vegetarian/American)* 85
Address: 1993 S. Kihei Rd., Kihei, South Maui
Phone: 808-879-9258 **$**

Vietnamese

Wine Bar

Wine List

Recommended Restaurants by Location

Central Maui

A Saigon Café *(Vietnamese)* 15
Address: 1792 Main St, Wailuku, Central Maui
Phone: 808-243-9560   **$ $**

Alive & Well *(Organic/Vegan)* 17
Address: 340 Hana Hwy., Kahului, Central Maui
Phone: 808-877-4950   **$**

Amigo's *(Mexican)* 19
Address: 333 Dairy Rd., Kahului, Central Maui
Phone: 808-872-9525   **$**

Ba-Le Sandwiches *(Vietnamese)* 22
Address: 270 Dairy Rd., Kahului, Central Maui
Phone: 808-877-2400   **$**
Address: 1824 Oihana St., Wailuku, Central Maui
Phone: 808-249-8833   **$**

Beach Bums Bar & Grill *(American/Barbecue)* 25
Address: 300 Ma'alaea Rd., Ma'alaea, Central Maui
Phone: 808-243-2286   **$ $**

Bistro Casanova *(Mediterranean/Italian)* 28
Address: 33 Lono Ave, Kahului, HI 96732
Phone: 808-873-3650   **$ $ $**

Brigit & Bernard's Garden Café *(German)* 32
Address: 335 Hoohana St., Kahului, Central Maui
Phone: 808-877-6000   **$ $**

Buzz's Wharf *(American/Pacific Rim)* 33
Address: 159 Ma'alaea Boat Harbor Rd., Ma'alaea,
          Central Maui
Phone: 808-244-5426   **$ $ $**

Café Marc Aurel *(American)* 37
Address: 28 N. Market St., Wailuku, HI 96793
Phone: 808-244-0852   **$ $**

Café O'Lei *(Pacific Rim/American)* 38
Address: 62 N. Market St., Wailuku, Central Maui
Phone: 808-986-0044   **$ $**
Address 1333 Maui Lani Parkway, Kahului, Central Maui
Phone: 808-877-0073   **$ $**

Costco Food Court *(American)* 52
Address: 540 Haleakala Highway, Kahului, Central Maui
Phone: 808-877-5248   **$**

Da Kitchen *(Local/Plate Lunch)* 54
Address: 425 Koloa St, Kahului, Central Maui
Phone: 808-871-7782   **$**

Dad's Donut Shop *(Bakery)* 55
Address: 1910 E. Vineyard St., Wailuku, Central Maui
Phone: 808-244-3303   **$**

Down to Earth *(Health Food Store)* 59
Address: 305 Dairy Rd, Kahului, Central Maui
Phone: 808-877-2661   **$**

Dragon Dragon Chinese Restaurant *(Chinese)* 59
Address: 70 E. Kaahumanu Ave., Kahului, Central Maui
Phone: 808-893-1628   **$ $**

Gianotto's Pizzeria *(Pizza)* 75
Address: 2050 Main St., Wailuku, Central Maui
Phone: 808-244-8282   **$**

L&L Hawaiian Barbecue *(Local/Plate Lunch)* 91
Address: 270 Dairy Rd., Kahului, Central Maui
Phone: 808-873-0323   **$**
Address: 790 Eha St., Wailuku, Central Maui
Phone: 808-242-1380   **$**

Main Street Bistro *(Pacific Rim)* 99
Address: 2051 Main St., Wailuku, Central Maui
Phone: 808-244-6816   **$ $**

North Shore

South Maui

Jawz Tacos *(Mexican)* 83
Address: 1279 S. Kihei Rd., Kihei, South Maui
Phone: 808-874-8226 **$**

Joe's Bar & Grill *(American)* 84
Address: 131 Wailea Ike Place, Wailea, South Maui
Phone: 808-875-7767 **$ $**

Joy's Place *(Vegetarian/American)* 85
Address: 1993 S. Kihei Rd., Kihei, South Maui
Phone: 808-879-9258 **$**

Kai Wailea *(Sushi)* 86
Address: 3750 Wailea Alanui Dr., Wailea, South Maui
Phone: 808-875-1955 **$ $ $**

Kihei Caffe *(American)* 87
Address: 1945 S. Kihei Rd., Kihei, South Maui
Phone: 808-879-2230 **$**

Koiso Sushi Bar *(Sushi)* 89
Address: 2395 S. Kihei Rd., Kihei, South Maui
Phone: 808-875-8258 **$ $**

L&L Hawaiian Barbecue *(Local/Plate Lunch)* 91
Address: 247 Pi'ikea Ave., Kihei, South Maui
Phone: 808-875-8898 **$**

Longhi's *(Italian)* 95
Address: 3750 Wailea Alanui Dr., Wailea, South Maui
Phone: 808-891-8883 **$ $ $**

Lulu's *(American)* 96
Address: 1941 S. Kihei Rd., Kihei, South Maui
Phone: 808-879-9944 **$ $**

Matteo's Pizzeria *(Italian/Pizza)* 108
Address: 100 Wailea Ike Dr., Wailea, South Maui
Phone: 808-874-1234 **$ $**

Maui Masala *(Indian)* 110
Address: 2395 S. Kihei Road, Kihei, South Maui
Phone: 808-875-9000 **$**

Maui Tacos *(Mexican)* 111
Address: 247 Pi'ikea Ave., Kihei, South Maui
Phone: 808-875-9340 **$**

Maui Tacos *(Mexican)* 111
Address: 2411 S. Kihei Rd., Kihei, South Maui
Phone: 808-879-5005 **$**

Monsoon India *(Indian)* 116
Address: 760 S. Kihei Rd., Kihei, South Maui
Phone: 808-875 6666 **$ $**

Moose McGillycuddy's *(American)* 117
Address: 2511 S. Kihei Rd., Kihei, South Maui
Phone: 808-891-8600 **$ $**

Mulligan's on the Blue
(American) 118
Address: 100 Kaukahi St., Wailea, South Maui
Phone: 808-874-1131 **$ $**

Pita Paradise *(Mediterranean)* 128
Address: 1913 S. Kihei Rd., Kihei, South Maui
Phone: 808-875-7679 **$**

Pizza Madness *(Pizza)* 128
Address: 1455 S. Kihei Rd., Kihei, South Maui
Phone: 808-270-9888 **$**

Ruth's Chris Steak House *(American)* 132
Address: 3750 Wailea Alanui Dr., Wailea, South Maui
Phone: 808-874-8880 **$ $ $ $**

Sansei Seafood Restaurant & Sushi Bar
(Sushi/Pacific Rim) 133
Address: 1881 S. Kihei Rd., Kihei, South Maui
Phone: 808-879-0004 **$ $ $**

Seawatch *(American)* 136
Address: 100 Wailea Golf Club Dr., Wailea, South Maui
Phone: 808-875-8080 **$ $ $**

Shaka Pizza *(Pizza)* 137
Address: 1770 S. Kihei Rd., Kihei, South Maui
Phone: 808-874-0331 **$**

Upcountry

West Maui

Lulu's *(American)* 96
Address: 1221 Honoapiilani Hwy, Lahaina, West Maui
Phone: 808-661-0808 **$ $**

Mai Tai Lounge *(Pacific Rim)* 98
Address: 839 Front St., Lahaina, West Maui
Phone: 808-661-5288 **$ $**

Mala *(Pacific Rim)* 101
Address: 1307 Front St., Lahaina, West Maui
Phone: 808-667-9394 **$ $ $**

Maui Brewing Company Brew Pub *(American)* 108
Address: 4405 Honoapiilani Hwy, Kahana, West Maui
Phone: 808-669-3474 **$ $**

Maui Tacos *(Mexican)* 111
Address: 840 Wainee St., Lahaina Square, Lahaina, West
        Maui
Phone: 808-661-8883 **$**
Address: 5095 Napilihau St., Napili, West Maui
Phone: 808-665-0222 **$**

Moose McGillycuddy's *(American)* 117
Address: 844 Front St., Lahaina, West Maui
Phone: 808-667-7758 **$ $**

Mulligan's at the Wharf
(American) 118
Address: 658 Front St., Lahaina, West Maui
Phone: 808-661-8881 **$ $**

Nikki's Pizza *(Pizza)* 120
Address: 2435 Ka'anapali Pkwy, Ka'anapali, West Maui
Phone: 808-667-0333 **$**

Old Lahaina Lu'au *(Lu'au)* 121
Address: 1251 Front Street, Lahaina, West Maui
Phone: 808-667-1998 **$ $ $ $**

Ono Gelato *(Lu'au)* 122
Address: 815 Front St., Lahaina, West Maui
Phone: 808-495-0203 **$**

Pacific'O *(Pacific Rim)* 123
Address: 505 Front St., Lahaina, West Maui
Phone: 808-667-4341 **$ $ $ $**

Penne Pasta *(Italian)* 125
Address: 180 Dickenson St., Lahaina, West Maui
Phone: 808-661-6633 **$ $**

Pineapple Grill *(Pacific Rim)* 126
Address: 200 Kapalua Dr., Kapalua, HI 96761
Phone: 808-669-9600 **$ $ $ $**

The Plantation House Restaurant *(Pacific Rim)* ... 129
Address: 2000 Plantation Club Dr., Lahaina, West Maui
Phone: 808-669-6299 **$ $ $**

Roy's Bar & Grill *(Pacific Rim)* 130
Address: 4405 Honoapiilani Hwy., Kahana, West Maui
Phone: 808-669-6999 **$ $ $**

Ruth's Chris Steak House *(American)* 132
Address: 900 Front St., Lahaina, HI 96761
Phone: 808-661-8815 **$ $ $ $**

Sansei Seafood Restaurant & Sushi Bar
(Sushi/Pacific Rim) 133
Address: 600 Office Rd., Kapalua, HI 96761
Phone: 808-669-6286 **$ $ $**

Sea House Restaurant *(American/Pacific Rim)* 135
Address: 5900 Lower Honoapiilani Rd, Napili, West
        Maui
Phone: 808-669-1500 **$ $ $**

Tropica *(Pacific Rim/American)* 146
Address: 2365 Ka'anapali Pkwy., Ka'anapali, West Maui
Phone: 808-667-2525 **$ $ $ $**

Ululani's Hawaiian Shave Ice *(Shave Ice)* 147
Address: 819 Front Street, Lahaina, West Maui
Phone: 360-609-5678 **$**

'Umalu *(Pacific Rim/American)* 148
Address: 200 Nohea Kai Dr., Ka'anapali, West Maui
Phone: 808-661-1234 **$ $ $ $**

Recommended Restaurants by Budget

$ Average Entrée $10 & Under

Alive & Well *(Organic/Vegan)* 17
Address: 340 Hana Hwy., Kahului, Central Maui
Phone: 808-877-4950

Aloha Mixed Plate *(Local/Plate Lunch)* 18
Address: 1285 Front St., Lahaina, West Maui
Phone: 808-661-3322

Amigo's *(Mexican)* 19
Address: 41 E. Lipoa St., Kihei, South Maui
Phone: 808-879-9952

Address: 333 Dairy Rd., Kahului, Central Maui
Phone: 808-872-9525

Address: 658 Front St., Wharf Cinema Center, Lahaina,
      West Maui
Phone: 808-661-0210

Ba-Le Sandwiches *(Vietnamese)* 22
Address: 1221 Honoapiilani Highway, Lahaina, West
      Maui
Phone: 808-661-5566

Address: 270 Dairy Rd., Kahului, Central Maui
Phone: 808-877-2400

Address: 247 Pi'ikea Ave., Kihei, South Maui
Phone: 808-875-6400

Address: 1824 Oihana St., Wailuku, Central Maui
Phone: 808-249-8833

Café Des Amis *(Mediterranean/Indian)* 34
Address: 42 Baldwin Ave., Paia, North Shore
Phone: 808-579-6323

Café @ La Plage *(American)* 35
Address: 2395 S. Kihei Rd., Kihei, South Maui
Phone: 808-875-7668

Cilantro *(Mexican)* 48
Address: 170 Papalaua St., Lahaina, HI 96761
Phone: 808-667-5444

CJ's Deli & Diner *(American)* 49
Address: 2580 Keka'a Dr., Ka'anapali, West Maui
Phone: 808-667-0968

Coconut's Fish Café *(American)* 50
Address: 1279 S. Kihei Rd., Kihei, South Maui
Phone: 808-875-9979

Costco Food Court *(American)* 52
Address: 540 Haleakala Highway, Kahului, Central Maui
Phone: 808-877-5248

Da Kitchen *(Local/Plate Lunch)* 54
Address: 425 Koloa St, Kahului, Central Maui
Phone: 808-871-7782

Address: 2439 S. Kihei Rd, Kihei, South Maui
Phone 808-875-7782

Address: 658 Front St., Lahaina, West Maui
Phone: 808-661-4900

Dad's Donut Shop *(Bakery)* 55
Address: 1910 E. Vineyard St., Wailuku, Central Maui
Phone: 808-244-3303

Down to Earth *(Health Food Store)* 59
Address: 305 Dairy Rd, Kahului, Central Maui
Phone: 808-877-2661

Eskimo Candy *(American)* 63
Address: 2665 Wai Wai Pl, Kihei, South Maui
Phone: 808-879-5686

Fat Daddy's Smokehouse *(American/Barbecue)* 64
Address: 1913 S. Kihei Rd., Kihei, South Maui
Phone: 808-879-8711

Gianotto's Pizzeria *(Pizza)* 75
Address: 2050 Main St., Wailuku, Central Maui
Phone: 808-244-8282

Grandma's Coffeehouse *(Coffeehouse)* 75
Address: 153 Kula Hwy, Kula, Upcountry
Phone: 808-375-7853

T. Komoda Store and Bakery *(Bakery)*.....................142
Address: 3674 Baldwin Ave., Makawao, Upcountry
Phone: 808-572-7261

Tasaka Guri Guri *(Guri Guri)*..................................143
Address: 70 E. Ka'ahumanu Ave., Kahului, Central Maui
Phone: 808-871-4513

Ululani's Hawaiian Shave Ice *(Shave Ice)*.................147
Address: 819 Front Street, Lahaina, West Maui
Phone: 360-609-5678

**Upcountry Fresh Tamales
& Mixed Plate** *(Mexican/Local/Plate Lunch)*.............149
Address: 55 Pukalani St., Pukalani, Upcountry
Phone: 808-572-8258

Who Cut the Cheese? *(American)*.............................150
Address: 1279 S. Kihei Rd., Kihei, South Maui
Phone: 808-874-3930

$$ Average Entrée $20 & Under

A Saigon Café *(Vietnamese)* 15
Address: 1792 Main St, Wailuku, Central Maui
Phone: 808-243-9560

Antonio's *(Italian)* 21
Address: 1215 S. Kihei Rd., Kihei, South Maui
Phone: 808-875-8800

Aroma D'Italia Ristorante *(Italian)* 21
Address: 1881 S. Kihei Rd., Kihei, South Maui
Phone: 808-879-0133

Beach Bums Bar & Grill *(American/Barbecue)* 25
Address: 300 Ma'alaea Rd., Ma'alaea, Central Maui
Phone: 808-243-2286

Bistro Molokini *(American)* 29
Address: 3850 Wailea Alanui Dr., Wailea, South Maui
Phone: 808-875-1234

BJ's Chicago Pizzeria *(American)* 31
Address: 730 Front St., Lahaina, West Maui
Phone: 808-661-0700

Brigit & Bernard's Garden Café *(German)* 32
Address: 335 Hoohana St., Kahului, Central Maui
Phone: 808-877-6000

Bubba Gump Shrimp Co. *(American)* 32
Address: 889 Front St., Lahaina, West Maui
Phone: 808-661-3111

Café Kapalua *(American)* 35
Address: 2000 Village Rd., Kapalua, West Maui
Phone: 808-665-4386

Café Mambo and Picnics *(Mediterranean)* 35
Address: 30 Baldwin Ave., Paia, North Shore
Phone: 808-579-8021

Café Marc Aurel *(American)* 37
Address: 28 N. Market St., Wailuku, HI 96793
Phone: 808-244-0852

Café O'Lei *(Pacific Rim/American)* 38
Address: 2439 S. Kihei Rd., Kihei, South Maui
Phone: 808-891-1368

Address: 62 N. Market St., Wailuku, Central Maui
Phone: 808-986-0044

Address 1333 Maui Lani Parkway, Kahului, Central Maui
Phone: 808-877-0073

Cane and Taro *(Pacific Rim/Sushi)* 39
Address: 2435 Ka'anapali Pkwy, Ka'anapali, West Maui
Phone: 808-662-0668

Casanova *(Italian)* 43
Address: 1188 Makawao Ave., Makawao, Upcountry
Phone: 808-572-0220

Colleen's *(American/Pacific Rim)* 50
Address: 810 Haiku Rd., Haiku, Upcountry
Phone: 808-575-9211

Cool Cat Café *(American)* 51
Address: 658 Front St., Lahaina, West Maui
Phone: 808-667-0908

Dog & Duck *(Pub)* 58
Address: 1913 S. Kihei Rd., Kihei, South Maui
Phone: 808-875-9669

Monsoon India *(Indian)* 116
Address: 760 S. Kihei Rd., Kihei, South Maui
Phone: 808-875 6666

Moose McGillycuddy's *(American)* 117
Address: 2511 S. Kihei Rd., Kihei, South Maui
Phone: 808-891-8600

Address: 844 Front St., Lahaina, West Maui
Phone: 808-667-7758

Mulligan's at the Wharf / Mulligan's on the Blue
(American) 118
Address: 658 Front St., Lahaina, West Maui
Phone: 808-661-8881

Address: 100 Kaukahi St., Wailea, South Maui
Phone: 808-874-1131

Penne Pasta *(Italian)* 125
Address: 180 Dickenson St., Lahaina, West Maui
Phone: 808-661-6633

Ruby's 131
Address: 275 W. Ka'ahumanu Ave., Kahului, Central Maui
Phone: 808-248-7829

South Shore Tiki Lounge *(American)* 138
Address: 1913 S. Kihei Rd., Kihei, South Maui
Phone: 808-874-6444

Thailand Cuisine *(Thai)* 144
Address: 70 E. Ka'ahumanu Ave., Kahului, Central Maui
Phone: 808-873-0225

Address: 1819 S. Kihei Rd., Kihei, South Maui
Phone: 808-875-0839

$$$ Average Entrée $35 & Under

Big Wave Café *(Pacific Rim/American)* 27
Address: 1215 S. Kihei Rd, Kihei, South Maui
Phone: 808-891-8688

Bistro Casanova *(Mediterranean/Italian)* 28
Address: 33 Lono Ave, Kahului, HI 96732
Phone: 808-873-3650

Buzz's Wharf *(American/Pacific Rim)* 33
Address: 159 Ma'alaea Boat Harbor Rd., Ma'alaea,
            Central Maui
Phone: 808-244-5426

Cascades Grille & Sushi Bar *(Pacific Rim/Sushi)* 44
Address: 200 Nohea Kai Dr., Ka'anapali, West Maui
Phone: 808-667-4727

Cuatro Restaurant *(Latin/Asian Fusion)* 52
Address: 1881 S. Kihei Rd., Kihei, South Maui
Phone: 808-879-1110

David Paul's Island Grill *(Pacific Rim)* 56
Address: 900 Front St., Lahaina, West Maui
Phone: 808-662-3000

Five Palms Restaurant *(American/Pacific Rim)* 67
Address: 2960 S. Kihei Rd., Kihei, South Maui
Phone: 808-879-2607

Hakone *(Japanese/Sushi)* 76
Address: 5400 Makena Alanui Dr., Makena, South Maui
Phone: 808-875-5888

Hali'imaile General Store *(Pacific Rim)* 77
Address: 900 Hali'imaile Rd., Makawao, Upcountry
Phone: 808-572-2666

Isana Restaurant *(Korean/Sushi)* 82
Address: 515 S. Kihei Rd., Kihei, South Maui
Phone: 808-874-5700

Kai Wailea *(Sushi)* 86
Address: 3750 Wailea Alanui Dr., Wailea, South Maui
Phone: 808-875-1955

Kobe *(Japanese Steakhouse)* 88
Address: 136 Dickenson St., Lahaina, West Maui
Phone: 808-667-5555

Longhi's *(Italian)* 95
Address: 3750 Wailea Alanui Dr., Wailea, South Maui
Phone: 808-891-8883

Address: 888 Front St., Lahaina, West Maui
Phone: 808-667-2288

$$$$ Average Entrée $35 & Up

Index

Register This Book!
(We'll Even Bribe You Twice)

As strange as it may sound, we really would like you to register this book so that we can let you know about important updates: new restaurants, closed restaurants, big changes at one of our favorite (or least favorite) places. Things change in the Maui Restaurant scene and that is why we want to keep you informed and updated.

This is a *free service* for our readers, but even so, we know that it takes a little effort to go over to a computer, type in a web address and fill in a few fields.

That is why we are going to offer you an ethical bribe. Actually, two bribes:

Win a $25 Gift Card

Every month from December 2009 thru December 2010, we will be giving away a $25 gift certificate for Amazon.com in an online sweepstakes we are running. When you register that you are an owner of **Top Maui Restaurants 2010** using the special link below, you will be entered to win in that month's sweepstakes.

Get a Trial Membership to TopMauiTips.com

This membership site for people who are planning their vacation to Maui has been in the works for three years and was finally opened to the public in December 2009. The site is loaded with articles that are packed with useful, actionable tips to get the most out of your trip to Maui. Whatever activity you are considering, whatever questions you have, chances are they are addressed in this thoroughly-researched membership site. And now, you can have a complimentary trial membership when you register this book.

Register your book today at:
www.TopMauiRestaurants.com/2010

How You Can Keep Up to Date on the Maui Restaurant Scene

Restaurants come and go here on Maui and we are dedicated to helping our readers navigate this ever-changing environment. There are a number of things that we have done and are planning to do that will help you get the most out of your Maui vacation.

We have recently launched our blog www.MauiRestaurantsBlog.com where you can read the latest dining news and also rate your personal experiences at any restaurant in Maui. Every restaurant has its own page and you can read what other diners have to say and see how others have rated each restaurant. (For our restaurant reviews, however, this book is the only place that you will be able to read what we think.)

There has also been some discussion about an Internet-syndicated radio show, but as of press time, we don't have details. When we know more, we will send an email to everyone who is subscribed to our list. To subscribe, register online using the link below.

We also host occasional reader appreciation Mai Tai parties at our home in South Maui. This is a great chance for us to get to talk with our readers and for our readers and other Maui foodies to talk with us…all while enjoying one of Molly's delicious Mai Tais. If you are in town when we host one of these parties, you are invited. You just have to RSVP to one of our invitations.

To receive those invitations—and other foodie-oriented stuff—from us, please register your copy of *Top Maui Restaurants 2010*.

To register your book, please visit
www.TopMauiRestaurants.com/2010